SHOWDOWN
AT SHEPHERD'S BUSH

ALSO BY DAVID DAVIS

Play by Play: Los Angeles Sports Photography, 1889–1989

SHOWDOWN
AT SHEPHERD'S BUSH

The 1908 Olympic Marathon
and the Three Runners Who
Launched a Sporting Craze

DAVID DAVIS

Thomas Dunne Books
St. Martin's Press
New York

THOMAS DUNNE BOOKS.
An imprint of St. Martin's Press.

SHOWDOWN AT SHEPHERD'S BUSH. Copyright © 2012 by David Davis. All rights
reserved. Printed in the United States of America. For information, address St.
Martin's Press, 175 Fifth Avenue, New York, N.Y. 10010.

www.thomasdunnebooks.com
www.stmartins.com

Library of Congress Cataloging-in-Publication Data

Davis, David.
    Showdown at Shepherd's Bush : the 1908 Olympic marathon and the
three runners who launched a sporting craze / David Davis.
        p. cm.
    ISBN 978-0-312-64100-9 (hardcover)
    ISBN 978-1-250-01239-5 (e-book)
    1. Marathon running—History.   2. Olympics—History.   3. Olympic
Games (4th : 1908 : London, England)   4. Pietri, Dorando, 1885–1942.
5. Longboat, Tom, 1887–1949.   6. Hayes, Johnny, 1886–1965.
7. Long-distance runners.   I. Title.
    GV1065.D38 2012
    796.42'52—dc23

                                                                    2012010297

First Edition: June 2012

10   9   8   7   6   5   4   3   2   1

To Harold and Sylvia Davis
&
Nathan and Sylvia Grosof

To me, [the marathon] is more than a race. It's a very personal thing—a sense of supreme well being. When you've trained for a race, you've brought the body God gave you to the finest attunement it can possibly know. Your muscles are strong. Your mind is clear and clean. You are conscious of the power of your heart and lungs. You can feel your blood flowing, the oxygen actually serving as fuel. In short you are really and truly living. . . . It's a supreme feeling of perfection and closeness to the infinite I can't express very well, but this is the way I attain it and I hope I always can.

—CLARENCE DEMAR, seven-time winner of the Boston Marathon[1]

To write properly about the Olympic Games of the twentieth century is to write about almost everything in the twentieth century. About plastics and politics and racism and the demise of the rigid Bible morality and the rise of situation ethics. About avarice and airplanes and vitamin pills and chauvinism and free love and selling refrigerators on television and urban renewal and electricity.

—WILLIAM OSCAR JOHNSON[2]

SHOWDOWN
AT SHEPHERD'S BUSH

INTRODUCTION

At the dawn of the twentieth century, mankind was getting into motion. Trains crisscrossed continents, ocean liners churned across the seas, subways burrowed underneath cities. The first generation of automobiles was arriving even as the Wright brothers were conquering the air. Flickering black-and-white images on a white screen were bringing entertainment to the masses.

The earliest practitioners of the marathon race, invented in 1896, introduced a different kind of motion. At a time when competitive runners rarely ventured past five miles, and at a time when knowledge of the human body was primitive, they were pioneers of endurance. They were seen as superhuman or crazed or both. They had to be in order to survive roads so dusty that their lungs were clogged; shoes so thin that mere slips of leather separated their bloodied feet from rocky, uneven surfaces; training methods so archaic as to invite permanent physical damage.

But they persevered to become, as Boston Marathon historian Tom Derderian put it, "the explorers, test pilots and astronauts of their era, boldly running where none had run before, and, in their perceptions and the public's, risking their lives and future health to do it."[1]

At the 1908 Olympics in London, when all of about fifty marathons had ever been raced, a man collapsed and almost died in front of 80,000 stunned spectators, including the Queen of England. The moment turned Dorando Pietri, from Italy, into one of the most famous athletes in the world and, after his recovery, one of the first celebrities to be known by a single name: Dorando.

Irving Berlin penned his first hit song about him, and Enrico Caruso sketched him. Sir Arthur Conan Doyle embraced him, while "Mr. Dooley," the fictional barkeep invented by journalist Finley Peter Dunne, pontificated about him. Charles Dana Gibson, Ezra Pound, and F. S. Kelly wrote about him; Madison Square Garden sold out because of him.

Two of Dorando's opponents, Johnny Hayes and Tom Longboat, became equally famous. An Irish-American lad straight out of the tenements of New York City, Hayes was a Horatio Alger character sprung to life, championed by none other than President Theodore Roosevelt. Tom Longboat's record-smashing victories and controversial losses made him the most legendary Canadian athlete until Wayne Gretzky came along (the two were born just miles apart). His athletic prowess afforded him mainstream respect, while his Native Indian heritage triggered hateful prejudice in and out of the sporting arena.

In the period before the start of World War I, the trio jumpstarted the first "Marathon Mania." They raced each other (and other opponents) in arenas and stadiums across the United States, transforming the marathon into a crowd-pleasing spectacle and a legitimate athletic event. Along the way, they helped resurrect the flagging Olympic Movement and establish the standard distance for the marathon: 26 miles, 385 yards.

The exploits of Dorando, Hayes, and Longboat are largely forgotten today. But their legacy can be found in the exuberant spirit of contemporary marathoning, a global phenomenon that attracts elite athletes and weekend warriors alike, and one that inspires all of us to keep moving.

ONE

O n the morning of July 24, 1908, the rains that had bedeviled the London Olympics surrendered to blue skies and a sodden heat. An excited hum disturbed the dawn as streams of Londoners exited the Wood Lane Underground station and hurried toward the Olympic Stadium as if drawn by hypnosis. The smart set chugged past in the newest, coolest toy—a motorized vehicle.

Sir Arthur Conan Doyle stood in the press area of the Stadium, preparing to cover the day's proceedings for the *Daily Mail* newspaper. On tap were wrestling and swimming finals, as well as the pole vault, but to Conan Doyle and the 80,000 spectators, reporters, Olympic officials, and royalty jammed inside the enormous sporting cathedral, as well as the tens of thousands of bystanders gathering along the twenty-five miles of roads leading to the Stadium, only one event mattered.

GREAT MARATHON RACE, read the headline in the *Standard*.

CROWNING EVENT OF THE OLYMPIC GAMES, the *Graphic* proclaimed.

Conan Doyle didn't require the deductive powers of Sherlock Holmes to understand what was at stake. The home team had endured a disastrous Olympics to this point. Foul weather led to poor attendance during the first week, and then the United States's well-trained squad had stomped the Brits' best on the track. Worse, their blustering Irish-American leader, James E. Sullivan, had whipped the press into hysterics by charging that the hosts were not behaving like honorable sportsmen.

To representatives of the British Empire, which prided itself as the birthplace of modern sports and the adjudicator of all matters concerning fair play and sportsmanship, this was the ultimate insult. Sullivan might as well have thumbed his nose at the Queen of England, who was, this very moment, journeying to the Stadium to observe the finish of the marathon.

Today was the last full day of what the press were calling "The Battle of Shepherd's Bush." The previous week's humiliations and escapades would be forgotten and forgiven, Conan Doyle surmised, with a British victory in the marathon. What's more, the pundits on both sides of the Atlantic favored the chances of the twelve-strong English team. If Alex Duncan and James Beale could repeat their magnificent showing in the April Trials, when they navigated over muddy roads and through freezing sleet on much the same course, the gold medal would be theirs. Victory by one of the lads from the territories, from Canada or South Africa, would suffice, Conan Doyle conceded, so long as the bloody Stars and Stripes didn't show on the flagpole again.

The sun penetrated Conan Doyle's tweed suit, and he retreated into the shade. It was going to be a hot one.

Adjacent to the press area, a parade of Olympic officials, led by Pierre de Coubertin, was finding their seats. A diminutive man with a frothy, jet-black mustache that threatened to engulf his face, the baron should have been in his glory. He had almost single-handedly engineered the revival of the Olympics in 1896, giving the ancient Games an international twist. A confirmed Anglophile, Coubertin had entrusted the 1908 Olympics to London on short notice, after Rome was forced to bow out. The London Games' lead organizer, Lord Desborough, had proved himself worthy, cutting a favorable deal to ensure the construction of the grand Stadium—the first such structure to be built for the modern Games—and attracting the world's top athletes.

But myriad shortcomings were overshadowing Coubertin's Olympian achievement. The 1900 Olympics, located in his hometown of Paris, had been a dreadful flop. So, too, were the 1904 Olympics in St. Louis. He considered the 1906 Athens Games to be nothing more than a flagrant attempt by Greece to usurp his vision and become permanent Olympic host. And now, the near-daily controversies involving the United States and the English teams were further undermining his authority. Every evening, Sullivan was haranguing the press and lobbying for Coubertin to be replaced.

As Coubertin glanced at the program for the marathon, it was apparent that his future, and the future of the Olympic Movement, was up for grabs.

On the day that he became an overnight sensation, Dorando Pietri woke in a nondescript room in a nondescript house in the Soho area of London. He stayed in bed for a few moments, letting his body awaken to the moment.

Few journalists recalled Dorando Pietri from two years ago, when the skinny Italian ran with the leaders at the Athens marathon before cramping up and dropping from the race. His credentials as Italy's top distance runner, and one of the best on the continent, meant little to the gathered media in London. Every newspaper in England and North America misspelled his name. When the experts weighed the chances of the field, he was ignored in favor of the consensus picks: Britain's Alex Duncan, Fred Lord, Fred Appleby, and Jack Price; South Africa's Charles Hefferon; and, of course, Canada's Tom Longboat.

The twenty-two-year-old Italian had waited two years for redemption. He was so determined that he had run two marathons in the past forty-five days to ready himself for London. Today, he vowed, he would prove that he was the world's top endurance runner. Today, he vowed, he would become an Olympic immortal.

He said a quick prayer, thinking of his parents and his first and only love, Teresa, back home in Carpi, then went to breakfast with his brother, Ulpiano. He dug into a steak and sipped cup after cup of hot coffee.

He nodded to his brother. *"Vincerò o morirò,"* he said.

Dorando repeated the phrase: *"Vincerò o morirò."*

"I will win or I will die."[1]

Johnny Hayes woke to sunshine. It took him a moment before he recognized his surroundings: the Chequers Inn in the town of Uxbridge, his third hotel in as many weeks. He and the six other American marathoners had just moved here so they could be near the start of the race.

He went down and consumed a light breakfast—steak, toast, and tea—and listened to final words of advice from coach Mike Murphy. "Mind, you gentlemen, this heat'll bake the starch right outta ya," the bowler-wearing sage from the University of Pennsylvania warned. "Stay the pace, and run your race."

The twenty-two-year-old Hayes nodded. He didn't talk much. Standing just under five foot four, he was probably the smallest man in the field. But "Little Johnny" was anything but frail. He had grown up in the rough-and-tumble tenements of New York, the son of Irish-American immigrant parents who had died before he reached age nineteen. He had watched his younger siblings get dragged off to an orphanage, and, to earn a living, worked one of the dirtiest, most dangerous jobs in the city—digging underground to build New York's newfangled subway.

Running marathons came as something of a relief. The race, Hayes found, was about absorbing enormous pain, physical and mental, and then driving through it to the finishing-post. He got good quickly. Between 1906 and 1908, he attained three top-five finishes at the prestigious Boston Marathon and a victory at the Yonkers Marathon.

The press disparaged the chances of Hayes and the other American marathoners. They were a young bunch, and they had done their training in Brighton, far from the London spotlight. Johnny and the other Irish-American marathoners, Mike Ryan and Tom Morrissey, talked about how much satisfaction they'd get in stomping the Brits on their own turf but, truth be told, they weren't much troubled by the English runners.

As he grabbed his gear and prepared to leave for the start, Johnny Hayes was worried about only one opponent: Tom Longboat.

From his room at the White Hart Hotel, the most famous and controversial athlete at the 1908 Olympics peered down at the spectators and policemen crowding the streets below. Tom Longboat stood almost 5 foot 11 and weighed 140 pounds, topped by an unruly shock of black hair. His bronze, muscular legs, which were featured in newspaper photographs, had carried him to the world's record at the 1907 Boston Marathon. He was a Canadian celebrity as well as a hero among his fellow Onondaga Indians on the Six Nations Reserve west of Toronto. He hadn't lost a race over fifteen miles in three years and was the overwhelming favorite in today's race.

But the Yanks were at it again. Even today, on the morning of the marathon, James E. Sullivan was claiming that Longboat was a professional athlete and should be barred from the all-amateur Olympics. The negative publicity was clouding what Longboat and Tom Flanagan, the runner's manager and promoter, saw as a golden opportunity. If Longboat were to follow up his Boston triumph with a victory in London, he would be crowned the greatest distance runner of all time. There would be no athlete as famous in the world—not baseball's "Georgia Peach," Ty Cobb, nor the African American heavyweight boxer, Jack Johnson. A post-Olympics bonanza of exhibitions, endorsements, and personal appearances awaited.

There was another problem besides Sullivan's accusations. Flanagan had brought Longboat to train in Ireland before the Olympics. In his last session, Tom had collided with a buggy. His knee was sore, and the rest of his body felt sluggish, like maybe he'd left his legs on the road to Kilmallock.

A knock on the door. "You up, Big Chief? Time to get ready," said Lou Marsh—Flanagan's assistant—on the job as always.

Longboat grimaced as he pivoted toward the door.

Showtime.

Due west of the Olympic Stadium, the village of Windsor bustled with a festive atmosphere. Children on holiday dodged horse-drawn carriages. Special trains leaving from Paddington Station chugged into the Royal Station and deposited spectators, journalists, athletes, and officials. The statue of Queen Victoria gleamed like a magnificent bronze sentry, and Union Jack flags sprouted on storefronts like tricolored mushrooms.

Jack M. Andrew took little notice of the swelling crowd. The organizer of the marathon walked down Windsor's steep cobblestone main street to double-check that the runners would be able to spot the distance-indicator at the one-mile mark. Overenthusiastic fans had stolen others along the course; thankfully, this sign was positioned perfectly.

Determining the marathon route had been the most challenging aspect of Andrew's job. This was the first international marathon ever raced in London (or England, for that matter), and he had agonized over every inch of the course. With the start from the grounds of Windsor Castle and the finish inside the Stadium, he had created the longest marathon in Olympic history. It was such an odd and random distance: Whoever heard of a marathon measuring 26 miles, 385 yards?

Andrew put on his straw bowler, the words CHIEF CLERK spelled out on the ribbon, and glanced at his pocket watch. The start couldn't come soon enough.

Dorando Pietri rode the special competitors' train from Paddington Station to Windsor. He was led to an area that had been turned into temporary dressing rooms for the runners. The pungent odor of liniment lingered in the air.

Dr. Michael Bulger and a small staff of physicians checked Dorando's heart and cleared him to race. Dorando changed into his running togs: a white shirt, leather shoes, and his signature pair of bright red pantaloons that extended nearly to his knees. The number 19 was affixed to his chest.

He walked outside. The sun's rays broiled his jet-black hair, and he placed a white pocket handkerchief atop his head, with knotted corners to secure it.

He caught sight of his adversaries—Hefferon, Lord, Duncan. They looked fit. And there was the legendary Longboat, smiling and chatting with several people. He was stolid, much larger than Dorando expected.

No one spoke to him.

I will win or I will die.

T he American team arrived late and dressed quickly at the
Windsor railway station. Johnny Hayes slipped into the American uniform: white shorts with red piping on the side and a white shirt
with a red-white-and-blue, stars-and-bars emblem across his chest. He
wore number 26.

He conferred with George Cameron, one of two cyclists who
would accompany him during the race. He checked the sky, and
the thinnest of smiles creased his stoic face. The sultry heat was a
blessing because it negated the one element he lacked as a runner:
speed.

He repeated Murphy's advice like a mantra: *Stay the pace, and run
your race.*

T om Longboat slowly put on his kit: an all-white uniform with a
gigantic red maple leaf on his chest. He pulled on dark socks and
leather ankle boots and tied a belt around his waist. Atop his head
he placed a white skullcap. He was assigned number 72.

As soon as he stepped outside, the overflowing crowd yelled out
his name. One fan screamed to take his photograph.

He obliged, flashing his infectious grin, then turned to greet an
old acquaintance, George V. Brown, from the Boston Marathon committee. Newspapermen scurried to ask Longboat about James E. Sullivan's latest broadside.

Tom's attendant, Lou Marsh, hustled him away.

.   .   .

Officials with green ribbons around their straw hats escorted the runners past the spectators and through Sovereign's Gate into the peaceful calm on the grounds of Windsor Castle. They strolled past Princess Mary and her children taking shelter beneath a shady tree.

Jack Andrew arranged the fifty-five men into four rows on a gravel pathway just beyond the East Terrace of the Castle, near the memorial for Queen Victoria's favorite dog, Dacko. The runners readied themselves and stared ahead at the road leading toward the town of Windsor.

There was, suddenly, silence. Princess Mary pressed an electric button and, moments later, the runners burst off in a pack.

The 1908 London marathon—the final skirmish in the Battle of Shepherd's Bush and the most controversial race in Olympic history—had begun.

TWO

In the days and months and years following the 1908 London Olympics, much that was written about Dorando Pietri turned out to be false. Many mistakes were minor, as when newspapers reversed his name and called him "Pietri Dorando" or "P. Dorando," or misspelled his name as "Durando." It was reported that he was born and raised on the sun-kissed isle of Capri, just south of Naples, when in fact he hailed from Carpi, a small city in the northern part of the country.

Other times the stories were apocryphal. Like the time Dorando, working as a baker's boy in a pastry shop, was given an urgent package to deliver. He missed the train as it was leaving the station and, instead of waiting for the next one, simply ran the fifteen or so miles to the next town. Then, he turned around and ran home.

Or, so it was stated.

Myth defined Dorando Pietri as surely as his epic misjudgments on the track defined his running career. Perhaps that's what happens when you take center stage at the most controversial race in Olympic history. Perhaps that's what happens when you become the first-ever global sports icon.

What is known about Dorando Pietri's life before he became famous, and before the facts became enshrouded in semi-truths, is that he grew up in small-town Italy. He was born on October 16, 1885, in Villa Mandrio, a hamlet of the village of Correggio.[1] The town lies in the Emilia-Romagna region of north-central Italy, about fifty miles from Bologna and ninety miles from Milan.

With its temperate climate and prime location, midway between the Adriatic and Ligurian Seas and tucked in the valley of the Po River just beyond the Apennine Mountains, this part of Italy is known even today for its culinary delights. The area is renowned for its Parmi-giano cheese, while the city of Modena is famed for its tangy balsamic vinegar. The region's Lambrusco grapes produce a rich, sparkling wine.

Dorando's parents, Desiderio and Maria Teresa Incerti, had no money to indulge in such delicacies. Desiderio coaxed a meager income as a sharecropper, growing fruits and vegetables on a tiny wedge of land, barely more than a tenth of a hectare, and then loading his wares onto a pushcart to sell. Maria Teresa cooked up simple fare to fend off the hunger pangs of their four sons, Dorando coming after Antonio Ettore and Ulpiano Oreste, and followed by Armando.

Their poverty was dire, and probably contributed to Dorando's short stature. He later told a reporter that, despite the impoverished conditions, "we four boys inherited a strong constitution, and, so far, not a member of the family ever has had a serious illness."[7] In the same breath, he boasted that his mother was a "short, broad shoul-dered, and sturdy woman."

At least the timing of his birth was propitious, coming on the heels of a new direction for the country. In the early part of the nineteenth century, Italy was nothing more than "a geographical expression," in the oft-quoted words of Austrian diplomat Klemens von Metternich, divided into local fiefdoms and ruled by various interlopers. By 1871, the effort to unify the kingdom of Italy was finally completed, with Rome as its capital.

Nationhood sparked a prideful renaissance throughout Italy, but it did not prevent the country from suffering a severe economic down-turn shortly after Dorando was born, caused in no small part by the bountiful harvests produced by post–Civil War America. Farmers abandoned the countryside, fleeing to jobs in Turin and Milan, but also to South America, the United States, and other parts of Europe.

Approaching fifty, Desiderio had little education. He possessed no marketable skills, no capital, no land. In October 1897, when Dorando was twelve, the gray-haired and stern-faced Desiderio had little choice but to uproot the family and move to Carpi.

When the Pietri family arrived, Carpi was a flourishing city of perhaps 20,000 people, best known as a small-scale manufacturing hub of straw hats and derbies, shaped from the pliable willow wood and poplar found in the nearby Po River basin. The Pio Castle, named for the family that reigned for two centuries, sat in the center of town, fortified by an immense circular wall that gave protection from the outside world.

The family moved into a tiny place at Via della Mura di Levante ("Street of the East Wall"), some distance from the town center. There, by the gate leading to the road toward Modena, Desiderio and Maria Teresa opened a small fruit and vegetable shop.

Their two oldest sons soon left Carpi in search of better opportunities. To supplement the family's meager income, Dorando dropped out of school and took a job as a baker's assistant. His Italian biographer, Augusto Frasca, indicates that Dorando started working as an apprentice at the Pasticceria Roma (the Rome Pastry Shop) in 1899, when he was about fourteen. The business, owned by Pasquale Melli and his family, was prominently located on the Piazza dei Pio, Carpi's central plaza.

Dorando learned to bake bread, pastries, and sweets, and handled deliveries throughout the city. Despite the white-hot heat emanating from the ovens, the setting was more than satisfactory. Photographs show Dorando looking thin, but content, in a well-worn white apron. And why not? A boy accustomed to a steady diet of stale bread crusts suddenly had "the choice between an abundance of eggs, sugar, and *zabaglione* [a custard dessert spiked with sweet wine]. It let him smile at life."[3]

The job at Pasticceria Roma gave Dorando his first taste of an existence beyond subsistence, leading to the discovery of his athletic potential. Well before myth enveloped him like the florid black mustache that was soon to be plastered across his face, Dorando would find an outlet for his supreme endurance along the well-worn streets of Carpi.

Johnny Hayes stripped off his clothes and, with barely a pause, flung himself into the water. When he surfaced, he whistled to his brother, Willie, to join him in the murky depths of the Hudson River.

Freckle-faced and pale, with short-cropped hair neatly parted, Johnny was compact sized. He and Willie, a year younger, had snuck off to the river with a few friends. The sewage-infested waters were rank, but at least they offered temporary respite from another scorching summer day.

Treading water and peering at the shoreline, Johnny could feel the teeming hum emanating from America's first great metropolis. With its twelve-story skyscrapers, and an underground subway on the way, New York City at the turn of the twentieth century promised boundless opportunity, even to the poor immigrant families who inhabited the many dilapidated tenements.

The path from rags to riches in America was, seemingly, straightforward for youngsters like Johnny and Willie. Find a trade, work hard, be honest, avoid vice, and you will reap just rewards. At least, that was the message found in the dime novels of Horatio Alger.

With the sun setting, Johnny and Willie returned to shore and, as usual, jogged home barefoot to reality. Hell's Kitchen was a sweltering corridor of cacophonous noise and noxious odors; the swells riding past in their horse-drawn carriages kicked up dust that stuck to the boys' wet clothes.

Just rewards and rags to riches seemed a long way off.

Michael and Nellie Hayes had been married less than a year when their first son, John Joseph Hayes, was born on April 10, 1886.[4] Willie quickly followed, in 1887, and then came four younger siblings—Harriett (born in 1890), Alice (1891), Daniel (1894), and Phillip (1897).

The Hayeses moved often as the family grew, from 88th Street near First Avenue to 42nd Street to 45th Street. Their rented rooms were much the same everywhere they went: a small and dark space, without indoor toilet, hot water, or electricity, wedged between the overcrowded apartments of other immigrant families. The whisper-thin walls could not staunch the winter winds blowing off the river nor protect them from the fetid stench of human and animal excrement in the streets and alleys. On the warmest nights, Johnny slept on the fire escape.

Shortly after Johnny was born, reporter Jacob A. Riis journeyed through the city's ethnic slums with a notebook, a camera, a tripod, and enough magnesium-based flash powder to photograph the squalid conditions he chronicled. In these buildings, Riis wrote:

All the fresh air that ever enters these stairs comes from the hall-door that is forever slamming, and from the windows of dark bedrooms that in turn receive from the stairs their sole supply of the elements God meant to be free, but man deals out with such niggardly hand. The sinks are in the hallway, that all the tenants may have access—and all be poisoned alike by their summer stenches. Hear the pump squeak! It is the lullaby of tenement-house babes.[5]

Solace came in two forms: the church and the bottle. According to Riis, there were "111 Protestant churches, chapels, and places of worship of every kind below Fourteenth Street, 4,065 saloons. . . .

Where God builds a church the devil builds next door—a saloon, is an old saying that has lost its point in New York. Either the Devil was on the ground first, or he has been doing a good deal more in the way of building."[6]

To Michael Francis Hayes, the putrid conditions represented a fresh start. Johnny's father was born and raised in Nenagh,[7] a small city in County Tipperary, Ireland. The surrounding hillsides by the River Shannon turned into waves of emerald green in the summer and produced bountiful harvests: beets and wheat, flax for Irish linen, and, it was said, barley for the Guinness brewery. Blacksmiths and harness-makers stayed busy, and the Moylan's factory produced carriage coaches for the gentry.

It made for a good life—if you owned any land, that is. For Michael, prospects were bleak. His father, John, ran a small bakery from the family home on Silver Street. The elder Hayes prepared loaves of soda bread every morning, loading them onto a waiting horse-and-carriage and delivering them to his customers. There was no room in the modest operation for Michael.

The political situation was another affront. The regimen of British oppression, according to William O'Dwyer, the future mayor of New York City, "reaped [sic] havoc on the people of Ireland—or what was left of them—on their language, customs, culture, laws, art and, above all else, their self-esteem and dignity. The conquerors were truly masters, riding to the hounds over peasants' crops and treating them as waste beneath their feet."[8]

The practical solution was to emigrate. Everyone knew somebody— an aunt, a neighbor, a teacher—who had gone to America. Soon after the railroad reached Nenagh in 1862, the port cities of Cork and Liverpool became easily accessible. From there, one set sail across the Atlantic.

The story, as told in Nenagh, is that, in the spring of 1880, twenty-two-year-old Michael Hayes took the family cow to market and, instead of returning home with the money, bought a railway ticket to Queenstown. There, he boarded the SS *Egypt* in Liverpool, a four-masted steamer with room for about 1,400 people in steerage, bound for the new world.

About ten days later, on April 19, 1880, Michael arrived at the Castle Garden immigration station on the southern tip of Manhattan. Two years later, he had become an American citizen. Soon afterward, he met—or was set up to meet—Ellen O'Rourke from Poughkeepsie, a small town in the Hudson Valley midway between New York and Albany. Less than a year later, Nellie (as she was known) gave birth to their son John, named after Michael's father, as Irish tradition dictated.

Nellie O'Rourke was born in America. Her parents, Peter and Mary O'Rourke, were likely among those who fled Ireland in the aftermath of the potato famine that ravaged the countryside during the mid-1800s. This first wave of immigrants spooked longtime Manhattanites and the Boston Brahmin, who mocked the new arrivals' thick brogues and disapproved of their Catholicism. The immigrants were stereotyped as drunken louts apt to break into song or fisticuffs. The NO IRISH NEED APPLY signs that employers and landlords posted summed up this abhorrence, as did Thomas Nast's nasty caricatures of the indolent Irish in *Harper's Weekly*.

This did nothing to discourage a second wave of Irish immigrants, including Michael Hayes, and soon their sheer numbers overwhelmed the bluebloods. In the fastest-growing city in the nation, more than half of the population of New York City's 1.5 million people was born outside of the United States, according to the 1890 census. Some 40 percent of New Yorkers were of Irish extraction.[9]

The Irish wielded their numerical advantage like a policeman's baton, especially in New York and Boston, where they wrested control of the cities' political machines. John Kelly became the first Irishman to run New York's Tammany Hall, in 1874, and his countrymen filled the firemen and police department ranks and reached toward the middle class. Perhaps the most compelling evidence of their newfound influence could be found on Fifth Avenue, where St. Patrick's Cathedral, named for Ireland's patron saint, opened its doors in May 1879 as "the glory of Catholic America."[10]

This was the New York City that Johnny Hayes was born and raised in. Prejudice and stereotyping remained, as did crushing poverty. But somewhere between the saccharine optimism of Horatio Alger, the gloomy reality of Jacob Riis, and the patronage doled out by Tammany Hall, there was opportunity.

Thomas Charles Longboat was born on the Six Nations Reserve, located about seventy miles southwest of Toronto.[11] He entered into the world as an Onondaga as, by tradition, tribal identification passed down from his mother's side. The Onondaga share the territory of the Reserve with the Mohawk, Seneca, Oneida, Cayuga, and Tuscarora tribes. (Collectively, they are known as the Iroquois.)

Tom was part of the Wolf Clan, and his Indian name was Cogwagee, translated as "everything." The exact date of his birth remains in dispute. Many historians cite his birthdate as June 4, 1887, and Tom Longboat Day is celebrated annually on that day in Ontario. But Longboat himself, in his signed induction papers before World War I, gave the date as July 4, 1886.[12] It would not be the only time that mainstream Canada and the runner would find themselves at odds.

The undulating terrain of the Reserve—part meadow, part bush, part swamp—provided for the tribe's immediate needs. Tom's father, George, and his mother, the former Betsy Skye, farmed their small plot of land in the tribal village of Ohsweken. They grew the staples:

corn, beans, and potatoes, and had a few chickens, to supply eggs, and a cow for milk, butter, and cheese.

They were too poor to afford a plow-horse. Everything they dug, planted, and harvested was done by hand. Water for drinking, cooking, and cleaning came from the communal pump on the Reserve. They fished in the nearby Grand River.

Tom and two siblings, Lucy and Simon, were squeezed into the family's tiny log cabin constructed from pine, no bigger than eighteen feet long and fourteen feet wide. When Tom first achieved fame, a *Toronto Telegram* reporter ventured to the Reserve to see the Longboat home:

> Built of rough, hewn logs, now rotting away in spots, the crevices partially filled with mortar and topped by a roof, the shingles of which are warped by the weather of many a changing season, the Longboat home could hardly be equaled for simplicity or the lack of needless ornamentation. . . . [A]s if to emphasize its scorn for useless grandeur a shingle has replaced a pane of glass in the window, while the single stovepipe that serves as a chimney has been eaten away on one side till the smoke escapes on a level with the peak of the roof and threatens at any moment to further celebrate Tom's victories by making a bonfire of the whole stately edifice.[13]

At five, Tom watched in silent horror as his father died suddenly. He never spoke about this publicly, and the cause of death has never been reported, but George Longboat's death left a massive void. Certainly, it added pressure on an already struggling household. Tom helped out his mother as best he could: chopping and hauling wood for the stove, ferrying the heavy water pails to the house, feeding the livestock, planting and harvesting corn. When he grew older and bigger, he cut hay and picked apples for the white farmers to earn extra money. Later, he went to Burlington or Hamilton to work in the canneries after the harvests. Everywhere he went, he ran or walked.

What buttressed the family was their faith. Like many on the Reserve, Tom identified himself as *Haudenosaunee*, roughly translated as "People of the Longhouse." According to tradition, the longhouse represented how the Iroquois tribes should live together in harmony, under the roof of a narrow, bark-covered structure. (The Onondaga were situated in the middle of the longhouse and charged with keeping the fire burning.) The People of the Longhouse worshipped an Almighty creator known as the "Great Spirit," along with other, supernatural spirits; their religious festivals revolved around the planting, farming, and harvesting seasons.

Tribal coexistence with mainstream Canada was more challenging. Long before European settlers came to North America, the Iroquois occupied vast tracts on either side of Lake Erie, extending south to what would become New York state and stretching beyond the Mohawk River Valley to the Genesee River. The Onondaga were based in the geographical center of Iroquois lands around present-day Syracuse.

When the white men did come—the Dutch first, followed by the French and the British—the Iroquois established a flourishing trade with them, exchanging beaver pelts for guns and beads. Trading posts and colonies followed as the French and the British vied for supremacy of the Northeast corridor. The Indians were deemed to be under the protectorate of Britain after the Treaty of Utrecht in 1713. By 1763, at the conclusion of the French and Indian War, France had surrendered its claims to Canada, and Britain was left in control of the area.

The British soon faced another threat: American settlers, on the eve of the Revolutionary War, pushing west into the hinterlands of New York and Pennsylvania. The bloody skirmishes along the frontier caught the attention of General George Washington, who ordered Major General John Sullivan to eliminate the menace. Sullivan's Continental forces scorched the tribal villages to the earth in the summer of 1779.

Many Iroquois retreated north, to southern Ontario, beyond the new borders of the United States, where the British still ruled. In 1784, Mohawk leader Joseph Brant negotiated a land grant with England's King George III. The vast territory—said to be 6 miles wide on either side of the Grand River, extending from its source at Lake Erie—became the Six Nations Reserve and the permanent home of the Iroquois. A century later, the Reserve had shrunk to about 45,000 acres, primarily located south of the Grand River. Some 3,500 Iroquois lived on the Reserve.

By the late 1800s, around the time Tom Longboat was born, the centuries-old traditions of the Iroquois nation, at once insular and independent, were under siege. England, America, and other imperialist powers were crafting a series of ill-advised, racist laws to govern their Native populations. Their reasoning? The white man, having conquered the aboriginal people through military and numerical superiority (not to mention the spread of deadly diseases), was destined to lead the primitive races.

In Canada, the Indian Act gave the government blanket authority over the Native population. Shaping Indian youth into upstanding citizens became a priority, with the goal of eradicating the customs of the Iroquois, teaching them a vocational trade, and transforming the "practically unrestrained savages"[14] into so-called civilized adults.

Richard Henry Pratt, the longtime superintendent at the Carlisle

Indian Industrial school in Pennsylvania, explained the reasoning this way: "Carlisle's mission is to kill THIS Indian, as we build up the better man. We give the rising Indian something nobler and higher to think about and do, and he comes out a young man with the ambitions and aspirations of his more favored white brother. We do not like to keep alive the stories of his past, hence deal more with his present and his future."[15]

When Tom was around twelve, he was forcibly removed from home and family and taken to the Mohawk Institute Residential School, a three-story red brick building on the outskirts of Brantford. The school was run by the New England Company, part of the Church of England, to promulgate "the Gospel of Jesus Christ amongst the heathen natives."[16]

Tom's thick black hair was cropped short, his clothes discarded and replaced by a uniform. He was not allowed to speak in the Onondaga tongue, even with fellow tribe members, and he was forced to read, write, and speak in English. He had to sing Christian hymns and worship a deity that he did not comprehend.

Work was draining and constant. Tom rose at 5:30 in the morning and labored in the fields until noon. In the afternoons, he had school lessons. Nights were devoted to prayer. Discipline was administered by the rod; there was no summer vacation. During the winters, as the winds sweeping off Lake Erie lashed the school, the children shivered under their thin blankets.

According to one account from 1895, students "had porridge for breakfast every day and also for supper five times a week."[17] That earned the Mohawk Institute its not-so-endearing nickname: "The Mush Hole."

The inner turmoil the children suffered was perhaps more profound than their hunger pains. "You felt the separation from your culture, [y]our own homes and languages," remembered one boy. "They wanted the children to be ashamed of their culture and origin."[18]

Tom vowed not to accept the cruel punishments and the stifling atmosphere of the Mohawk Institute. He stewed in silence and decided to run away at the earliest opportunity.

THREE

J ohnny Hayes switched schools often, and his formal education came in shards.[1] He helped out his mother and supervised the younger siblings. In the days before child-labor laws, he sometimes worked alongside his father at Cushman's bakery, enduring the searing flashes of heat as the breads were removed from the ovens.

He was a serious young man, forced to mature quickly, but he found release through sports. He first learned to run playing with the other neighborhood kids on the 42nd Street hill near First Avenue. The rough-and-tumble neighborhood was known as Cochran's Roost, in honor of Paddy Cochran's old gang stronghold, and its main feature was the horrid odors of the slaughterhouses by the East River. There, Johnny used his size—or lack thereof—to outmaneuver the bigger kids in games of tag and handball.

Occasionally, the Hayeses visited Nellie's family in Poughkeepsie. Johnny welcomed the fresh air of the countryside, and he loved to tear loose along the open plank roads of the Hudson Valley. He'd race Willie south toward Wappingers Falls, or north toward Hyde Park, home to the swank summer residences of New York City's wealthiest. Afterward, they'd jump into the Hudson River to cool off.

Scrawny and undersized, Johnny was discovering his limitations. He wasn't built for sprinting, where the larger and stronger boys held an advantage. But he found that he could run vast distances, over long periods of time, whether it was in Poughkeepsie or on the streets of New York. When the other boys were clutching their sides and doubled over, Johnny was getting warmed up.

So, too, sports in America was warming up.[1] With the dark memories of the Civil War fading and the creation of something called leisure time, a disparate group of politicians, religious leaders, businessmen, educators, and civic boosters were turning athletics into a moral crusade, a movement often described as "muscular Christianity." Fitness advocates like Theodore Roosevelt and Dr. Luther Gulick, the lead ambassador for the Young Men's Christian Association (YMCA) in the United States, were convinced that exercise was an essential, moral tool for a population fleeing the rigors of farm labor for the sedentary city life. Gulick directed one of his YMCA instructors to concoct an indoor activity that could be played during the winter. Soon, James Naismith was posting the thirteen rules for something called "Basket-ball." Four years later, William Morgan, another YMCA staffer, invented volleyball.

Simultaneously, the country's entrepreneurial bent created another avenue for sports. The Cincinnati Red Stockings, the nation's first professional baseball team, launched a national barnstorming tour in 1869 that netted big profits; the National League, baseball's first pro league, formed in 1876. Former pitching great-turned-entrepreneur Albert G. Spalding and his brother, Walter, formed an eponymous sporting-goods company that established itself as the original Nike. Spalding manufactured and sold affordable uniforms, tennis racquets, and shoes for the masses. A new breed of celebrity athletes emerged; fans couldn't get enough of ballplayers like Mike "King" Kelly, known as the "$10,000 Beauty" (and said to be the model for Ernest Thayer's "Casey at the Bat").

The growth of sports could only have happened with the myriad innovations of the Industrial Age, when "[a] world of stone and wood, powered by animals, wind and water was completely remade into something entirely new, forged of steel and iron, and powered by steam, coal, and oil," according to historian Gavin Weightman.[3] The flurry of construction that created an efficient railroad system enabled, say, the New York Giants to travel to Boston to play the Braves. Spectators now could gather during the winters and at night at indoor palaces like Madison Square Garden—heated by coal, built of steel and iron, illuminated by Thomas Edison's electric lights. Advances in rubber manufacturing led to durable tires for bicycles.

Improvements in the printing press—and the inventions of the typewriter, the telegraph, and the linotype machine—produced cheap, daily newspapers that enabled fans to follow their teams' fortunes. Publisher Richard Kyle Fox created the first sports page within the shocking pink sheets of his *National Police Gazette*; soon, Joseph Pulitzer was launching the first sports department at a daily paper, the *New York World*, and watching circulation soar. Publications like *Outing*, a monthly helmed by editor Caspar Whitney, and *Physical Culture*, from fitness guru Bernarr Macfadden, extolled the virtues of competition and a healthy diet.[4]

Trappings of British exclusivity remained at the Ivy League colleges and at private organizations like the New York Athletic Club. But the Irish diaspora was creating its own sports culture for newly minted immigrants like Michael Hayes. Many still practiced traditional Gaelic games, like handball and hurling (a cross between field hockey and lacrosse). At the so-called Hibernian carnivals, the burliest men competed to see who could throw fifty-six-pound weights the farthest. Smaller men competed in cross-country races of five miles. In New York, the Irish-American Athletic Club (I-ACC) built Celtic Park in Queens, an athletic paradise complete with a running track, a football field, seating for 10,000 people, and a clubhouse for social events.

The Irish also cashed in professionally. In the manly arts, Paddy

Ryan, John L. Sullivan, and "Gentleman Jim" Corbett ruled the heavy-weight ranks from 1880 to 1895, with the "Great John L." donning green shorts before dishing out his vicious brand of bare-knuckled punishment. (The fighters took pleasure in reminding journalists that the word "donnybrook" came from the Dublin neighborhood renowned for its brawls.) Baseball in the dead-ball era was dominated by Irishmen like John "Muggsy" McGraw, Wee Willie Keeler (who "hit 'em where they ain't"), Mike "King" Kelly, Hugh Duffy, "Iron Man" McGinnity, "Big Ed" Walsh, the Delahanty brothers.

"By the turn of the [twentieth century], it had become equally clear that none could run like them, nor fight like them," commented historians Nathan Glazer and Daniel Moynihan. "When it came to diving off the Brooklyn Bridge or winning pennants for the Giants, it took an Irishman."[5]

Johnny and Willie loved to go to Celtic Park to watch the fastest athletes on the track and the behemoths in the weight events. Their favorite spot was the Polo Grounds in upper Manhattan, where their beloved New York Giants played baseball, the sport fast becoming the national pastime and described by Mark Twain as "the very symbol, the outward and visible expression of the drive, and push, and rush and struggle of the raging, tearing, booming nineteenth century."[6]

Like many kids, Johnny aspired to play baseball and to be a Giant. But his path to sports fame would come through an unorthodox race, the marathon, that did not exist before 1896.

I n 1903, the students set fire to the campus of the Mohawk Institute, destroying the main building and several barns.[7] Tom Longboat was not involved in the arson. Not long after he was forced to enroll at Mohawk, and displaying for perhaps the first time the awesome combination of speed and stamina that would make him a world-famous runner within the decade, Tom fled the Mohawk Institute and returned to his family's home on the Six Nations Reserve.

School authorities found him and dragged him back to Brantford. He simmered, then escaped again and hid out with an uncle. This time, he was left alone.

Later, after he had become the most celebrated athlete in Canada, the Mohawk Institute asked Tom Longboat to speak at the school about his experiences. He declined. "If I was ever to go back, I would just tell them how I was abused," he told his son. "If I had my way, I wouldn't even send my dog to that place."[8]

Back home on the Reserve, Tom was growing into a lanky, gangly teen. The family did not own a horse, and the Reserve had yet to see its first automobile, so Tom used the only form of transportation he could access: his two legs.

He ran everywhere: to the river, to visit family and friends, to look for work at nearby farms. He was a familiar sight, pounding along the winding roads that turned to soggy mush every spring after the snows melted. He soon could reach Brantford, about twelve miles away, in a sustained burst. He ran barefoot unless he could cadge a pair of shoes.

His prowess was not unique. Tribes throughout North America, especially the Hopi and the Tarahumara in the southwest, venerated endurance running. Iroquois messengers ran from one end of the Mohawk Confederacy to the other, bringing news from the Atlantic Seaboard to the Niagara frontier. Naturalist author Ernest Thompson Seton recalled seeing a Cree, who "on foot, had just brought dispatches from Fort Qu'Appelle (125 miles away) in 25 hours."[9]

By tradition, warriors ran into battle. Hunters ran down prey by tracking them to exhaustion. They ran to test the limits of their bodies, and they ran for spiritual reasons, to "induce rain to fill the dry arroyos . . . and to control the course of the sun. . . . The object was not to win but to push your body to exhaustion; only then would life's vitality be lent to the recalcitrant forces of nature."[10]

Later, Tom was quoted as saying that there were other runners on the Reserve who were as talented as he was, that somehow he had followed a different path and competed in races outside the Reserve, against the world's best in the United States and in Europe. He never said whether that was a positive thing.

Tom also played *Deyhontsigwa'ehs* for his Onondaga team. The Iroquois considered *Deyhontsigwa'ehs*, the centuries-old stick-and-ball game known today as lacrosse, to be a sacred experience. Every element of the sport linked players to the Creator. Sticks were hand carved from branches of hickory trees,[11] with pockets crafted from leather. Balls were made of deerskin or rawhide, stuffed with hair. The players wore only a tight breech cloth. As if to mimic the infinite almighty, *Deyhontsigwa'ehs* was contested without boundaries or a time clock.

In a sport that demands speed, strength, and endurance, Longboat excelled. He may have been a better lacrosse player than a runner. In one match, against another Native Indian team in Buffalo in 1906, "It fell to Tom to check Devil Krause, a big Indian who was a very dirty player," recalled an observer. "He laid into Tom, but Tom came right back at him and gave him a good trimming. Tom's speed and staying powers struck me as the feature of the game."[12]

Lacrosse offered one of the few occasions where white Canadians and Native Indians faced off as equals, with the first lacrosse game between them dating to 1844. Soon afterward, a Montreal dentist named William George Beers transformed the ancient game by codifying the rules, reducing the dimensions of the field, limiting the number of players, and imposing time restrictions.

According to Beers, "only a savage people could, would or should play the old game. Only such constitutions, such wind and endurance could stand its violence. The present game, improved and reduced to rule by the whites, employs the greatest combination of physical and mental activity white men can sustain in recreation, and is as much superior to the original as civilization is to barbarism, base ball to its old English parent of rounders, or a pretty Canadian girl to any uncultivated squaw."[13]

Beers's comment comes across as racist today, but this was the prevailing viewpoint of mainstream Canada. This same attitude would soon ensnare Tom Longboat. While his supreme talent was undeniable, many felt his "primitive" gift required the structure and guidance of the white man.

Just entering his teens, Dorando Pietri stood five foot three beneath an unruly mop of jet-black hair. He always seemed to be in motion, whether he was hustling to deliver a package from the Pasticceria Roma or trailing his older brother, Ulpiano, on forays outside the walls of Carpi. He ran everywhere he went.

He got no encouragement, or understanding, from his parents. For a *contadino* like Desiderio Pietri, sports had never been an option. "Father had no time for athletics," Dorando later said. "In fact, they did not know what athletics were in those days."[14]

Modern sport in postunification Italy trailed the United States and much of Europe. It was a nascent endeavor, with the northern part of the country leading the way. Soccer, an import from Britain, was developing a passionate following. Locals called it *Calcio*, or "kickball," from an early version of the sport, and villages fielded their own squads. Organized matches followed, with Club Juventus forming in 1897 in Turin, and the predecessor of A.C. Milan, originally a cricket and football club, organizing in 1899.

The sport that captured the imagination of all Italians—rich and poor, old and young, male and female—was cycling. Introduced as a "two-wheeled, foot-cranked velocipede" in the 1860s, the bicycle was considered a technological marvel. Before they flew airplanes, Orville and Wilbur Wright built and repaired bicycles in their shop in Dayton, Ohio. Before he designed and produced automobiles, Henry Ford studied the physics of motion as a bike mechanic. John Dunlop, a Scottish veterinarian based in Belfast, invented pneumatic (air-filled) tires because he wanted to remove the bumps his son encountered whenever he rode his tricycle.[15]

The spinning wheels represented freedom and speed at a time when personal transportation was defined by horses, mules, and one's two legs. One early enthusiast, Sir Arthur Conan Doyle, wrote in 1896: "When the spirits are low, when the day appears dark, when work becomes monotonous, when hope seems hardly worth having, just mount a bicycle and go out for a spin down the road, without thought on anything but the ride you are taking."[16]

From Milan, Edoardo Bianchi and his pioneering machines (among the first to feature same-size wheels) won international acclaim when Giovanni Tommasello captured the Grand Prix de Paris in 1899. Cycling was such a phenomenon that it inspired the start-up of Italy's first sports newspaper, La Gazzetta dello Sport. The daily journal publicized all of the provincial races and sponsored two prestigious contests that are active today: the Milan–San Remo race (started in 1907) and the multi-staged Giro d'Italia, first held in 1909.

The first time Dorando Pietri saw a bicycle in motion he was transfixed. He couldn't afford to buy one, but in Carpi he had an outlet for his enthusiasm. In 1879, eight local men had created the Società Ginnastica La Patria (roughly translated as the "The Fatherland"). The purpose of La Patria, as the club was known, was to "preserve the development of the physical forces of youth and cultivate the spirit of brotherhood among citizens of every class, in the supreme interest of the nation."[17]

Dorando followed his older brother, Ulpiano, and joined *La Patria*. He hounded club members to borrow their bikes. Within a few years, *La Patria* would provide Dorando with a base for his athletic career, one shaped not by the bicycle but by the revival of the ancient Olympic Games.

Today, it's difficult to imagine the sports landscape without the Olympic Games. No other event—not the World Cup, the World Series, or the Super Bowl—matches their global impact. The number of countries represented at the 2008 Beijing Olympics was 204. There are 192 member states in the United Nations.

The world's biggest cities spend millions of dollars bidding for the right to host the Olympics; the selected host city spends billions of dollars constructing stadiums and swimming pools and providing security for what is a two-week event. Television networks compete for the right to broadcast the Games because they generate huge ratings and advertising dollars. Corporations like Coca-Cola and Nike line up to associate themselves with the Olympic brand, in no small part because its legion of heroes—Jim Thorpe, Paavo Nurmi, Kitei Son, Jesse Owens, Sonja Henie, Abebe Bikila, Muhammad Ali, Jean-Claude Killy, Olga Korbut, Frank Shorter, Nadia Comeneci, Joan Benoit, Katarina Witt, Johan Olav Koss, Shawn White, Usain Bolt, to name but a few—transcends gender, race, religion, nationality, and class, and resonates from Beijing to Berlin to Barcelona to Beverly Hills.

And yet, when Pierre de Coubertin first lobbied for the Olympics in 1892, the idea was nothing short of audacious.[18] The nascent sports culture in North America and Europe that was attracting the likes of Tom Longboat, Johnny Hayes, and Dorando Pietri did not include large-scaled and international events. The first Davis Cup (1900), Tour de France (1903), and World Cup (1930) were in the future, as were the first Rose Bowl game (1902) and the first World Series (1903).

Coubertin, a French baron, was enamored of the spirit of the ancient Games at Olympia, located on the western edge of the Peloponnesian peninsula, about 200 miles west of Athens. The Games were contested every four years, beginning in 776 BC, with a month-long truce declared throughout Greece so that athletes and spectators could travel peacefully to the verdant vale.

There, the fastest and the strongest faced off before crowds of tens of thousands. The all-male athletes competed in the nude—women were barred from Olympia—and the five-day schedule grew to include jumping events, javelin and discus throws, wrestling, boxing, chariot contests, and *pankration* (a violent sport that was the original version of mixed-martial arts). Winners earned a wreath made of olive branches and were handsomely rewarded when they returned home, with lifetime stipends and other benefits. Their patrons made religious sacrifices and paid tribute to the gods by building ever-more splendid monuments.

The Games at Olympia continued after Greece was folded into the Roman Empire. They ceased in 394, on the command of Theodosius the Great, on the grounds of paganism. The grounds fell into disrepair due to earthquakes, invasion, and neglect, and the site was abandoned in the seventh century.

In the late nineteenth century, archeologists uncovered the ruins of Olympia, which ignited a fresh fascination with the Games. Coubertin became one such advocate; his effort to reignite the Olympic flame was so all consuming, and so defined him, that the baron later claimed to be the "sole author of the whole project," as if he had conjured the spirit of Olympia from the dustbin of antiquity with one twirl of his walking stick. That was a gross exaggeration. But while he did not single-handedly birth the modern Games, it was Coubertin who handpicked the International Olympic Committee (IOC) to organize and manage the structure of the competition, and it was Coubertin who arranged for the inaugural Olympics of 1896 to take place in Athens. A more accurate description might be found in a nickname: *Le Renovateur*—"The Reviver."

Coubertin's motivation for restoring the Olympics continues to be debated. What's known is that Coubertin, an Anglophile whose sacred text was *Tom Brown's Schooldays,* used his family's wealth to coalesce interest in reviving the Olympics among like-minded advocates in Europe and America. On one such recruiting trip to New York City, he was introduced to a failed mayoral candidate, the recently widowed Theodore Roosevelt, who had grown up asthmatic at a time when the illness was considered life threatening. Exercise became his salvation, and, like Coubertin, he had the means to pursue "the strenuous life"—horseback riding, rowing, hunting, boxing. Coubertin and Roosevelt bonded and, upon his return home, Coubertin inundated Roosevelt with his voluminous writings.

Coubertin's inspiration for the Games, as a modern spectacle with global impact, came from the most popular form of mass entertainment during the latter half of the nineteenth century. World's Fairs were the equivalent of today's technology conventions, Middle Eastern bazaars, art walks, and amusement parks rolled into one sprawling package.[19] In 1878, a teenaged Pierre and 16 million other patrons of the Universal Exposition in Paris gawked at Lady Liberty's gigantic head, Auguste Bartholdi's topper to the Statue of Liberty that was being readied for transport to America, and the telephone device developed by Alexander Graham Bell at his family's home in Ontario (not far from where Tom Longboat was born).

At the 1889 World's Fair, with over 32 million attendees, Coubertin presented a study about athletic education. That received scant attention compared to Gustave Eiffel's soaring iron tower, at nearly 1,000 feet the highest structure built by man, and Annie Oakley, guns a-blazing, performing at Buffalo Bill's Wild West Show. In 1893, Coubertin was one of 27 million visitors to Chicago's "White City," where the World's Columbian Exposition commemorated the 400th anniversary of Christopher Columbus's voyage to America.

Coubertin's Olympics would meld the sense of wonderment and progress found at the World's Fairs with the top-flight competition, solemn rituals, and harmonic peace derived from ancient Greece. From the World's Fairs came the concept of rotating host cities; from Olympia, the idea of a quadrennial event. His Olympics, Coubertin insisted, "would bring the representatives of the nations of the world face to face every four years, and it may be thought that their peaceful and chivalrous contests would constitute the best of internationalism."[20]

Coubertin's initial effort to restart the Olympics, in 1892, failed, but on the morning of June 23, 1894, after wining and dining a congress of handpicked sports and education leaders in Paris, his proposal to revive the Olympics succeeded. Enthusiasm was so widespread that, rather than wait to inaugurate the Games in 1900, as Coubertin had planned, Athens was awarded the Olympics for 1896. A motto—*Citius, Altius, Fortius* ("Swifter, Higher, Stronger")—was adopted.

At the closing banquet, Coubertin toasted the occasion: "I raise my glass to the Olympic idea which, like a ray of the all-powerful sun, has pierced the mists of the ages . . . to illuminate the threshold of the twentieth century with joy and hope."[21]

FOUR

In September 1894, as he was planning the inaugural Olympics, Pierre de Coubertin received a letter from noted linguist and fellow Olympic enthusiast Michel Bréal. Coubertin should consider adding a long-distance running event to the 1896 Olympic program, Bréal wrote, one that would start in the village of Marathon and conclude at the Pnyx hill, near the Acropolis, in Athens.

Such a test would resonate with historic overtones by emphasizing "the character of Antiquity," Bréal noted. "If we knew the time the Greek warrior took, we would be able to establish the record. For my part, I would beg the honor of presenting a Marathon Cup [to the winner]."[1]

Bréal, it appears, was confusing Olympic history with ancient myth. No marathon race was ever held at Olympia; the longest running event at the ancient Games measured perhaps twenty-four lengths of the track, or approximately three miles. Bréal also appears to be referring to a courier named Pheidippides, who was a footnote in one of the most famous military battles in history. In 490 BC, Greece came under attack by King Darius of Persia, who crossed the Aegean Sea and, with an estimated 25,000 Persian soldiers, set up camp on the plain of Marathon, northeast of Athens. King Darius intended to march to Athens and destroy the city in reprisal for its support of the Ionian revolt against him.

The panicked, vastly outnumbered Athenians dispatched Pheidippides, a trained messenger, to Sparta, some 150 miles distant, to ask for assistance. The courier returned, in mere days, with the grim news that the Spartans were unable to help and that Athens would have to go it alone.

About 10,000 Athenian soldiers immediately marched to Marathon. In a furious onslaught, they whipped Darius and his outsize force, with the reported loss of only 192 lives. A different herald then allegedly raced from the battlefield to Athens, a distance of about twenty-five miles, to announce that the Greeks had miraculously prevailed in Marathon.

"Rejoice, we conquer!" he supposedly announced, before collapsing and dying on the spot.

Or so the legend goes. The historian Herodotus does not mention this Marathon–Athens run in his definitive account of the battle. Nor does he write about the death of any courier. The tale is probably a myth.[2]

But Coubertin was delighted to connect a glorious event from ancient Greek history with his modern Games, no matter its origin or veracity. He took Bréal's suggestion and added the Marathon–Athens run to the 1896 Olympic program, changing the final destination to the Panathenaic Stadium in Athens, despite the fact that no amateur athlete was training for, much less competing in, endurance races of approximately 25 miles. The next longest race on the Olympic program measured 1,500 meters (or, just under one mile).

With the marathon, Michel Bréal and Pierre de Coubertin had concocted an anomaly, one that would attract only the inexperienced, the ignorant, and the intrepid.

As the 1896 Athens Olympics drew near, Pierre de Coubertin pleaded with his international colleagues to supply athletes and spectators. He was staggeringly ineffective. Fifteen countries sent competitors to Greece, with England's team totaling ten men, the United States's fourteen, Italy's one, and Canada's none. Only the host, ninety-eight strong, fielded a substantial squad.

The U.S. team was a patched-together collection of club athletes and college students, with four from Princeton and six from Harvard, including one dropout, South Boston's James Connolly. The Boston Athletic Association (B.A.A.) supplied funds and a coach, John Graham, to supervise the men. They arrived in Athens two days before the Games to find a city burning with Olympic fever. Banners and bunting emblazoned with the initials o.a. (the Greek abbreviation for "Olympic Games") hung from stores.[3] The names of Miltiades Gouskos and Sotirios Versis, local favorites in the shot put and discus, found their way into every conversation. The marble benches of Panathenaic Stadium gleamed a brilliant white after an expensive face-lift.

On the afternoon of April 6, Coubertin repaired to the section of the Stadium reserved for IOC officials and watched approximately 250 athletes congregate in the middle of the infield. With spectators straining to hear—there were no microphones, loudspeakers, or Jumbotrons—Greece's King George I rose to address the crowd: "I declare the opening of the first international Olympic games in Athens. Long live the nation! Long live the Greek people!"[4]

The applause had scarcely faded away when, with a leap of nearly forty-five feet in the triple jump, James Connolly was crowned the first Olympic champion since 369. The most anticipated event of the day was the discus, with Versis expected to prevail. But Princeton's Robert Garrett snatched the upset on his final throw.

This set the tone for the rest of the Games. Intermittent rain and cold weather held down attendance, while athletes from the host country disappointed. As dawn broke on April 10, the fifth day of competition, all of Athens seethed with frustration. One hope remained: the marathon.

The hosts had embraced Bréal's creation. They held two trial races over the Marathon–Athens course—they are now considered to be the first true marathons ever held—and entered thirteen runners.[5] The course was measured to be forty kilometers, or just under twenty-five miles.

Some observers worried that anyone foolhardy enough to run such a distance would keel over and die, just like the mythic herald. But many viewed it as a test of character for a fledgling nation grasping for its identity. To the winner would come many spoils: A fetching young lady, identified only as "Mlle. Y,"[6] was promised to the first-place finisher (provided he was Greek). Local restaurateurs guaranteed the victor free meals for life—offers that were seconded by tailors, barbers, and hatters.

The day before the race, during a driving rainstorm, officials transported the competitors by horse-and-carriage to Marathon. They spent a fitful night together at a local inn and drank plenty of wine. The next morning, the competitors were given breakfast: milk and a couple of beers apiece. They changed into their uniforms and shoes and, at 2 p.m., lined up at Marathon Bridge to await the signal from the starter, one Major Papadiamantopoulos. Accompanying them were escorts on bicycles, soldiers on horseback, and a medical wagon.

Alongside the thirteen Greek men were four foreigners, including Harvard's Arthur Blake, who had finished second in the 1,500 meters. France's Albin Lermusiaux had competed in the 100-meter sprint. He summed up his strategy for the marathon this way: "One day I run a leetle way, vairy queek. Ze next day, I run a long way, vairy slow."[7]

The cool temperatures encouraged a fast start. Lermusiaux, wearing white gloves, maneuvered to the front at the gun, trailed by Blake and Edwin Flack, an Australian accountant who had won the 800- and 1,500-meter races.

Lermusiaux opened up a big advantage and held the lead through the first half of the race. Flack and Blake followed. But their inexperience running such a long distance soon showed. Just past the midway point, as the stony road veered uphill, the quick pace took its toll. Blake, with "a pair of legs like dividers," collapsed after fifteen miles. At the eighteen-mile mark, Lermusiaux could run no more. Flack moved into first and, with about five miles remaining, appeared poised to win.

Lurking behind the leaders was small, sunburned Spiridon Louis, a twenty-four-year-old water carrier from nearby Marousi, who daily jogged alongside his mule lugging barrels of water to Athens. After pausing for a pick-me-up glass of red wine, Louis approached Flack and refused to let him surge ahead until, near the village of Ampelokipi, the Australian crumpled.

Ahead in Athens, nearly three hours after the start, a crowd of over 100,000 waited anxiously in the stadium and on the surrounding hillsides. Waving blue-and-white flags, they resembled "bees clustering over a comb,"[8] according to one eyewitness.

A cannon shot thundered through the sky, followed closely by a rumor that Flack was ahead. A mournful silence descended.

Then, in a blur, Major Papadiamantopoulos rode into the stadium and hurried to the royal box. King George stood and began waving his gold-embroidered cap. Faster than you could say, "Papadiamantopoulos," word spread: Hellene! Hellene! ("A Greek! A Greek!")

A mass of bodies approached the stadium. At the head of the pack was Louis—dusty, parched, and bedraggled—his cracked shoes almost worn through, more survivor than champion. To a throaty roar he entered Panathenaic Stadium.

Greece's Prince Constantine and Prince George leaped from the royal box to the field and ferried Louis to the finish. He crossed the tape in 2:58:50, putting him nearly 8 minutes ahead of countryman Charilaos Vasilakos. Hungary's Gyula Kellner, the only foreigner to finish, was third.

Louis's victory was like a lightning bolt sent directly from Mount Olympus. Grown men Frisbeed their hats into the air and hugged one another, while women wept and waved linen handkerchiefs. White pigeons were released to the heavens. As the spectators exulted, Pierre de Coubertin stood applauding, a broad grin visible beneath his florid black mustache.

The long-distance test invented from ancient myth, an event that attracted the largest sports crowd to that point in history, had ensured the successful launch of the modern Olympics.

Spiridon Louis never competed in another marathon. He declined all marriage and job offers and retired to Maroussi with the silver cup donated by Michel Bréal. Photographs taken the day after the race showed Louis attired in a *fustanella*, a traditional folk costume with a poofy white skirt that flared like a pompadour.

Coubertin and Bréal envisioned the marathon as a signature event for the 1896 Athens Olympics. They did not intend for the marathon to spread beyond, well, Marathon. What they had invented, athletically, was unique. It was sui generis. It did not come from the playing fields of Eton or from the imagination of a YMCA instructor. It was not drawn up in the New York Athletic Club or sponsored by the Spalding company or sanctioned by the Amateur Athletic Union. It did not have an official distance.

But word of Louis's dramatic victory—his very survival—was met with wonderment. "The innate endurance of the Greek peasants prevailed in the great test," travel writer Burton Holmes remarked, "over the scientific training of the 'American Invincibles.'"[9]

And what one writer has called "the most audacious of races" soon secured a foothold in the burgeoning sporting scene. Marathons were held in France (for professionals only), Hungary, Norway, and Denmark in 1896, with Germany (1898), Italy (1898), and Sweden (1899) soon to follow.[10]

No doubt spectators were drawn to it because of its perceived peril: a runner might die in front of them. But the marathon came along at a time when mankind was rushing to explore its limits, whether that meant taking flight in an airplane or building an underground subway system or racing to discover the Arctic. And, while the marathon was a race against other competitors, it was also a contest against the elements (the weather, the terrain), the clock, and each runner's physical and emotional capabilities.

Dorando Pietri was ten when the ancient Olympics were revived. The marathon received much of the attention, in Italy and elsewhere, with Louis's humble background spotlighted. That resonated with Dorando: Louis had sacrificed his body to bring athletic glory to his village and his country. It was the stuff of heroes, and Dorando was impressed. He tried to fathom exactly how far Louis had run. Forty kilometers—he had scarcely traveled forty kilometers in his entire life.

For Tom Longboat and Johnny Hayes, word about the marathon came not from Athens or Paris, but from their own backyard. Johnny was ten when the first marathon in the new world took place. On September 19, 1896, New York City's Knickerbocker Athletic Club held a twenty-five-miler that started at the town square in Stamford, Connecticut, where twenty-eight hardy souls gathered wearing "loose, knee-length drawers . . . to fulfill the Victorian need for modesty," and "low-cut leather running shoes," according to historian Pamela Cooper.[11]

Hamilton Gray, the reigning ten-mile champ, was the favorite, but the Pastime Athletic Club's John McDermott stole the spotlight. He and Gray cruised south through Connecticut and along the muddy byways of Westchester before McDermott left Gray behind shortly after passing through New Rochelle. He finished with a flourish, circling the Columbia Oval in the Bronx to exuberant cheers.

According to the *New York Times*, the debut U.S. marathon was a crowd-pleaser: "Men dashed from their seats and down beside the track to get a look at the Americo-Marathon victor. There was a pandemonium of joy. Judges stopped their work; athletes found time to become spectators."[12]

Meanwhile, trainer John Graham had returned from the 1896 Olympics bowled over by the Greeks' exuberant reaction to the marathon. He broached the idea of staging a marathon in Boston that would commemorate the midnight rides of Paul Revere and William Dawes from 1775, warning American revolutionaries of an imminent British attack. Members of the B.A.A. agreed to back Graham's effort.[13]

Graham was unable to arrange a route from Concord, so he and businessman Herbert Holton mounted bicycles and headed west from the B.A.A.'s plush five-story headquarters on the corner of Boylston and Exeter streets. They followed the Boston & Albany railroad tracks, past Newton and Wellesley College and Natick, until, with the cyclometer nudging twenty-five miles, they found themselves in the hamlet of Ashland.

That would be the starting point, with the ending to take place at the Irvington Street track near the B.A.A. clubhouse in Boston's Back Bay. The course roughly mimicked the topography of the Marathon–Athens route, with alternately flat and hilly sections, one later described as "14 miles of fun, eight miles of sweat and four miles of hell."[14]

Graham enlisted the local regiment to organize a bicycle and ambulance corps to follow the action, with cyclists carrying drink and lemons for the runners. He also arranged for the spectators waiting at the finish to get updates on the leaders via telephone communication along the course.

Raved the *Boston Post* on the eve of the race: GREAT INTEREST IN THE EVENT ALL ALONG THE TWENTY-FIVE MILE COURSE—SOMEWHAT LIKE THE ORIGINAL MARATHON HIGHWAY.[15] (The course actually measured 24.7 miles.)

On Patriots' Day, or just over a year to the day after Louis's victory, fifteen men lined up in front of Metcalf's Mill in Ashland. No starter's gun was available, so two-time Athens Olympic winner Tom Burke yelled, "Go!" to begin the race at 12:19 p.m.

A crowd of 25,000 people lined the roads and urged Hamilton Gray and Harvard's Dick Grant to an early lead. But the Pastime's McDermott, who had journeyed from New York, knew to pace himself well. The Irish-American lithographer passed Gray and Grant between Wellesley and Newton and, after stopping for a hasty massage, overcame cramps and a pair of bloody and blistered feet to take the first Boston Marathon, this time by more than a mile in 2:55:10. Ten of the fifteen starters finished the race.

The Irvington Street oval was so crowded that "the fences were black with boys, young men and women," according to the *Globe*.[16] The crowd greeted the victor with "deafening" cheers and hoisted him on their shoulders. Concluded the reporter: "It was by the hardest kind of reasoning that [McDermott] escaped and ran to the B.A.A. clubhouse."[17]

L ike Spiridon Louis, John McDermott is now a footnote in marathon history. But after his popular win, Graham and the B.A.A. decided to turn their marathon into an annual tradition on Patriots'

Day. The second Boston Marathon drew twenty-five runners, the third race seventeen.

The 1900 edition, with twenty-nine starters, added international flavor as three runners from Hamilton, Ontario—Jack Caffery, Billy Sherring, and Fred Highson—swept to a one-two-three Canadian flush. Caffery's time of 2:39:44 shattered the course record. "Nothing was left to the Bostonians but the credit of being able to cook pork and beans to perfection," crowed the *Hamilton Spectator*.[18]

The results shocked the local pundits, but insiders knew that Hamilton, a gritty steel city nicknamed the "Birmingham of Canada," was becoming a long-distance running mecca. Back in 1894, the *Hamilton Herald* had sponsored the Around the Bay race, now recognized as North America's first endurance race of the modern era. Caffery had won the nineteen-miler in 1898; Sherring triumphed the following year.

In 1901, Caffery repeated in Boston, with William Davis, a Mohawk Indian from Hamilton, second. On July 4, 1901, James E. Sullivan organized a marathon as part of the athletic program at the Pan-American Exposition in Buffalo, New York (the World's Fair best known for being the place where President William McKinley was assassinated).

Sullivan was the head of the Amateur Athletic Union (AAU) and the nation's power broker for amateur sports. In Buffalo, he scheduled the twenty-five-miler to start and finish in the arena, reasoning that "The Stadium without a Marathon race would be like a Romeo without a Juliet."

It was a blisteringly hot day, "totally unfit for such a long race," according to Sullivan.[19] In front of a partisan crowd bent on enjoying the nation's 125th birthday, Yonkers' Samuel Mellor staggered home first in over 3¼ hours. Runner-up again was Davis.

Mellor beat forty-one competitors to win the 1902 Boston Marathon, then became the first American to win Hamilton's Around the Bay. The 1903 Boston Marathon attracted fifty-six starters, with John Lorden, an Irish immigrant from East Cambridge, prevailing and Mellor second.

An American-Canadian marathon rivalry was developing in the Northeast corridor, stretching from New York City to Boston to Ontario, one that excited Johnny Hayes and Tom Longboat. They couldn't help but notice that the pioneering marathoners came from backgrounds similar to their own. These were blue-collar men— construction workers, bricklayers, printing-press operators—who managed to log miles before or after work and on weekends.

These rugged men endured primitive, arduous conditions. Runners wore nothing more than a slice of kangaroo leather over a stiff rubber sole. They pounded on uneven and rough roads and suffered through nasty blisters, cuts, and sore feet. Joseph Forshaw, a runner from St. Louis, took to greasing his shoes and socks with beef tallow to prevent damage.

Nutritional science was a novel concept and, in the days before electrical refrigeration, fresh fruits and vegetables were unavailable year-round. Trainers discouraged, or outright barred, runners from drinking water before and after workouts and during races, even when the roads were dusty, causing the athletes to cramp up and gasp for air. If a runner was in extremis, he downed a shot of whiskey or brandy.

What training methods existed relied on inaccurate (or incomplete) knowledge of human physiology. Doctors warned about the dangers of a condition known as "athlete's heart" without understanding that a slowing pulse rate was beneficial. Weightlifting was deplored. A rigorous workout entailed running 10 to 15 miles a day, three times a week; the idea of building endurance, of logging 125 miles a week (or more), as is common among today's elite marathoners, would have been ridiculed.

Carbo-loading and exercising at altitude (to maximize oxygen consumption) were unheard of in 1900. One training guide recommended that, "A long-distance runner should start out with a sweater on and run till he gets warmed up; he must not perspire, as by then taking off his sweater he would catch cold. It is very easy for a man to catch cold if he perspires freely."[20]

In the summer of 1900, the second edition of the modern Olympics came to France. Pierre de Coubertin had hoped to boost the status of the Games by linking them to the World's Fair in Paris. This was a grave mistake. Coubertin lost control of his invention, and the sports were but a "humiliated vassal" to the Exhibition, as he accurately described it.[21] Bizarre events—croquet, ballooning, the firemen's drill, angling for live fish—were included. Women were allowed to compete, much to Coubertin's everlasting horror, and many competitors left Paris unaware that they had participated in the Olympics.

Away from Athens, the second Olympic marathon had none of the impact of the inaugural race. It started on the Bois de Boulogne track, then looped around the city, before crossing the Seine and returning to the Racing Club. With an afternoon start time and temperatures topping 100 degrees, the sixteen runners suffered amid torrid conditions. Michel Théato, a local baker's deliveryman, took control after the midway point and finished first in a time of 2:59:45, amid conflicting reports that he used shortcuts en route to the finish.

The 1900 Games represented a gigantic step backward for Coubertin and the Olympic Movement. With the third edition of the Olympics scheduled for the United States in 1904, Coubertin could only hope that America's sports enthusiasts would rally the Games.

FIVE

I n Italy, Dorando Pietri remained fascinated by the sport of cycling. He appeared to have the perfect frame for the sport, compact and muscular, but his work afforded him little time to practice. Still, he ventured south to Modena to participate in the weekly cycling races. He used the money he earned at the café to pay a modest rental fee for the bike.

In August 1903, he took second in a ten-kilometer race at the Piazza d'Armi in Modena. Encouraged, he returned later that month for a twenty-five-kilometer event. But in the middle of the race, he was dragged to the ground in the fifth lap, apparently having gotten tangled up with a motorcycle. He was taken to the hospital and laid up for ten days, with bruised bones and abrasions.

So ended Dorando's cycling career.[1] He next turned to running, saying later that his older brother inspired his first steps. "Ulpiano was the first athlete in our family," he noted, "and while he never had a chance to compete in any big events he was the champion long-distance man of our club. It was through his example I took up running, finding the exercise beneficial, as I am a pastry cook by trade and that is not one of the most healthy occupations."[2]

True, running allowed Dorando to eat as many pastries as he was able and still maintain a trim figure. But on the dusty roads outside the fortified walls of Carpi, he was discovering his métier. His body had a unique resiliency that enabled him to train, mile after mile. He was like a windup toy, summoning up stores of energy from deep within his body. He enjoyed encountering the fatigue that beset his lungs and his legs, almost simultaneously, and then running beyond that, conquering the mental barrier of distance running. Soon, he would learn to channel this and adapt it for the rigors of the marathon.

On the Reserve, Tom Longboat heard the marathon buzz with the success of William Davis, a Mohawk Indian who was part of the Hamilton running scene. Davis had taken back-to-back seconds in two marathons within a three-month span in 1901. His commitment to training, and his courage in challenging the Americans on their turf, impressed even the tribal elders. Many likened his prowess to the legendary Deerfoot, the Seneca Indian from upstate New York who had competed as a professional "pedestrian" during the 1860s, often in one-hour timed races.

Davis's breakthrough came at a time when Native athletes were making their way into mainstream sports. The success of the Carlisle Institute football team in Pennsylvania was turning Aboriginal athletes Albert Exendine, Frank Mt. Pleasant, and Jim Thorpe into national stars. Louis Sockalexis, a Penobscot Indian from Maine, had a short-lived career with the Cleveland Spiders of the National League in the late 1890s. Charles Albert Bender, a Chippewa from Minnesota and the Carlisle Institute, made his pitching debut with the Philadelphia Athletics in 1903. They faced prejudice, stereotyping, and worse, but at least they had opportunity: African-Americans were still barred from professional baseball and were not welcome at most athletic clubs.

Always, Native American athletes were reminded of their heritage. Bender, a future Hall of Famer, was saddled with the sobriquet "Chief," as was catcher John Meyers, the Cahuilla Indian who began his career with the New York Giants in 1909. At the 1901 Boston Marathon, newspapers described Davis as the "copper-skinned athlete" and the "dark-visaged Indian-Frenchman." When he passed local favorite Ronald McDonald, the *Globe* reported, "[McDonald] was made instantly aware of the presence of his rival by the Indian war whoops and catcalls which those following the contest gave voice to."[3]

Davis would soon become more than a role model for Longboat. For now, Tom's ambitions were modest. Running was a mode of transportation, a way to travel to jobs, such as apple picking and other farming work and at the canneries located off the Reserve to support his family. It was also a balm, his own personal escape. He moved at his own pace, fast and hard in short bursts, other times languid for long periods. Always, he ran relaxed. When he felt sore, he rested or went on long walks. The workouts helped his lacrosse game, and vice versa.

Others took note of his dedication. "Tommy practiced running two years [on the Reserve]," a guide later told a Toronto newspaper. "He run every morning. He run every night."[4]

In the summer of 1901, Johnny Hayes watched his mother, Nellie, collapse due to severe abdominal pain. She was rushed to Bellevue Hospital from their home at 846 East 140th Street. She died less than two weeks later, on August 26, never having left the hospital. She was thirty-eight.[5]

The cause of death was cirrhosis of the liver. In all likelihood, Nellie died of chronic alcoholism of the type that Jacob Riis so eloquently described in *How the Other Half Lives*. She was buried at Calvary Cemetery in Queens.

Johnny was saddened even as he was relieved that his mother no longer suffered. There was little time for mourning. Michael Hayes worked long hours and was out of the house before dawn for his job at Cushman's bakery. Johnny helped out when he could and squeezed in evening classes at school. He and his younger brother, Willie, minded their four younger siblings, getting them ready for school and managing the shopping, cooking, and cleaning chores. Relatives helped out when they could, including Nellie's family in Poughkeepsie.

Johnny found solace through running. In this, he happened to be well placed. If Boston was the capital of the marathon, then the New York metropolitan area was the center of road racing. The New York Athletic Club held track meets on its grounds at Travers Island, and the Irish-American Athletic Club attracted the top athletes to its Queens facility. The Pastime and Mohawk clubs hosted regular races on the Jerome Avenue course in the Bronx.

In the fall of 1903, at the age of seventeen, Johnny became a member of the St. Bartholomew's Athletic Club, located near his old stomping grounds on East 42nd Street. The St. Bart's Parish House offered sports and other programs at little or no expense, and its gymnasium, crowded with gymnastics equipment and a handball court, was a magnet for neighborhood youth. Johnny received personal coaching for the first time, under the leadership of the club's physical director, Alfred Harvey, and joined the cross-country team.[6]

The camaraderie boosted his spirits at a dark time in his life, and success was not far behind. On April 3, 1904, at the Pastime Athletic Club's annual handicap race, Johnny clocked 38:07 to finish a surprising fourth (out of fifty-four runners) on a six-mile course. In leading St. Bart's to a second-place team showing, Johnny won the novice prize. Three weeks later, he finished fifth in a five-miler hosted by the Mohawk club (with brother Willie in sixth).

That same month, the Pastime's Michael Spring defeated sixty-seven starters and clocked under 2:40 to win the 1904 Boston Marathon. Johnny had seen the twenty-one-year-old Spring perform at local meets, wearing the Pastime's familiar Brazilian cross emblem;

he was a Jewish kid from Brooklyn who worked for the Edison Company. Later, Spring and another local marathoner, Sam Mellor from Yonkers, were named to the U.S. Olympic squad for the upcoming Olympic Games in St. Louis.

It gave Johnny, just eighteen, a new direction for his life. One day soon, he vowed, he'd be ready to tackle the marathon.

A s St. Louis prepared for the 1904 Olympics, the sports world was hurtling forward into the modern age. In France, where the newspaper L'Auto was struggling to increase circulation, its publisher decided to inaugurate a multipart bicycle race in the summer of 1903. Voilà, the Tour de France was born.

That October, after the two competing professional baseball leagues declared a truce, the champions of the American League and the National League met in the first World Series. Cy Young's upstart Boston squad downed Honus Wagner and the Pittsburgh Pirates, five games to three, in baseball's first-ever fall classic. The World Series was not held in 1904, but it became an annual event in 1905, when John McGraw's New York Giants defeated Connie Mack's Philadelphia Athletics, 4–1.

In May 1904, the governing body of soccer, the Fédération Internationale de Football Association (FIFA), was formed in Paris. The Australian Open, which became the fourth leg of tennis's Grand Slam, debuted the following year.

President Roosevelt was using the bully pulpit of the White House to summon college presidents for an emergency meeting about the future of collegiate football. Roosevelt was a passionate fan, and his son, Ted, played for Harvard's freshman team. He believed that "in life, as in a football game, the principle to follow is: Hit the line hard; don't foul and don't shirk, but hit the line hard!"[7]

But Roosevelt had seen football devolve into a crude version of British rugby, with an endless series of violent, grappling scrums. No helmets were worn, and, in 1905, twenty-three young men died from football-related injuries. Parents, legislators, and educators were calling for the abolishment of what one University of Chicago professor described as a "boy-killing, man-mutilating, money-making, education-prostituting, gladiatorial sport."[8]

Fresh off mediating a peace settlement in the Russo-Japanese War, Roosevelt rallied college presidents to reform the sport. From this came the origin of the modern game, including the introduction of the forward pass and the establishment of the ten-yard first down. Ultimately, it led to the formation of the governing body of college sports: the National Collegiate Athletic Association (NCAA).

On April 30, 1904, President Roosevelt pressed a gold telegraph key in the White House to, as he put it, "unfurl the flags and start the machinery"[9] at the World's Fair in St. Louis, designed to commemorate the 100th anniversary of the Louisiana Purchase. (The anniversary date was actually 1903, but the Fair was delayed a year.)

As in Paris in 1900, the World's Fair would also host the Olympic Games. Pierre de Coubertin did not leave France to attend the 1904 Games.[10] He left the planning of the sports program to James E. Sullivan. America's "sports czar" broke ground by introducing boxing and freestyle wrestling events to the Olympics. For the first time, the top three finishers were awarded gold, silver, and bronze medals. African-American athletes won their first medals, with Milwaukee Athletic Club hurdler George Poage taking two bronzes and Cleveland's Joseph Stadler winning two jumping medals.

Again, the monthslong competition was but a sideshow to the World's Fair. Worse, Sullivan orchestrated a "Special Olympics" among the Native peoples working at the fairgrounds. The mix included Filipino natives, Sioux Indians, African Pygmies and Zulus, and Patagonian Tehuelches. They were not trained athletes and, not surprisingly, performed poorly, but Sullivan trumpeted the results as evidence of the white race's supremacy. "The whole meeting proves conclusively that the savage has been a very much overrated man from an athletic point of view," he noted. "Lecturers and authors will in the future please omit all reference to the natural athletic ability of the savage, unless they can substantiate their alleged feats."[11]

If Sullivan's "Savages' Day" was ignominious absurdity, the marathon in St. Louis was madcap folly. The zany cast featured one Félix Carvajal, a five-foot-tall postman from Cuba. En route to St. Louis, he reportedly lost his money in a craps game in New Orleans. He somehow made it to Missouri and lined up in long trousers, heavy street shoes, and a cheap frilly shirt. Shot-putter Martin Sheridan promptly sheared off Carvajal's pants at the knees. Len Tau and Jan Mashiani, South African tribesmen working at the fairgrounds, had never run the marathon. They were entered in the race and became the first two Africans to compete at the Olympics. The foreign contingent was filled out by nine inexperienced Greeks and Albert Corey, a French-born butcher making his home in Chicago. None of the Canadian stars, like Jack Caffery, Billy Sherring, or Bill Davis, bothered to come to Missouri.

The United States fielded a deep eighteen-man squad, including the three most recent Boston Marathon champs—Spring, Lordon, and Mellor. But in the shank of an August afternoon, with temperatures reaching 90 degrees, the sun-splashed course felt as stifling as a barbecue pit. Organizers showed an astonishing lack of foresight by providing only two water stops: at a water tower at the six-mile mark and at a well located twelve miles from the stadium. One runner, William Garcia from San Francisco, was found passed out with severe hemorrhaging of the stomach after ingesting too much dust. He survived after an emergency operation.

The brutal conditions won out. Fewer than half the runners managed to finish the race. Thomas Hicks, British born but an American citizen, took the lead at the 14.5-mile mark. What happened next was practically murder and marked the first reported case of performance-enhancement drug use at the Olympics.

Wrote Hicks's handler, Charles Lucas, who followed Hicks throughout the race in an automobile:

> Ten miles from the finish, Hicks began to show positive signs of collapse. When he asked for a drink of water, it was refused him, and his mouth was sponged out with distilled water. He managed to keep up well, until seven miles from the Stadium, and then the author was forced to administer one-sixtieth grain of sulphate of strychnine, by the mouth, besides the white of one egg. Although French brandy was in the possession of the party, it was deemed best to abstain from further stimulants so long as possible.[12]

Hicks continued to plod toward the stadium. According to Lucas:

> As Hicks passed the twenty-mile post, his color began to become ashen pale, and then another tablet of one-sixtieth grain strychnine was administered him, and two more eggs, besides a sip of brandy. His entire body was bathed in warm water, including his head, the water having been kept warm along the road by being placed on the boiler of a steam automobile. After the bathing with warm water, he appeared to revive and jogged along once more. Over the last two miles of the road, Hicks was running mechanically—like a well-oiled piece of machinery. His eyes were dull, lusterless; the ashen color of his face and skin had deepened; his arms appeared as weights well tied down; he could scarcely lift his legs, while his knees were almost stiff. The brain was fairly

normal, but there was more or less hallucination, the most natural being that the finish was twenty miles from where he was running.[13]

Hicks somehow maintained his lead, but ahead was more tom-foolery. Unbeknownst to Lucas, Fred Lorz of New York's Mohawk Athletic Club had entered the stadium in front of Hicks and re-ceived an ovation from the crowd. Lorz had actually dropped out of the race at the nine-mile mark and been given an automobile ride. After the car broke down, Lorz got out and ran to the stadium. The crowd saw him as the victor, and he was about to be awarded the gold medal when Hicks staggered into view.

Pale, dehydrated, and barely conscious, Hicks finished in 3:28:53, the slowest-winning time of any Olympic marathon. He lost ten pounds during the ordeal. After a night's rest, he returned to health and was awarded a special silver cup.

Hicks's victory gave the United States its first Olympic marathon gold medal (and kept alive the streak of the host country prevailing in the event for the third consecutive Games). Cuba's Carvajal placed fourth despite stopping to eat fruit along the way. Tau finished ninth, after being chased off course for a mile by a dog.

For pretending to have finished first, the AAU banned Fred Lorz for life. There was no talk of Thomas Hicks being stripped of his gold medal because, in 1904, drugs in sports were not illegal. Trainers and athletes were experimenting with substances as fast as the scientists unmasked their properties in the laboratory. The energy-boosting capability of amphetamine, first synthesized in 1887, was well recognized, and coca compounds were both legal and pop-ular. Johnson & Johnson marketed a drink called "Vino-Kolafra," made from cola nuts and sherry wine, and advertised in mainstream magazines as a "stimulant which serves its purposes without any ill effects, and the taking of which does not become a fixed and pernicious habit."[14]

Strychnine in tiny doses acts as a stimulant for the central nervous system, with what researchers claimed as "positive effects on fatigue and physical exercise."[15] The poisonous alkaloid can be fatal in large doses or when mixed with other compounds; an unknown number of professional cyclists collapsed and died at the turn of the twentieth century, reportedly because of strychnine use.

Thomas Hicks was lucky to have survived the triple threat to his body: sustained physical exertion, heat, and doping. His handler, Lucas, saw it differently. The victory, he wrote, "from a medical standpoint, demonstrated that drugs are of much benefit to athletes along the road, and that warm sponging is much better than cold sponging for an athlete in action."[16]

The day after Hicks's victory, James E. Sullivan deplored the marathon. "The marathon race was a decided success from an athletic point of view, but I think they should be dropped from the list of events," he told the St. Louis Republic. "I think they are man-killing."[17]

Sullivan may have wanted to distance himself from the marathon because the race was outside the bailiwick of the AAU. The marathon was also seen as Coubertin's invention, and the two men were now openly feuding. The twin disappointments of Paris and St. Louis—what historians accurately dubbed the "farcical Games"[18]—had fractured and diminished Coubertin's Olympic movement, and Sullivan was calling for new leadership.

Coubertin and Sullivan were nearly the same age. Both men had dedicated their lives to the promotion of sports; both believed that sports was a positive and even necessary force within society. Both decried professionalism and gambling interests. Both counted President Teddy Roosevelt as an ally.

They clashed over the philosophy and the direction of the Olympics. A pocket-sized aristocrat from France, Coubertin was a cosmopolitan idealist who, with his Anglophile leanings, saw sports as just one component of a gentleman's education. He envisioned the Olympics as a multisport, international festival that highlighted harmony, sportsmanship, and the rituals and traditions of ancient Greece.

Sullivan never finished high school. The stout son of immigrants from County Kerry, he believed that track and field should occupy the center of international sports meetings. He bristled at anything smacking of England and was determined that American athletes should approach every competition with one goal: to win. As one who had used athletics to escape poverty, he believed that "athletics should be for the masses and not for the classes."[19]

"You say you do not understand my ways and manners," Sullivan wrote to Coubertin in one of their few surviving letters. "Perhaps not. I don't think you have tried to understand me thoroughly; if you did I think we could become firm friends."[20]

The two never reconciled. Adding to Coubertin's headaches was the lobbying by Greece for the right to host the Olympics on a semipermanent basis, with the Greek royal family rallying support among politicians, press, and sports leaders. Coubertin was in no position to fend off both Sullivan and the Greeks. As a compromise, Coubertin and the IOC granted Athens the "Intercalated" Games for 1906, in between the four-year cycle of the Olympiad.

Only the selection of Rome as the host city of the 1908 Games brought solace to Coubertin: "I wanted Rome because there alone, after its excursion to utilitarian America, would Olympism be able to don once again the sumptuous toga, woven of art and philosophy, in which I always wanted to clothe her."[21]

SIX

The pronouncement that Rome would host the 1908 Olympics, as well as word that Athens would stage an "interim" Games in 1906, buoyed sports throughout Italy. With support from Pope Pius X and King Victor Emmanuel III, Pierre de Coubertin and IOC general secretary Count Eugenio Brunetta d'Usseaux began drawing up the program for 1908, with track-and-field events scheduled for the Piazza di Siena in the Villa Borghese Gardens and swimming in the Tiber River.

In Carpi, where Dorando Pietri had abandoned cycling because of injury, he had figured out how his stout legs might bring glory to his athletic club. It is believed that Dorando's first public exposure as a runner occurred in Carpi's main square on a crisp September day in 1904.[1] A celebrated newsboy-turned-athlete named Pericle Pagliani, from the Lazio running club, had announced that he would run at the Piazza dei Pio. His intent was to surpass the distance record for a half hour and, perhaps, pick up a few extra lire in bets and tips.

Dorando stood outside the pastry shop to watch the action in the piazza. As Pagliani started off and the crowd began to respond with a low rumble, Dorando grew excited. He threw off his apron and chased after Pagliani. Soon, he found himself on Pagliani's heels as Italy's finest distance runner completed the circuit. Pagliani was reportedly upset at Dorando's dogged pursuit, but the townspeople cheered Dorando's verve.

That same August, another athlete, Gaetano Cagliari, came to

Carpi. His goal was to run four laps, a distance of less than seventeen kilometers, in an hour. On the second lap, Cagliari called out for a drink, thinking that someone on a bicycle would bring him liquid refreshment. Instead, he found Dorando running alongside him and proferring a soda bottle.

Cagliari slaked his thirst, but he could not shake Dorando. Said Cagliari: "At the finish of the fourth lap there were a hundred meters separating us—but it was him ahead of me! I don't remember the time, but I won the bet thanks to him." The two later paired up to win a race in Modena. Cagliari remembers that Dorando was "a phenomenal eater; after the race he could eat for four."[2]

Dorando's first recorded race occurred in Bologna in early October 1904, when he finished second to Aduo Fava in a 3,000-meter contest. A string of races followed as Dorando, sponsored by *La Patria*, hit Italy's running circuit. In Genoa on October 23: third in a 12-kilometer race. In Milan on November 13: third to Pagliani over 25 kilometers. In Bologna on November 20: second to Fava in 25 kilometers.

Often, he took home a watch—something he could pawn for pocket money. Other times, he was slipped money for expenses. Watching Cagliari and Pagliani, he learned to perform, to entertain the crowd. He ran clutching a handkerchief, which he used to wipe away sweat and moisture from his face, as well as two cork grips. The latter were held in place by rubber bands that went around the back of his hands. Dorando and other runners from that era believed that the cork helped them maintain their hands in a comfortable, fist-like grip and improved their concentration. (Apparently, some athletes used hollowed-out cork tubes as a flask, filling them with brandy to nip from during their runs.)

Dorando redoubled his efforts over the winter. He ran outside the walls of Carpi, always thinking of how to approach the next race. He grew a mustache, gained weight, and walked with a confident air. He met the love of his life, Teresa Dondi, the woman he would marry after the 1908 Olympics.

It was a happy time for him, and, beginning in June, Dorando began to establish himself as the top distance man in Italy. He won at distances of 10K, 20K, 25K, and 36K; he won in Milan, Modena, Carpi, Vercelli, Rome, Savona, and Piacenza. At one point, he won eight consecutive starts, vanquishing Pagliani twice and everyone else. His parents' tiny home was awash in silver trophies. He was nineteen years old and dominant.

That fall, after romping yet again in the town of La Spezia, Dorando ventured to France to test himself at the 1905 Paris marathon, sponsored by the sports newspaper *L'Auto*. Over 100 distance aces from France, Britain, Belgium, and Spain, including cross-country titlist Gaston Ragueneau, vied to capture what was essentially the European marathon championship (although the distance was reduced to thirty kilometers) as well as a prize valued at 500 francs.

La Patria sponsored Dorando—and paid his travel expenses to Paris—and he wore the club's colors. The race marked the first time that he represented Italy in competition; when he lined up at the starting line at the Park of Princes in a drizzling rain, he was never prouder. Dorando stayed bundled up inside a long beige raincoat until moments before the start. Right before the gun, he dramatically stripped it off.

This would be his day, as it was his season, and he took the lead "from the first meter to the first crossing of St. Cloud Bridge," according to biographer Augusto Frasca.[3] At the checkpoint in Rueil, he had a twenty-meter lead, an advantage he gradually stretched until, at the close, Dorando had crushed runner-up Emile Bonheure of France by nearly six minutes. His time was 1:55.

He telegraphed news of the victory to the local papers in Carpi and to *Gazzetta dello Sport*, thanking them for their coverage. It was a gesture he would repeat throughout his career and showed a media savvy that belied his limited education. Parisian newspapers, however, circulated rumors that Dorando had competed as a professional. The charges were vague. He had reportedly raced against other professionals in Italy. If proven, Dorando would have lost his amateur status and been declared ineligible for the Olympics. Organizers moved to strip him of his title but, somehow, Dorando maintained his amateur rank.

Three weeks later, Dorando was conscripted for his compulsory two-year stint in the military. He left behind his parents, his job, his burgeoning romance with Teresa, and his running career and reported for duty in Turin, about 150 miles from Carpi.

In 1904, Johnny Hayes was finding his stride with St. Bartholomew's cross country team. He took third in the junior cross-country championships in November. John Daly captured the senior division title, and the *New York Times* noted that "Ireland produces men who are as fleet of foot as the Celtic race is quick and sprightly of wit."[4] The following spring, Johnny won St. Bartholomew's six-mile cross-country handicap in 32:33.

His success was interrupted by another death in the family. This time, it was his father, Michael Hayes, who was stricken ill and taken to Bellevue Hospital. Four days later, the baker was pronounced dead from a cerebral hemorrhage.[5] He was buried alongside his wife, Nellie, in Calvary Cemetery.

Nineteen-year-old Johnny was now parentless and the nominal head of the household, with brother Willie serving as his trusty lieutenant. But they had limited control over the family's future. Shortly after the deaths of his two parents, Johnny's younger siblings were apparently taken away and placed in an orphanage (reportedly at a facility run by Catholic nuns in Blauvelt, New York).[6]

Johnny had no time to feel sorry for himself. He and Willie stayed together and bunked with relatives. The two scrounged for work, anything that would keep them afloat. They hit pay dirt deep underground.

New York City was building an electric subway system, financed by such bankers as August Belmont, to ease congestion in the nation's largest and busiest metropolis. The first line, the Interborough Rapid Transit (IRT), was completed in 1904 and whisked passengers north from City Hall to Grand Central Terminal, then west under 42nd Street to Times Square, before heading uptown under Broadway to the Bronx.

Johnny got a job as a sandhog—an underwater digger—with the Degnon Construction Company, one of the city's busiest contractors.[7] Started by the son of an Irish immigrant, the Degnon Construction Company employed 4,000 people and was building five subway lines in New York, including one that would connect Manhattan and Brooklyn via a tunnel below the East River.

The hours were long and the conditions hazardous for workers who toiled in compressed-air chambers, "where pressure could soar to 100 pounds per square inch."[8] The men used dynamite to dislodge rock and mud. Sandhogs shoveled the damp, heavy muck into wheelbarrows, then carted these up a ramp to waiting, mule-driven carts. The pay was between $2 to $4 per day.

Many men lost their lives. On the morning of March 27, 1905, construction worker Richard Creegan was blown out of the tunnel "on the spouting stream of a mud geyser" some twenty feet into the air, according to the Brooklyn Daily Eagle. "When he reached his highest altitude Creegan turned a not ungraceful somersault until his feet were pointing toward the air. Then the force of gravity got him and Creegan came down again."[9]

Amazingly, Creegan was rescued and pulled out of the river alive.

His three coworkers in the tunnel also survived, including one John Hayes. But the "Creegan Blowout" underscored how dangerous this type of work was. Soon enough, as Johnny blossomed into an elite marathoner, he would be steered away from the backbreaking work of digging tunnels and pushing wheelbarrows and into a safer environment.

I n May 1905, all of Canada prepared to celebrate Victoria Day, a holiday in honor of the late Queen of England's birthday. Small towns like Caledonia, just east of the Six Nations Reserve, held a daylong fair, complete with a five-mile race.

At seventeen, Tom Longboat didn't look like much of a threat when he toed the starting line.[10] He was a lean, gangly kid topped by an unruly mass of black hair. His feet were covered in battered, hand me down shoes. He didn't own a pair of the thigh-length shorts that male runners commonly wore in those prudish times. He used trousers that were cut off at the knees. The crowd laughed at his improvised getup.

Their amusement gave way to amazement as Longboat sped off at the start and grabbed an early advantage. His long legs churned with a relaxed swiftness through the first four miles. In the final mile, he began to tighten up. He was passed by one man, then had to fight off another to take second. He collapsed and rolled onto his back, gasping for air.

Bill Davis, the Mohawk marathoner, took notice. In Longboat, Davis saw a prodigy who could cover vast distances with coltish aplomb. He also saw an inexperienced runner who knew nothing about pacing and racing strategy. They began to work together, and Davis found in Longboat a sponge, eager for guidance. The older man counseled the youngster about training methods, about how to develop stamina as well as speed.

Longboat listened—and listened to his body—and began a unique regimen on the roads of the Reserve. Some days, he ran long distances at high speed, extending himself as much as possible. Days in between, he took long walks at a brisk pace and allowed his body to recover from the high-stress workouts.

He built up his endurance so that he could summon his speed during the endless miles on the road. By all reports, he was a joyous runner who loved the feeling of release, of freedom, when he ran hard, legs and arms churning, his breath coming quicker, lungs feeling the burn. Any and all troubles were left behind in his dust.

As a guide at the Reserve remembered, "He run down [at Caledonia in 1905] and got beaten. Then he come home and run more. He run around this block [of land]. It five miles and a half and Tommy got so he ran it in twenty-three and a half minutes."[11]

One year later, at the same race on Victoria Day in Caledonia, the opposition never had a chance. Stronger, fitter, and more experienced, Tom eased up at the end and still won by a quarter mile. He was smiling broadly at the tape.

His training methods were working, and he enjoyed the praise that he received, both on and off the Reserve. He had little time to relax: Bill Davis had big plans for him.

The void, Johnny discovered, never disappeared. The deaths of his parents, followed by the abrupt dissolution of the rest of his family, created a huge emptiness. Again, he turned to running for succor, pounding the roads until his body, and his mind, went numb. Then, he could begin to heal.

In the fall of 1905, Johnny was elected captain of the St. Bartholomew cross-country team. He finished fifth in the junior AAU cross-country championships, again trailing 1904 Boston Marathon champ Michael Spring. Three weeks later, he posted a swift 33:41 for six miles on Long Island. Then, two days before Christmas, he captured fifth at the city championships.

In competing against Spring and Sam Mellor, Johnny was able to measure himself against the top endurance runners in the country. He was plenty strong enough, his muscles bulging from the sandhog work, but he lacked the step-on-the-accelerator speed necessary to win the four- and six-milers. He decided to enter the 1906 Boston Marathon to see if the additional mileage would be a good fit.

He upped his training, after work and on weekends, and ran tune-up races in the spring, finishing eighth and fourth at meets held by the Mott Haven Athletic Club. A few days before the 1906 Boston Marathon, he left New York with two St. Bart's teammates.

The tenth running of the Boston Marathon began, by tradition, in Ashland, where official George Brown sent off a record 105 entrants,[12] including favorites Mellor and 1904 Olympic champ Thomas Hicks (fully recovered from his strychnine doping episode). Johnny started slowly, content to pace himself. He settled into the ninth position as the field drifted through South Framingham, Nattick, and Wellesley.

The race deepened, each mile he passed a victory of sorts. His body was fatigued. But his early cautiousness paid off as, down the stretch, he cantered by most of the fading front-runners. Johnny finished fifth in a respectable 2:55:38, 10 minutes slower than Tim Ford's winning mark.

Afterward, for two weeks, Johnny's entire body ached. His feet were sore and as red as McIntosh apples, and his ankles were swollen to twice their normal size. But he had conquered the distance and learned an important lesson. The marathon struck a unique balance between gauging how one's body was feeling during the race and responding to what the other competitors were doing on the course.

He returned to work as a sandhog, satisfied with his maiden effort. He told Willie that the marathon was the perfect race for him.

Dorando Pietri may have been a lowly soldier in the Italian Army, but his experience as a successful international athlete afforded him special treatment. The head of Italy's track-and-field federation, Mario Luigi Mina, arranged for Dorando to be assigned to the 25th Reggimento Fanteria in Turin, which was "renowned for giving athletes enough time and space to train and race," according to one biographer.[13]

Still, when Dorando walked into the Dabormida Barracks for the first time, "I almost lost my breath, it seemed like going into prison, all dark. . . . They took us to the bunkrooms where there were miserable mattresses stuffed with a handful of straw waiting for us, perched on two iron sawhorses and three miserable splints of wood. . . . I couldn't sleep a wink."[14]

He stayed focused on running when he was able to. On the last day of 1905, he attempted to break the national one-hour record, held by Ettore Ferri, on a 500-meter track at Turin's Parco del Valentino. He fell just short, logging 17.137 kilometers.

To participate in the 1906 Athens Games, Dorando needed permission to take a military leave. *La Patria* lobbied Italy's Ministry of War, only to be turned down. The press rallied around Dorando, with one newspaper sarcastically remarking, "The nation might suffer irreparable harm if this simple soldier went on leave, even for a single day! A rifle missing! Good heavens!"[15]

Finally, he received ministerial permission in mid-March. Dorando was able to squeeze in a 26K tune-up before heading to Rome for the Olympic qualifying marathon on April 2. This was Dorando's first full-length marathon, on a course that measured 42K, but the lack of intensive training and the extra distance did not bother him. Outfitted in a white shirt from the Atalanta Turin club, red shorts, heelless shoes, and a cloth bathing cap, he took the lead shortly after the start from Piazza di Siena and pounded out a decisive victory in 2:42:06, nearly 5 minutes ahead of Ferri.

Commented *La Vita* newspaper: "The champion from Patria di Carpi arrived completely fresh, took a tour of Piazza di Siena with a relaxed pace, and arrived at the finish line with a superb sprint."

Perhaps his biggest thrill came after the race, when he was personally congratulated by King Victor Emmanuel III and presented with a commemorative sash by Queen Elena. "He descended [from the royal box] in leaps," *La Vita* commented, "as if the 42 kilometers had only been a brief constitutional, and took another tour of the piazza at a run, waving and laughing."[16]

The confectionary worker had punched his ticket to Athens. Given a monthlong leave from the army, Dorando returned to Carpi a full-blown sensation. His parents made sure he ate enough. Teresa pampered him. During training, he envisioned how the race in Athens would play out. He saw himself dominating and winning, just like he had been doing in Paris and Rome, then returning to Carpi with the Olympic gold medal. The victory would be doubly satisfying because of the location at the ancestral home of the ancient Games.

On April 20, he and fifty-odd Italian athletes left the port of Brindisi on the steamship *Sicilia*, with Dorando reportedly seasick the entire time. The Italians landed in Patras and then went to Athens via railroad. Dorando stayed with the Italian Consul in Athens.

Beginning on April 4, just days before Dorando and the Italian team journeyed to Athens, a series of explosions shot liquid fire skyward and decapitated the pointed cone of Mount Vesuvius in southern Italy. A fiery serpent of lava flowed from the volcano; over the course of several days, ash and sand covered the surrounding area like an immense gray snowbank. Hundreds were killed, and the nearby city of Naples emptied in panic.[17]

En route to Athens, the U.S. Olympic team arrived in Naples on April 13 and toured the scenes of desolation near Mount Vesuvius. Trainer Matthew Halpin noted that, despite the choking dust, the men enjoyed a good workout in a park "under somewhat difficult conditions, there being four inches of lava on the ground."[18]

They arrived in Athens to a brass band and copious quantities of fine port wine. The exuberant welcome eased their travel woes and revealed a city that gleamed as brightly as the white marble of venerable Panathenaic Stadium. King George I and his family spared no expense to fête their guests, including his own sister and brother-in-law, England's King Edward VII and Queen Alexandra. The hosts even prepared a proto-Athlete's Village, called the *Zappeion*, which the Americans quickly abandoned for a hotel after one too many servings of boiled, rubbery goat meat.[19]

As in 1896, the marathon was viewed as both the climactic event of the Games and an opportunity for the hosts to gain a measure of redemption. Local merchants offered a variety of enticements to the winner if, like Spiridon Louis a decade previous, he should turn out to be Greek: a marble statue, three free cups of coffee daily for life, a free shave every day.

Greece boasted thirty-one entrants for the marathon, or more than half of the fifty-two-man field, on a course that was longer than in 1896 (the distance was probably closer to twenty-six miles). They faced runners from "15 geopolitical entities," which made it "the most international [field] of any marathon staged thus far."[20] Great Britain had two entries, including John Daly from Ireland, who reportedly was miserable because he was forced to compete wearing England's colors.

The U.S. marathon quartet was chosen both for their recent successes and, since the Games conflicted with the 1906 Boston marathon, their availability. Mustachioed Billy Frank, originally from Pennsylvania, was an established distance man for the I-AAC, and Cambridgeport's Robert Fowler was a veteran of the 1904 Games.

From the Midwest came wiry Joseph Forshaw of the Missouri Athletic Club.[21] Forshaw had been a sickly child whose fainting spells were "cured" by an exercise regimen devised by his father that included protein shakes of raw eggs and sherry. Inspired by the 1904 Olympics held in his hometown, Forshaw won the first marathon he entered: a twenty-five-miler in St. Louis in 1905. He trained before and after working at the family store, where he sold stoves and furnace parts.

The folks in Hamilton, Ontario, had hoped to raise enough money to send Canada's top two marathoners to Athens, double Boston winner Jack Caffery and Billy Sherring, the two-time winner of the Around the Bay race. According to one oft-repeated tale, what trickled in wasn't enough to send either of them, but Sherring took the $75 and, on a tip, bet it on a nag named Cicely at long odds. Cicely came home first, giving the railway brakeman enough money for a berth on a cattle boat to Athens.[22]

Whether or not the story is true, Sherring astutely arrived two months before the race, with enough time to acclimatize his body. He got a job on the railway to pay for his meals and board and trained exclusively along the Marathon-to-Athens route.

SEVEN

The day before the 1906 Athens marathon, Dorando Pietri was taken in a horse-and-carriage to the village of Marathon with a basket of food. He stayed with other runners at the home of the Greek foreign minister, Georgios Skouzes, and tried to quiet his excited nerves.[1]

The American quartet arrived at night and, after a steak dinner, was taken to a dingy schoolroom. They found sleep impossible when thousands of bugs attacked them in the middle of the night. Joe Forshaw remembered that they went outside and dozed there until dawn. They awoke to a frightfully hot day, with all of Greece impatient for the "race that their history has created, a race much higher than the common human nature, a race so dangerous and tragical and so famous."[2]

The road to Athens was cleared, with 1,000 horsemen positioned to keep order. Nurses and doctors were stationed every five kilometers. Despite the heat and the afternoon starting time, a crowd estimated at 150,000 people lined the roadway, forming what Canada's Billy Sherring described as "a living wall on both sides of the road for every yard of the 26 miles."[3]

At 3 p.m., the fifty-two competitors lined up in Marathon for the start. Dorando was calm, but he was breathing quickly. He eyed his opponents. The scrawny Sherring was grimly focused in a white sleeveless jersey emblazoned with an enormous green shamrock, while Forshaw and Billy Frank held a brief exchange. Ahead was Francesco

Verri, Italy's triple gold medal-winning cyclist, waiting to accompany Dorando during the race.

The massive crowd urged on the nearly three dozen Greek runners as Australia's George Blake pushed the pace from the start, despite the heat. Frank and Ireland's Daly positioned close behind. At around the five-mile mark, Dorando moved up alongside Frank. The field strung out, and soon Americans Fowler and Spring were forced to retire.

Dorando stayed with the leaders on the road until just before the halfway point. Suddenly, he was stricken with severe stomach pains, perhaps because of dehydration, perhaps because of the temperature. Doubled over with pain, he slowed to a walk, gasping for air, as Verri tried to assist him.

He struggled on for several kilometers, but the cramps were too intense. At the twenty-four-kilometer mark, Dorando dropped out and climbed onto the ambulance truck, his gold-medal aspirations blistered in the Athenian heat.

"I felt strong until the twelfth kilometer," he said later, "but I needed refreshment because of the dusty route and the high temperature. I had myself soused with cold water and this, according to the doctors, was the cause of my ailments. All of a sudden I felt an attack of strong abdominal pains. . . . This kind of event is new to me. I've never experienced abdominal pains."[4]

Sherring, meanwhile, paced himself well, lurking near Blake and Frank during the early miles. At the fifteenth mile, he left Blake behind. At the eighteenth mile, he muttered, "Well, good-bye, Billy," and dusted Frank.

Pounding out mile after mile, Sherring sipped water and ate oranges. A cannon shot was fired as he approached the columned entrance of Panathenaic Stadium. Upward of 50,000 spectators awaited, with tens of thousands packing the surrounding hillside.

The Hamiltonian mustered an exhausted grin and ran to the winning post with a sweat-soaked fedora balanced precariously atop his head.

He was joined on the final stretch by Greece's Prince George, who came down to the track and, towering over the 5-foot-7, 110-pound Canadian, trotted alongside and applauded the steely determination of Athens' second Olympic marathon winner. Commented one observer: "The Marathon race is a rash and courageous race, and that antelope of Canada, armed with the strength of its climate, with preparatory exercises and the feeling of vast space, has beaten all the other nations."[5]

Sherring's time, 2:51:23, was nearly 7 minutes faster than second-place finisher Johan Svanberg from Sweden. Frank managed third. Forshaw was twelfth. Afterward, Forshaw wrote, the runners were given "all the champagne we could put away."[6]

Sherring's prerace training on the course, and his experience in North American distance racing, paid off as big as the bet he had reportedly placed on Cicely the horse. Not eligible to win three free cups of coffee for life, he earned a 1.3-meter high statue of the goddess Athena and a black statuette entitled DYING PHEIDIPPIDES, in tribute to the famous courier.

Previously, James E. Sullivan had tolerated the marathon, no doubt because it was considered Pierre de Coubertin's creation. But after witnessing the race at its birthplace, and watching how tens of thousands of spectators flocked to the Stadium and the roads to watch the runners in action, he was swayed. The marathon, Sullivan conceded, is "the most important race of the Olympic Games."[7]

King George I and his sons planned to host another "interim" Olympics in Athens in 1910. But the Games would not return to Greece until 2004. The IOC no longer recognizes the 1906 Games as "official." Their reasoning? The competition occurred outside the four-year cycle and without Coubertin's imprimatur.

Whatever their formal status, their significance is unquestioned. The 1906 Games stabilized and reenergized an Olympic Movement that was floundering after the debacles of Paris and St. Louis. The 1906 Games were also the most international Olympics to that point. For the first time, athletes competed not as individuals but as members of their national teams. Sullivan outfitted his U.S. squad with the first-ever American uniform: knee-length white trunks, with red piping on the sides, and a white T-shirt adorned with a chest-high emblem shaped like a shield, consisting of red-and-white vertical stripes and thirteen white stars against a blue background.

To Sullivan, competing for national pride was the raison d'être of the Olympics. After the U.S. team cleaned up in the medals race, Sullivan crowed about the results in a cable to Teddy Roosevelt: "Final score stadium events: America eleven firsts, six seconds, six thirds; total 75 points; Great Britain and all her possessions four firsts, six seconds, three thirds; total 39 points. . . . Great athletic victory for America."[8]

Replied Roosevelt: "Hearty congratulations to you and the American contestants. Uncle Sam is all right."[9]

The 1906 Games are historically significant for another reason. At about the same time Dorando Pietri was dropping out of the marathon, IOC secretary general Count Brunetta d'Usseaux was informing his colleagues in Athens that the Italian government was withholding the funds necessary to stage the next scheduled Games. The eruption of Mount Vesuvius, and the devastation around Naples, was the proverbial last straw. Rome was pulling out as host city of the 1908 Olympics.

The gravity of the situation impelled Brunetta d'Usseaux to

sound out Lord Desborough of Taplow, a champion fencer and the head of the newly formed British Olympic Association. Would London be willing to replace Rome as host of the 1908 Olympics?[10]

Desborough discussed this development with his épée teammates. Over glasses of port and champagne on the *Branwen*, a luxury schooner that served as their living quarters in Athens, they pondered what to them was both a challenge and an opportunity. They were cocksure that, if they were to apply their knowledge, social connections, and wealth to the Olympics, they could stage the ultimate international sporting event for the modern age, one that would, not so incidentally, showcase the British Empire's hegemony under King Edward VII. By the time they left Athens, only one question remained unanswered: Was two years sufficient notice for England to properly organize the 1908 Olympics?

For the moment, news about the withdrawal of Rome, and the possible ascension of London, was kept from the press and the athletes.

Dorando Pietri returned to Carpi a chastened runner even though his collapse in Athens wasn't all that unlikely. Only fifteen entrants had been able to deal with the heat and finish the marathon. He was young—not even twenty-one—and this was only his second marathon. And, while he had established himself as one of Europe's top distance men, this was his first showing against the more experienced North American marathoners. Finally, his military duties had curtailed training. This caught up with him again later that summer, when he was forced to drop out of another marathon, this time on the Arona–Pallanza course.

With his ignominious showing in Athens, Dorando was shunted aside by the press in favor of the cyclist Verri and gymnast Alberto

Braglia, from nearby Modena, who won two silver medals (including one in the prestigious all-around). Dorando consoled himself with thoughts of the immediate future. In two years, he would again have the chance to represent Italy at the Olympics, this time in Rome. Not only would he know the Piazza di Siena course better than every foreigner, but the home crowd would surely scream his name every step of the way. In the summer of 1906, he returned to Turin to resume his military service vowing to redouble his training.

Billy Sherring came home to a hero's welcome in Canada, his victory worth far more than three cups of coffee. Friends presented him with a house and a lot valued at $5,000. The Ontario government, the city councils of Toronto and Hamilton, and the Toronto baseball team each voted gifts of $500. Altogether, Sherring received a reported $15,000 in money and goods.[11] This made him a professional and thus ineligible to defend his crown at the 1908 Olympics.

News of Sherring's triumph, and his ample reward, spread quickly. On the Six Nations Reserve, twenty-five miles southwest of Hamilton, Bill Davis was strategizing with Tom Longboat about his next outing. Davis was convinced that Longboat, with the proper training, could contend in the major fall races in the area, starting with the prestigious Around the Bay.

On October 18, 1906, Davis and Sherring watched as twenty-six runners lined up for the Around the Bay outside the *Hamilton Herald* offices. The crowd snickered at Longboat's pathetic appearance: a bathing suit with horizontal stripes and beat-up canvas shoes. The odds against the Native Indian were quoted as 100:1. The punters overwhelmingly backed John Marsh, an experienced Englishman who had captured a twenty-mile race earlier in the summer.

Marsh took the early lead as the runners weaved through the east end of Hamilton. The race soon developed into a two-man duel between Longboat and Marsh. As if to test his speed, Longboat occasionally burst ahead of Marsh, only to come back to his side. They reached the midway point and, into a stiff wind, turned toward home. With about four miles left, coming from Burlington Beach, they climbed a steep hill at the approach of Stone Road Junction. Just past the summit Longboat broke Marsh, leaving him behind as he sprinted to the *Herald* building.

His winning time was 1:49:25, about 2½ minutes faster than Marsh.[12] Tom might have broken Sam Mellor's record except that, with less than 1 mile remaining, he veered off course and ran nearly 100 yards the wrong way before he was corrected.

Said Sherring afterward, sounding relieved that he didn't have to face the youthful Longboat: "His gait is not very pretty, but he is powerful, has speed, and will make a great runner."[13]

Bill Davis was more than pleased and, less than two weeks later, brought Longboat to Toronto for the annual John J. Ward marathon. Ward was a tailor, a socialist, and a city powerbroker who lent his name to a variety of sporting events and teams. In 1906, the 15-mile race attracted seventy-some entrants on a blustery day. The course was straightforward: From the start at High Park, the runners went west for 7.5 miles along Lakeshore Road, out to the rifle ranges, and then back.

Longboat and Bill Cumming, representing Toronto's West End YMCA, turned the race into a two-man show. Again, Longboat toyed with his opponent, sprinting away and breaking him, ahead by more than 3 minutes, with a time of 1:31:00.

Back in Hamilton on Christmas Day, Longboat and Cumming hooked up once more, this time over ten miles. On the icy, rutted road, a buggy "besides which they were running capsized through slipping on some ice and fell on the runners."[14] They survived the crash, but Cumming could not survive Longboat's kick. Tom's time of 54:50 shattered the old mark by more than 2 minutes. The Toronto *Globe* headline on Boxing Day read: LONGBOAT ALWAYS WINS.

Four for four. Tom Longboat had entered four races in the span of seven months and won them all convincingly. He triumphed at five miles, at nineteen miles, at fifteen miles, and at ten miles. On his return to the Six Nations Reserve, newspapermen in Toronto, Hamilton, and Brantford clamored for interviews. His exploits took on mythic proportions. He was said to have scampered from Ohsweken to Hamilton faster than his brother traveled there via horse and buggy.

"Once, when there was a fair in our nearest village, seven miles away, an Indian boy was wagering himself to outrun any pony or pair in a race of two miles upward," poet Frank Prewett recalled. "Now, all of the well-off farmers fancied their ponies, yet the Indian boy beat them. He was left far behind at the start but he came back to the fair well in the lead. I learned later that the boy's name was Tom Longboat. He was slim and dark."[15]

Other, more disturbing information emerged. According to the Toronto *Globe*, gamblers approached Longboat before the Christmas Day race in Hamilton and asked him to throw the contest. When he didn't agree to do so, he was "run into by a buggy" in a "deliberate" attack.

Bill Davis was removed as manager, and Longboat's affairs were taken over by Harry Rosenthal, the first in a series of non-Native managers. Rosenthal was a sportsman who lived with his mother in Toronto.[16] He persuaded Tom to move to the city and arranged for his employer, the Gage publishing company, to hire Tom as an office boy. In exchange for handling the details of Tom's running career, including booking the races and making travel plans, Rosenthal wanted nothing. Presumably, his earnings would come from gambling on Tom at the races.

This was Tom's first time living in Ontario's biggest city, with its many churches (hence the nickname "Toronto the Good") and the smell of hogs from William Davies's processing plant on Front Street (and, inevitably, a second moniker: "Hogtown"). Working indoors full time and surrounded by English-speaking white Canadians, Tom experienced culture shock. He felt like an interloper without the security of the Reserve. But he also enjoyed his new, privileged status. The same Canadians who, months earlier, would have shunned him (or worse) now fought to buy him a meal or smoke a cigar with him.

He concentrated on what he knew best. In February 1907, Rosenthal arranged for Longboat to meet George Bonhag in an indoor three-miler. The odds were stacked against Longboat. The stocky Bonhag was the American record holder at the distance and an experienced Olympian. He excelled on the wooden boards—and came equipped with a pair of spiked shoes—while Longboat, who was just getting warmed up at three miles, wore leather shoes.

A crowd of 8,000 people shivered inside the 74th Regiment Armory in Buffalo as Bonhag and Longboat took to the eight-laps-per-mile track. The I-AAC veteran stuck to the inside, forcing Longboat to navigate the outside lanes. Tom shadowed his opponent the entire race, skirting the tight corners on the slippery surface, until a desperate kick gave Bonhag the victory by a whisker. Both men broke the record. "It was Tom's greatest race," Rosenthal said, in view of the handicaps Longboat faced.[17]

He pointed Longboat toward the 1907 Boston Marathon, but Rosenthal soon ran afoul of the Canadian AAU (CAAU), the nation's governing body of amateur athletics.[18] The CAAU was concerned that Rosenthal was "parading around the country with the Onondaga" for his gambling interests. The CAAU denied Longboat a permit to meet Frank Nebrich just days before they were to race at Madison Square Garden as part of the New York Athletic Club's winter meet. The decision was a rebuke to Rosenthal, who had negotiated for Tom's appearance, and he was forced to sever his ties with Longboat.

The CAAU steered Longboat to a respectable club, the West End YMCA, and he moved into a residential boardinghouse at 1186 Queen Street West in Toronto. The CAAU and the YMCA arranged for Fred Loft, a Mohawk Indian and, later, the founder of the League of Indians of Canada, to supervise Longboat's training. "Mr. Loft is a man who will take better care of Longboat than he has ever had before," CAAU president James Merrick said. "I do not think that he needs anything like the looking after that H. Rosenthal says he does and here is one thing certain: he will not be chased around the country as a betting proposition."[19]

The CAAU's last-minute cancellation of Longboat's race against Nebrich, however, roiled the powerful New York Athletic Club, which had advertised Longboat's appearance at Madison Square Garden, as well as James Sullivan of the AAU. (The CAAU and the AAU were not formally connected.) The AAU announced that Longboat was suspended from competing in the United States and thus ineligible for the Boston Marathon.

Canadian authorities angrily objected. "The CAAU says Longboat is all right, and that goes," said one official. "We are in control of Longboat and intend to continue so. Why should we allow the A.A.U. to take our affairs into their hands and dictate to us?"[20]

Just days before the 1907 Boston Marathon, the AAU met to decide Longboat's fate. He was ruled eligible to compete, but the AAU kept the matter alive in the press by declaring that Longboat would run "under protest."[21]

As Longboat prepared to leave for Boston with his West End clubmates, it was apparent that the biggest loser was Harry Rosenthal. He perhaps summed up the true motives of the AAU regarding Canada's brightest Olympic hope. "These Americans are simply shouting to shoo Longboat out of the Great Marathon Race in England next summer," Rosenthal told the Toronto Daily Star. "Longboat is going over for the big event and the Yankee distance men know that the Red Man will beat them so far that the second man will need binoculars to see the copper-hued Canuck."[22]

As Dorando Pietri and Tom Longboat were discovering, amateurism was a hot-button topic in sports in much the same way that performance-enhancing drugs stir controversy today. The separation of amateurs and professionals originated in British sports organizations during the Victorian era. These groups, controlled by the titled and the moneyed, hued to the so-called "mechanics clause," a protectionist way to bar working-class Joes from competing alongside the upper-crust.

From its exclusionary origins, amateurism morphed into an ethic. The powerbrokers of sport—Sullivan and the AAU, Pierre de Coubertin and the IOC, and their counterparts in Canada and Britain—viewed amateurism as gracing society with a moral purity. "The evils of professionalism, so called, are not merely the taking of money," wrote one advocate in the *New York Times* in 1907, "it is the spirit which this contending for money produces, the taking advantage of every subterfuge, of every device, honest or dishonest, in order to win. To straighten out the difficulties in their way the [athletic] clubs and the men are willing to misconstrue facts and misrepresent! This is the evil, dishonesty."[23]

The rules that amateur athletes like Dorando and Longboat encountered were incredibly restrictive. They were not permitted to earn money from their running prowess. They were not allowed to coach the sport or compete against professionals. They could receive money for travel expenses, but only a minimal amount. In America, Sullivan regulated the beat like a no-nonsense cop. One year, he suspended

288 athletes, including sprinter Arthur Duffey, who said they came to "fear" the AAU.[24]

Others smelled hypocrisy, pointing to Sullivan's profitable business ties with A. G. Spalding's sporting-goods company. Wrote journalist James Connolly, the first American to win a gold medal at the 1896 Olympics and a fierce critic of Sullivan, "When Johnnie Garrels, the Michigan University athlete, in an intercollegiate meet, made a world's record with the discus, it was rejected by Secretary Sullivan of the A.A.U. who said the discus used was not regulation. He should have said, 'Not a Spalding discus,' for that is what he meant."[25]

"Peerless Mel" Sheppard, the I-AAC's excellent middle-distance man, noted that banning athletes from coaching is "defeating the very basic principle of amateur athletics, which, as I understand it, should be considered strictly from the standpoint of providing recreation and athletics for everybody. And how can an aim of this sort be better accomplished than by starting at the very beginning—with the youngsters of the country? And who is more qualified to instruct these youngsters of the art and science of playing than those who are actively engaged in that very pastime themselves?"[26]

The system was replete with loopholes. Athletes who received watches and silver cups knew they could sell the baubles. (They were called "stock" watches, because they were returned to the jeweler's stock.) Well-heeled supporters might slip them money under the table or find them no-show jobs. They sometimes competed under assumed names to avoid detection. What the rules never addressed was exactly how an elite athlete could afford to train full-time while simultaneously holding down a job. This gray area was an abyss that would consternate administrators for decades, and one that would ensnare Tom Longboat in controversy up until the day he competed in the 1908 Olympic marathon.

EIGHT

Tom Longboat arrived in Massachusetts in April 1907 as the overwhelming favorite for the eleventh annual Boston Marathon, his record-breaking skein in Canada, as well as the hullabaloo over his amateur status, having made him a celebrity. His every move was dissected. How the cough he had developed would affect his time was debated. The *Boston Post* photographed him going over the course in an "American Mors gasolene [sic] car."[1] When he refused to meet with reporters, "they just faked up interviews," according to Lou Marsh of the *Toronto Daily Star*. "One photographer missed the redskin but his enterprising sheet dug up an old cut of an Indian football player and ran it over Tom's name."[2]

His heritage was always mentioned. He was, variously, "The Speedy Son of the Forest," "The Onondaga Wonder," "The Indian Iron Man," "The Streak of Bronze," "The Caledonia Cyclone," "Wildfire," and "Young Deerfoot."[3]

Longboat settled into digs in Springfield as Johnny Hayes slipped into town for his second attempt at the Boston Marathon, joined by hulking, red-haired Michael Ryan, another Irish-American runner from St. Bart's. Johnny was given little chance because he hadn't logged as many tune-up races as the previous year. But a healthy dose of cross-country runs in the fall, as well as intensive handball sessions and indoor calisthenics work with Indian clubs and dumbbells in the winter, gave him a solid training base.

Patriots' Day brought rain and a biting wind to frigid Boston for the noon start, but that didn't discourage the record 102 entrants or the 200,000 shivering spectators lining the course. When Longboat and Hayes toed the line at the race's new starting point, at Stevens Corner, the contrast was readily apparent: the lithe Longboat, now twenty, was 5 foot 11 and about 130 pounds. Hayes, twenty-one, was 120 pounds of coiled muscle on a compact frame of 5 foot 4.

Longboat jumped into the lead at the gun, joined by 1905 Boston winner Fred Lorz, 1906 Olympic bronze medalist Billy Frank, and Toronto's Charles Petch. Ever cautious, Hayes started slowly.

About four miles into the race, the outcome was decided by a fluke. Just after the front-runners crossed the railroad tracks at the South Framingham station, a long freight train rolled through. The gates came down, and the course was completely shut off for the trailing runners. Longboat, Petch, and Frank used the opportunity to lengthen their advantage.

Hayes was blocked from continuing, and he jogged haplessly in place as thirty seconds, forty-five seconds, ninety seconds passed. Finally, the train passed and Hayes was free to scurry after the leaders. FREIGHT TRAIN BUTTS IN, read the next day's *Journal* headline.[4]

It's doubtful whether the delay would have altered the result, for this was Tom Longboat's finest hour. In Wellesley, the "elongated aborigine"[5] waved to the college girls and was greeted with enthusiastic shrieks. He reeled in Jimmy Lee, the pacesetter, at the fourteen-mile mark, then went head-to-head with Petch until the heartbreaking Newton Hills, when a panting Petch faded. On Massachusetts Avenue, Longboat was handed a Canadian flag, and he waved it high in the air with a broad grin.

Toward the "black barrier of humanity"[6] at Exeter Street he swept, police vainly trying to hold back the crowds, until at last the finish and a thunderous ovation. His time was 2:24:24, a new Boston Marathon record that clipped more than 5 minutes from Jack Caffery's

1901 mark. Trailing by over 6 minutes was Johnny Hayes, who rallied past Petch and Lee for third.

At B.A.A. headquarters, Massachusetts governor Curtis Guild presented Longboat with a gold medal and a three-foot-high bronze statue of Mercury, the winged messenger god. Tom repaired to his hotel, had a bath, and ate a well-earned feast of chicken broth, blue-point oysters, tenderloin steak, and other viands. The bill came to $3.95.

His record time was greeted with wonderment. He was the first runner to combine speed with endurance over the entire marathon distance. He also held himself differently. He kept his hands by his hips, arms unfolded "like a half-opened jackknife when in action,"[7] as opposed to the then-common practice of keeping the arms up around one's chest. He didn't run up on his toes, like many did in that era. He took long powerful strides and glided flat-footed, scarcely seeming to lift his knees, but nonetheless expending less energy in the process.

"Never before in the annals of running, either amateur or professional, in this country or abroad, has Longboat's performance been approached," the *Globe* wrote. "It was a marvelous test of endurance, whether we consider it as a result of wise training or of racial capacity."[8]

"His work demonstrated beyond all question that he is the greatest distance runner the world has ever seen," thundered another. "He knocked to smithereens all records for all courses that had ever been made."[9]

Longboat was unaccustomed to speaking to the press and let his escort, West End YMCA director Charles Ashley, do most of the talking. But he allowed that he would "devote all his time, attention and perseverence [sic] to the conditioning of himself for the Olympic games which are to be held in London in 1908."[10]

.   .   .

Tom Longboat! You hear it everywhere," commented the *Toronto Telegram* as the city prepared to welcome home the marathoner.[11] West End Y enthusiasts mobbed the train at the Parkdale Station, but the big welcome came at Union Station in Toronto. Longboat and Petch were deposited in an automobile, then escorted by torchbearers and a procession of bands past thousands of cheering onlookers to City Hall.

In a brief ceremony, Mayor Emerson Coatsworth pinned a gold medal to Longboat's suit jacket, and then the crowd called for a speech. "I thank you kindly, Mr. Mayor," Tom said, before shyly falling silent.[12]

"I had a little talk with Tom about this," the West End Y's Ashley said, "and he wants me to thank you. He has repeatedly said that he wants to be an educated man. He aspires to be the true man, perfect not only in body, but in spirit and mind. That is the aim of Tom Longboat."[13]

Many in the Canadian press decided to count Longboat as one of theirs. "Whether Tom Longboat's address is Toronto, Brantford, Hamilton, Cayuga, or Caledonia, there is no doubt that he is a Canadian and we're proud of him," wrote the *Brantford Courier*, perhaps the closest thing to Longboat's hometown newspaper. "There is no excuse for not sending Longboat to represent Canada in the big Marathon in England."[14]

And yet, the newspapers did not fully embrace him. "With the typical square jaw and the loosely knit frame, the redskin reminds one of the school history's description of the redman," the *Montreal Gazette* commented. "Stubborn to a marked degree the famous runner is a very difficult subject for a trainer to handle."[15]

The *Toronto Daily Star* noted that, "His trainers are to be congratulated, not only on having such a docile pupil, but on being able to show such excellent results from their regime. It is to be hoped that Longboat's success will not develop obstinacy on his part and that he will continue to be manageable. If he does not lose his head or begin to break faith with the public, he has other triumphs in store and as much adulation as any mortal man could wish."[16]

The Toronto city council voted to authorize a $500 reward for Longboat, with the money earmarked for his college education after he retired from amateur running. Another $250 was raised for the same purpose through private donations.

However well intentioned, the fund backfired. American authorities questioned whether the $500 donation made Longboat a professional athlete and announced another investigation into his amateur status. The city of Toronto decided to hold on to the money.

Longboat soon faced other problems. He was arrested after getting into a fistfight at a Toronto tavern. He was also caught drinking and smoking and suspended from the West End club for breaking training rules. YMCA officials believed they "have done everything in their power for Longboat . . . but he is headstrong and secretive, and a day and night corps of attendants is necessary to keep him right."[17]

His arrangement with the West End abruptly ended. Longboat then wrote to athlete-turned-promoter Tom Flanagan: "DEAR SIR: I want to join the Irish Canadian Athletic Club. Enclosed find a dollar. THOMAS LONGBOAT."[18]

In Tom Flanagan, Longboat found a burly patron who, like Rosenthal, would arrange the details of his career—and one who would alternately champion and plague him even after his death. Born and raised in the town of Kilbreedy, in County Limerick, Tom grew strong-armed by "saving the hay," using scythes to cut the summer hay and then storing it in the barn. He wasn't as large, or as athletically successful, as his older brother John, who had earlier immigrated to New York City and become an Olympic champ in the hammer throw, but he was determined to make his mark in sports.

Tom Flanagan settled in Toronto and jointly owned the Grand Central Hotel with partner Tim O'Rourke. The pair cofounded the Irish Canadian Athletic Club, a successful outfit and worlds apart from the stodgy YMCA. Flanagan conducted his business at the tavern inside the Grand Central, where he arranged races for his charges and schmoozed the newspapermen. He believed that it was healthy for his runners to indulge in the occasional glass of ale. "As a cure for staleness I have always found beer to work without fail," he offered. "However, I am not the pioneer in this. Nearly all trainers of note prescribe beer. In fact, every single American athletic record is held by men who follow this principle."[19]

One of Longboat's new clubmates was Lou Marsh, a redheaded, blue-eyed youth from Campbellford, Ontario. Marsh started as an office boy at the *Toronto Daily Star* newspaper before rising through the ranks to become sports columnist. (Marsh also served as a referee in the National Hockey League while still employed as a journalist, the conflict-of-interest rules being very different back then.) Longboat and Marsh worked out together and became friends. But, later, Marsh would take Flanagan's side in his disputes with Longboat; Marsh's barbed words about Longboat would irreparably damage Tom's reputation.

Johnny Hayes was anything but discouraged by his showing in Boston in 1907. He had defeated several past winners and Olympians and had seen the redoubtable Longboat up close. While he respected the Canadian's remarkable showing, he was not intimidated. His 2:30:38 improved, by 25 minutes, his 1906 showing, and he took solace in the fact that, were it not for the freight-train interruption, he would have lowered his time further.

In his second marathon, he was starting to get a feel for the unpredictability, the sheer fickleness, of this maddening endurance test. A runner could train perfectly and arrive at the start in peak condition. But random elements—the temperature (too hot or too cold), the hills on the course, the condition of his shoes, what he ate for dinner the night before—affected the outcome. Marathoners had to be prepared for anything, even a passing freight train.

As Johnny and Mike Ryan rode back to New York, they discussed the future. Sullivan and the U.S. Olympic selection committee were starting to make arrangements for the 1908 Olympics. To distinguish himself from the biggest names in American marathoning— Spring, Mellor, Lorz, and Hicks—and to make the U.S. team, Johnny had to do something special. He needed a signature victory.

After his DNF (did not finish) in Athens, Dorando Pietri was finding that military life and training did not mix well. In February 1907, he took ill and spent twenty days in the infirmary. Finally, in April, he got a chance to work out. "The only thing that made me happy was to put on my outfit and run those roads," he wrote in his diary.[20]

The news that London was slated to replace Rome as host of the 1908 Games was another setback. Dorando was not going to get to compete in the Olympics as the national favorite. He would have to leave Italy to take on the world's best—as he had in 1906, with horrible results. He tried not to let the disappointment consume him. This was the Olympics, his ultimate dream, and he vowed not to let anything prevent him from the gold medal.

He also realized that he had much work to do. After his twin marathon failures in 1906, his confidence was down. He asked *La Patria* clubmates in Carpi, and Atalanta members in Turin, for advice. Did he need to up his training mileage? Was there something he should do differently during the race?

Dorando knew he wasn't ready to tackle another marathon, but he began to run competitively again. He won races in Turin at shorter distances throughout July and August, and followed those with a 12K victory in Modena and a 15K win in Bologna. That fall, he took the military championship at 1,000 meters. Slowly, his confidence returned.

I n London, William Henry Grenfell was tackling the job of organizing the 1908 London Olympics. Grenfell became Lord Desborough, First Baron of Taplow, in the summer of 1905, around the same time that he and several sports-minded colleagues created the British Olympic Association (BOA). It was soon obvious that he was the perfect gentleman for the job.

"If one were asked to name the most typical Englishman of his generation," the editor of *Vanity Fair* wrote, "one would be inclined to name Lord Desborough."[21] Born in 1855, Willie Grenfell set a mile record at the Harrow School that lasted for sixty years. He was president of the Oxford University Boat Club and rowed twice in The Boat Race (the annual match pitting Oxford against Cambridge), including the controversial dead heat of 1877. He had stroked with an eight across the English Channel, climbed the Matterhorn by three different routes, and twice swam the base of Niagara Falls, once during a snowstorm. He was president of the Amateur Fencing Association, the Marylebone Cricket Club at Lord's, the Bath Club, and the Lawn Tennis Association, among others. The private court he had constructed for *stické*—a racquet game played on lawn and enclosed by walls—became the standard size for the sport. At the age of fifty, he led Britain's épée team to a silver medal at the 1906 Olympics.[22]

His wife was Ethel "Ettie" Fane. From their country estate in Buckinghamshire, on the River Thames, Lady Desborough was the charming hostess at the center of "The Souls," a social clique of aesthetes who debated literary, political, and philosophical matters of the day. Arthur Balfour and George Curzon dropped by regularly, while J. M. Barrie, Henry James, H. G. Wells, Edith Wharton, Rudyard Kipling, Oscar Wilde, and a young Winston Churchill came for conversation.

Tall and broad shouldered, with an understated mustache, Lord Desborough was polite to The Souls, but he preferred to retreat to a well-worn leather chair by the fireplace in his wood-paneled library. Dozens of mounted trophies attested to his hunting and fishing skill: tarpon caught off the coast of Florida, lions shot in Africa, tigers in India, grizzlies in the Rocky Mountains. A wounded elephant once charged him, it was reported, "and fell dead to his rifle within six feet of where he stood."[23]

In the summer of 1906, after coalescing support to host the 1908 Olympics among the heads of England's sports organizations, Desborough focused on locating a proper venue for the Olympics. It was the element he considered to be most crucial for the success of the Games. No stadium existed in and around London that was capable of accommodating a variety of sporting events, as well as the expected droves of spectators. And, operating without government largesse, Desborough and the BOA had scant funds to build an arena.

The solution came in the form of Imre Kiralfy.[24] A Jewish-Hungarian émigré, Kiralfy started in show business at the age of four, performing traditional Magyar folk dances with his brother, Bolossy. The brothers came to the United States, and Imre collaborated with Thomas Edison and P. T. Barnum to produce lavish and wildly popular spectacles for the stage: an adaptation of Jules Verne's *Around the World in 80 Days*, *The Fall of Babylon*, *The Burning of Rome*.

The brothers had a falling-out, and Imre moved on to London. He soon was the city's busiest theater impresario, presenting a series of successful exhibitions at Earl's Court. He had also, in an idea that was ahead of its time, put on indoor soccer matches at the Olympia Theater, using green-dyed carpeting as the playing surface.

Kiralfy became a British citizen, a Freemason, and a devout supporter of his adopted country's imperialist bent. In 1904, when King Edward VII thawed relations with France, England's longtime enemy, leading to the Entente Cordiale, Kirlafy decided to celebrate the new pact by organizing the Franco–British Exhibition. Conveniently, he had acquired a swath of pasture land of about 140 acres, in an area of West London called Shepherd's Bush, what he described as "grass fields and cabbage gardens . . . lying half forgotten at the very doorstep of London . . . within twenty minutes of Charing Cross, which is the centre of the world."[25]

Desborough approached Kiralfy about staging the Olympics in conjunction with the Franco–British Exhibition. The showman immediately grasped how the Olympics would attract customers and sponsors to Shepherd's Bush and struck a deal with Desborough. Kiralfy would design, finance, and construct a multipurpose sports stadium. In exchange, his company would keep three-quarters of the paid receipts during the two weeks of the Games, including the live gate, program sales, and advertising revenue. Kiralfy also agreed to pay the British Olympic committee £2,000 for operating expenses.

Without a single bargaining chip except for the Olympic designation, Desborough had found an extraordinary solution. The 1908 effort would get a state-of-the-art stadium without having to spend one quid, at a location well serviced by several modes of public transportation. The only "cost" was agreeing to integrate the Games within the Franco–British Exhibition, an arrangement that had not worked well during the 1900 and 1904 World's Fairs.

When the British Olympic Council met in late December at the Bath Club, Percy Fisher of the Amateur Athletic Association, England's governing body of track and field, expressed concern that the competition would take place on a track that had yet to be constructed, and that such a surface "must, of necessity, be extremely slow."[26] Desborough politely countered that, with the 1908 Olympics less than twenty months away, they had no alternative. The agreement between the Council and Kiralfy for what would become the world's largest, most modern stadium was executed on January 14, 1907.

In May, Desborough and his right-hand man on the British Olympic Council, the Reverend Robert de Courcy Laffan, reviewed their plans with Pierre de Coubertin and the IOC in The Hague.[27] Essentially, London planned to host two programs. The first, comprising track and field, swimming and diving, cycling, and wrestling events, would begin in mid-July. This would be considered the "true" Olympic Games. The second, beginning in October, would feature autumnal and winter sports: soccer, rugby, field hockey, lacrosse, boxing, and, for the first time, figure skating (for men and women). Several events, including the racquets tournament and polo, were to be held in April, before the official Opening Ceremony. The Council was responsible for drawing up the rules and regulations for each sport and for supplying the officials to govern the Games.

On July 31, 1907, nearly six months after signing the deal with Kiralfy, Lord and Lady Desborough arrived in Shepherd's Bush to put into place the first stanchion of the Olympic Stadium. Over the next nine months, Desborough came often to West London to watch as Kiralfy, architect James Fulton, contractors George Wimpey Ltd., and a small militia of carpenters, steel- and ironworkers, welders, plumbers, roofers, and electricians labored over an engineering marvel the likes of which had never before been seen.

There was no small element of national pride in this. Lord Desborough and the privileged gentlemen who governed British amateur sport believed that what they had learned on the well-manicured lawns of Rugby, Eton, and Harrow schools and at Oxford and Cambridge—discipline, competitiveness, teamwork, adherence to the rules—shaped character and helped explain Britain's position as the world's super-power, with control of nearly one-fourth the globe.[28] Or, to reference the famous quote uttered after England's defeat of France in an earlier military campaign: "The battle of Waterloo was won on the playing fields of Eton."

Sport was viewed as a kind of cultural glue that bound together Britain's far-flung holdings. The English invented cricket, then ex-ported it to India and the Caribbean. They created rugby and took it to South Africa, Australia, and New Zealand. They concocted ten-nis, golf, and soccer, and soon these were played everywhere. They birthed the YMCA movement that spread globally. Their influence included the United States, despite American protestations to the contrary. Baseball was shaped by rounders and cricket, while football combined elements of soccer and rugby.

The construction of the Stadium and the organization of the 1908 Games, then, would serve as more than a beacon for British sport. It would be tonic for an empire that was, for the first time in decades, facing a serious rival on the global stage. Britain's former colony, the United States, was the fastest-growing nation and economy in the world, in no small part because of its immigrants, Irish and otherwise. It, too, was flexing imperialist muscle by defeating the Spanish in Cuba and assuming control of Guam, Puerto Rico, Hawaii, and, ulti-mately, the Philippines. The United States took over construction of the Panama Canal from French interests, and, in the winter of 1907, cheerleader-in-chief Teddy Roosevelt dispatched the Great White Fleet, an armada sixteen battleships strong, on an around-the-world deployment to show off America's naval power.

The 1908 Olympics were turning into something more than just sports competition. "The battle for world supremacy in athletics, and symbolic supremacy as the globe's most vigorous nation, would take place on English turf at London's Shepherd's Bush Stadium," historian Mark Dyreson wrote.[29]

NINE

In the fall of 1907, the city of Yonkers hosted its first-ever marathon. Located just north of New York City, hard by the Hudson River, Yonkers was a burgeoning industrial hub. The Otis company factory manufactured lifting devices for passengers, powered first by steam and then electricity, and installed them in the office and apartment buildings that were changing the skyline of the metropolis. Nearby, at his barn-turned-laboratory, chemist Dr. Leo Henricus Baekeland was creating Bakelite, the durable, synthetic plastic that would revolutionize the production of mass-consumer goods as well as the automobile and aviation industries.

Yonkers was also home to the Mercury and the Mohawk athletic clubs, which attracted New York's elite distance runners at cross-country meets over the hilly Westchester terrain. In 1907, the Mohawk decided to challenge Boston's hegemony over the marathon by sponsoring its own, on a doozy of a twenty-five-mile course. On Thanksgiving day, Johnny Hayes and his St. Bart's teammate, Mike Ryan, faced a small but tough field of 42 competitors that included local hero Sam Mellor, the Mohawk's own Fred Lorz, and Albert Corey and Sidney Hatch from the Midwest. Mayor John Coyne started the race in front of the Hollywood Inn social club, in the business section of the city, where an estimated 50,000 people gathered to watch the runners on a course that "was laid out in such a manner that the athletes could be seen from any stage of the journey," the *New York Times* reported.[1]

Hayes had learned from his two Boston Marathons, when his

pacing had proved to be too deliberate. This time, he lingered near the lead and didn't allow the front pack to stray far from sight. At around the four-mile mark, he encountered some random fortune. As he was running by the New York Orphan Asylum, he noticed a horseshoe lying in the road.[2] He took a quick detour to cover it, and the good omen held as the runners moved north, to Dobbs Ferry, and then to the Saw Mill River Road.

The course was a treacherous series of hills. One incline was so steep that a thirty-horsepower automobile trailing the runners could not climb it, and the car's occupants were forced to get out and walk. The discouraging rises winnowed the field, and after another precipitous grind at Woodland Avenue, others dropped out. Johnny stuck with the leaders and at the twenty-one-mile mark, muscled to the front. He was in an unaccustomed position, but he rode the energy of the crowd home, churning hard and finishing in style in 2:44:45. Lorz was second, more than 13 minutes behind, with Corey third and Ryan fourth.

Only nineteen of the forty-two starters finished. One runner, G. C. Cunningham of the New York Athletic Club, collapsed unconscious and was taken to the hospital for treatment. According to the *Yonkers Herald*, he was said "to have been given too much whiskey."[3]

In the aftermath of what the *Herald* called "the greatest athletic event Yonkers has ever known,"[4] Hayes was carried on his teammates' shoulders to the Hollywood Inn gymnasium. He received a large silver trophy at the Orpheum Theater that evening.

Hayes's first marathon triumph, over a tough course and against the nation's top runners, gave him leverage. He had witnessed, in Boston and in New York, the dirty secret of amateur sports, where star athletes, including Tom Longboat, received special treatment.

Prominent clubs like the New York Athletic Club fought over these men, often by promising them jobs in exchange for their services. Johnny was determined to grab the opportunity.

In a city where the Irish had risen by taking care of their own, Johnny knew exactly whom to approach. The original Irish-American Athletic Club was founded in 1879. A latter-day incarnation was revived in the fall of 1897 when, for $9,000, Patrick Conway and his partners purchased seven acres of barren land in the Sunnyside section of Queens "to develop athletics among the Irish race and promote Gaelic sports, such as football and hurling." They ponied up an additional $50,000 to create Celtic Park, which Conway, a blacksmith with a shop at East 60th Street in Manhattan and himself an emigrant from Limerick, described as "a playground for the Irish."[5] (Calvary Cemetery, the so-called "City of the Celtic Dead," where Johnny had buried both his parents, was minutes away.)

Future New York City mayor William O'Dwyer would remember spending Sunday afternoons at Celtic Park, taking "the 34th Street ferry [from Manhattan], the trolley ride to the neighborhood, and a six-block walk to the park itself. . . . There were bars, a dancing pavilion, a well-kept field and a grandstand. I saw Martin J. Sheridan, Pat McDonald, Matt McGrath, Johnny Joyce beat their own records there."[6]

One danger lurked for the athletes at Celtic Park: the New Jersey mosquito, a bloodsucking breed achieved by crossing "the woodpecker with the rattlesnake,"[7] according to miler Mel Sheppard.

Conway liked to tell reporters that the I-AAC "annexed athletic stars" from other clubs. Actually, at the height of its rivalry with New York Athletic Club, the I-AAC was aggressively acquisitive, snatching the best talent by appealing to Gaelic pride and by promising that they would have access to the best facilities in the metropolitan area. Sheppard recalled that, on the night he set an indoor world's record in the mile, club member Harry Hyman "took me to the train, bought me a berth and incidentally managed to get me out of the city before any of the representatives of the other clubs had had a chance to have a word with me. The next morning [I-AAC trainer Ernie] Hjertberg himself showed up at my home in Philadelphia bright and early, and then it was all over but the shouting. I was henceforth a member of the Irish American Athletic Club."[8]

Swedish-born Hjertberg, a former distance running champ, was a master of technique and strategy. He coached every type of discipline—sprinters and marathoners, high jumpers and long jumpers, hurdlers and hammer throwers—and personally tutored Martin Sheridan, considered the world's finest all-around athlete going into the London Olympics. Together, Hjertberg and Conway built the I-AAC into a powerhouse that captured the 1904 U.S. outdoor title and whose members won numerous Olympic medals in 1904, 1906, 1908, and 1912.[9]

The club's biggest stars, literally, were the so-called Irish Whales, led by behemoth hammer throwers John Flanagan, born and raised in County Limerick, and Matt McGrath, originally from Nenagh, the same town that Johnny Hayes's father came from. Flanagan, McGrath, and Sheridan (from County Mayo) moonlighted as New York City cops, which allowed them to retain their amateur status. (The I-AAC was not formally connected with Tom Flanagan's Irish Canadian Athletic Club.)

The I-AAC motto was *Láim Láidir Abú* ("Strong Hand Forever"), and its logo was a green Winged Fist, a not-so-veiled jab at the New York Athletic Club's Winged Foot and its exclusive membership. Intentionally or not, the Winged Fist symbolized the righteous political stance of many Irish immigrants, and events at Celtic Park raised funds for the independence campaign back home. (Thomas Clarke, a signatory of the Proclamation of the Irish Republic and later executed for his part in the 1916 Easter Rebellion, was a card-carrying I-AAC member.) Even so, the I-AAC valued talent over ethnicity. Crack Jewish athletes Myer Prinstein and Abel Kiviat, as well as John Taylor, the African-American sprinter from Penn, were on the squad.

Soon after his first-place showing at the Yonkers Marathon, Johnny Hayes was wooed by the I-AAC. He had enjoyed being captain of the St. Bart's cross-country team. The club and his teammates had encouraged him as he developed into a quality marathoner and supported him at his darkest hour, providing solace after his parents' deaths. But St. Bart's was a neighborhood club with limited facilities. The I-AAC represented the top rung of track and field. With the Olympics on the horizon, and with the opportunity to develop under Hjertberg, Johnny defected to don the green Winged Fist. He began training at Celtic Park under Hjertberg's tutelage, logging endless miles on the roads of Long Island City. Sunday mornings without fail, he did half the marathon distance.

Hayes asked the I-AAC for help in finding him a "dry job."[10] He later related that he was worried about contracting rheumatism while working in the damp tunnels underneath the East River. The I-AAC followed his instructions literally, setting up Johnny with employment in the dry-goods section of Bloomingdale's department store at 59th Street and Third Avenue.

The job was a ruse, a device to throw off the AAU and allow Johnny to concentrate on his primary job as an athlete. Whether Johnny showed up and worked at Bloomingdale's—or just drew a salary while training full time—remains a mystery. (Bloomingdale's refused to release Hayes's employment records.) But after Johnny returned from London, every article mentioned that he worked at the store and that owner Samuel Bloomingdale had built a rooftop track so that Johnny could train. It was the type of advertising that money could not buy.

In the summer of 1907, shortly after joining the Irish Canadian Athletic Club, Tom Longboat demonstrated that he was the world's fastest amateur distance runner. He shattered the national five-mile mark at Lansdowne Park in Ottawa in July, defeating a three-man relay team that included Lou Marsh. At the Police Games in Toronto in August, Longboat again beat Marsh, who was part of a five-man team, over four miles.

He whipped John Daly, the Irish champ and 1906 Olympian, over five miles at Hanlan's Point Stadium on the Toronto Islands, and then the other Marsh—John—in Hamilton. In October, he dominated an elite field to defend his Ward Marathon crown in Toronto, setting a new record in 1:41:40 (over twenty miles). The next month, he won a fifteen-mile road race sponsored by the *Montreal Star* newspaper in 1:26:55, before an estimated crowd of 200,000 people.

Longboat was paying off big-time as an investment for Tom Flanagan. The curly haired, nattily dressed operator held court in the saloon at his Grand Central Hotel, where he organized the very events that Longboat helped sell tickets to (with a hefty share of the proceeds going to Flanagan). Longboat had a room at the hotel and took his meals there. He was "entirely Flanagan's creature at this stage of his career,"[11] according to biographer Jack Batten.

Inevitably, their relationship attracted controversy. In November, A. N. Payne charged that he had paid Flanagan "a big sum for the services of Longboat"[12] for the July carnival in Ottawa. That same month, the CAAU announced an investigation into charges that Longboat had not worked since joining Flanagan's Irish Canadian club. Meanwhile, Alf Shrubb, the top-ranked professional distance runner, challenged Longboat to a race at any length, the implication being that he considered Tom to be a pro.

Montreal Star publisher Hugh Graham appealed to Longboat to hew to amateur rules. "Your own victories may gratify your personal ambition, but that should not be the end of it," Graham wrote with more than a touch of paternalism. "Your country can be not a little served by a continued example of clean sports. . . . If at the end of five years you are still in the athletic field, and it can be truthfully said of you that you have resisted temptations, kept temperance and managed yourself always on the side of clean sport, I shall be most pleased to hand you a cheque for $2000."[13]

To counter the growing accusations of Longboat's professionalism, Flanagan established his "Irish Indian" as the proprietor of a retail shop in Toronto. The Tom Longboat Athletic Cigar Store, located in the same building as the Princess Theatre, was oddly antithetical to the aerobic rigors of the sport. "Longboat sold cigars from tins with his photo on the lid at a price of four for a quarter," wrote one biographer. "He also hawked pictures of himself in running clothes but . . . Longboat had little aptitude for business, the joke circulating in running circles that he smoked most of the stock personally."[14]

The smoke wafted across the border, where the protector of amateurism's sanctity, James Sullivan, announced that Longboat was banished from competing in America. The AAU found that he "does not work for a living, that he is taken from town to town by [Tom Flanagan] . . . with brass bands, carriages and silk hats. This is the kind of amateurism that the A.A.U. intends to eradicate."[15]

When the Pastime club inquired as to Longboat's availability for a meet at Madison Square Garden, Sullivan thundered: "Longboat is a disqualified man in the Amateur Athletic Union. Don't for a moment think of advertising him as a competitor. He cannot take part in any games until the parent body reinstates him. If you violate those instructions I will ask the Registration Committee to withdraw its sanction for the meet."[16]

Many Canadians interpreted Sullivan's finger-wagging as another example of the big-stick United States telling its neighbor how to behave. This inflamed the CAAU, and the rapport between Sullivan and the CAAU deteriorated. Relations frayed further when the Montreal-based Amateur Athletic Federation of Canada allied with Sullivan against the established CAAU. It took the intervention of Lord Earl Grey, the Governor General of the country, to persuade the two sports organizations to put aside their differences and select a Canadian team for the 1908 Olympics.

Canada's so-called "Athletic War"[17] was ostensibly over the issue of amateurism, but caught in the middle was Tom Longboat. The runner had established himself as the nation's biggest sports star, bigger even than the oarsman Ned Hanlon, at a time when pride in the Canadian way was taking root. That status made him "the cat's paw," both for athletic administrators and the press.

In a 1907 profile that appeared in *Mind and Body* magazine, Longboat was portrayed as having the "sheer inability to feel fatigue . . . an Indian from toe-nail to top-knot, poor, illiterate, of an intelligence so low that he is treated by his trainers as nothing more than a running-machine. . . . That's what he is, nothing more. Tom Longboat can run 25 miles faster than any man living, but he cannot converse intelligently in English, he could not write a letter, he is a man of as primitive ideas as any of the red-skinned braves whose blood courses through his veins. . . . He does not know how to run—that is to say, he has no 'form' or finish, he knows none of the arts by which trained runners save themselves and gain speed."[18]

Flanagan propagated this perception. In October, he arranged for Longboat to make a solo run from Hamilton to Toronto. The exhibition was done merely to attract gamblers to a betting proposition: Could the runner cover the forty-two-mile distance in under 5½ hours?

The answer was a resounding no. Longboat collapsed several times en route, his feet a bloody and shredded mess, until finally he was taken by car to Toronto. It was a cruel and unnecessary publicity stunt gone awry and, as one biographer pointed out, "a single continuous run of this magnitude could well have produced severe physiological and psychological problems, at least on a short term basis."[19] Certainly, it ranked as one of Longboat's few athletic failures in 1907.

In the fall of 1907, Dorando Pietri's two-year military service ended. He was finally able to concentrate on his training—and just in time. Italy's qualifying trials for the 1908 Olympics were fast approaching.

That November, Dorando journeyed to Rome for the country's national championships. In a two-day span, he took second in the 1,000 meters, then won the 5,000 meters and the 20,000 meters, the latter by three minutes over rival Pericle Pagliani. He felt the rust from his army stint disappearing with each stride.

Dorando continued to receive support from La Patria. The arrangement probably broke amateur rules, but Dorando knew that such transgressions, if kept low-key, went unpunished. Fellow athlete Giacinto Volpati, who defended Dorando after the professional accusations following the Paris Marathon in 1905, viewed the "long-standing divide between amateurs and professionals" as fostering a hypocritical system. "Our fine amateurs are aristocrats, or at least they want to pass as such," he wrote. "They disdainfully refuse prizes in money, and the day after the race they sell their other prizes for hard cash. They're more professional than the true professionals, but pass themselves off under the eyes of the world as the 'immaculate,' those who practice sport only for love of glory."[20]

For now, Dorando circled one date on his calendar: June 3, 1908. That was the day of Italy's Olympic trials in the marathon.

TEN

At the stroke of midnight on December 31, 1907, a 700-pound glittering ball dropped at Times Square. It was the first time that New York City celebrated New Year's Eve with such hoopla.

On December 31, 1908, Wilbur Wright went aloft in his powered, heavier-than-air flying machine for nearly 2½ hours near Le Mans, France. In one swoop, he set a new flight record, won the Michelin Cup, and proved to remaining skeptics that mankind had conquered the skies.

Bookended by the awesome and the awe-inspiring, the 366 days of 1908—yes, it was a leap year—were "by whatever quirk of history or cosmology . . . one hell of a ride around the sun," according to author Jim Rasenberger.[1]

That May, in the desert outpost of Masjid-i-Suleiman (what is now southwestern Iran), British explorers struck oil, sending a gusher of black liquid seventy-five feet in the air. The timing of the first significant discovery of petroleum in the Middle East was perfect. In September, the first gasoline-powered Model T rolled out of Henry Ford's Piquette Avenue factory in Detroit. The four-seat, four-cylinder black roadster (it only came in one color) sold for $850. Ford threw in a windshield, headlights, and a speedometer for another hundred bucks.

The sports world, too, was in for one hell of a ride in 1908—in addition, that is, to the 20,000-mile, around-the-world automobile race that began in New York City and ended in Paris. Hawaiian waterman George Freeth was helping to revive the ancient Polynesian sport of wave-riding, or surfing, and giving exhibitions along the coast of southern Calfornia. The bravado of boxer Jack Johnson and the racist taunts that dogged his every punch had overshadowed his pugilistic mastery. His opponents knew better and, using his skin color as an excuse, ducked getting into the ring with him with the title at stake. Finally, in December 1908, he was given a chance to fight for the title; his knockout victory over Tommy Burns made him the first African-American heavyweight champ.

The year 1908 marked the debut of "Take Me Out to the Ball Game," a matter of sublime timing given that the New York Giants, the Chicago Cubs, and the Pittsburgh Pirates staged a riveting pennant race that climaxed with Fred Merkle's infamous base-running gaffe. An extraordinary one-game play-off between the Giants and the Cubs followed, with Chicago prevailing and then capturing the World Series over the Detroit Tigers. Nobody could have predicted the Cubbies' future in 1908—not Joe Tinker, Johnny Evers, Frank Chance, or Three Finger Brown—but this was to be their last World Series triumph in, well, forever.

James E. Sullivan also put his imprint on baseball in 1908. Even as he was preparing the U.S. team for the London Olympics, Sullivan was part of a committee hand-appointed by his boss, Albert Spalding, to determine the origin of baseball. The Mills Commission's findings, published by Spalding, revealed that General Abner Doubleday, a Civil War hero at Gettysburg, had invented the sport in Cooperstown, New York, in 1839. The news was shocking and also untrue—baseball had evolved from, among others, the British sports of cricket and rounders—but the report was cheered with the same patriotic fervor that the "investigation" was conducted. After all, the national pastime should be an all-American invention.

(Baseball's immaculate and patriotic conception, as well as Double-day's purported role, was later debunked, although not before the sport's Hall of Fame was established in Cooperstown.)

One hell of a ride around the sun? That perfectly describes the 1908 London Olympic Games.

James E. Sullivan asked President Teddy Roosevelt for $100,000 from the U.S. government to fund the 1908 American Olympic effort, claiming that "the sinews of athletic war, of national pride rather than individual honor are at stake."[2] Roosevelt declined, and Sullivan was forced to raise money for the Games through private donations.

Sullivan held three separate tryouts for the 1908 Olympic track team, with each athlete required to pay a $2 entry fee for the privilege. There was no single qualifying race for the marathon (as is the practice today). After consulting with Mike Murphy, the Penn coach, and Ernie Hjertberg of the Irish-American club, Sullivan established that the Boston Marathon would serve as the East Coast test, with the St. Louis marathon as the audition for the rest of the country. Afterward, American officials would select the Olympic runners.

Johnny Hayes approached the 1908 Boston Marathon with one purpose: to win it. He had the Yonkers victory under his belt and, in his third go-round in Massachusetts, knew the course as well as any Back Bay native. He was in top form under Hjertberg's tutelage and the backing of the Irish-American club. A week beforehand, Hayes, Hjertberg, and Mike Ryan headed to Lynn, about twelve miles outside of Boston. They stayed with one of Johnny's uncles and took their final training runs there.

Defending champion and course record-holder Tom Longboat was not in the United States, much less Massachusetts. Longboat had again riled American sports authorities, this time after Tom Flanagan brought him and three other Irish Canadian members to Boston's Park Square Coliseum for a mid-February exhibition. Longboat lowered Alf Shrubb's ten-mile record, but the AAU did not sanction the appearance. In March, the AAU declared that Longboat was a professional and ineligible for the Boston Marathon. "It was openly charged that there was a division of the gate receipts and the four runners participated,"[3] one newspaper reported.

Canadian officials immediately countered the charges by publishing a report that exonerated Longboat. "[The CAAU is] unable to discover that Longboat has profited in the slightest degree from athletics. The [Irish Canadian club] produced statements and vouchers of every trip made by Longboat since he became connected with the organization . . . and the committee was unable to find a single term that was not in strict accordance with the amateur rule."[4]

Still, in light of the American ruling, Longboat had little choice but to skip Boston. Flanagan kept him busy with exhibitions throughout Ontario. The *Montreal Star* reported that Tom bested a trotter horse named Sam McBee, over a ten-mile course from Hagersville to Caledonia. Longboat was "running like a deer,"[5] the newspaper noted.

With a berth on the U.S. Olympic team on the line, Longboat's absence did not diminish the importance of the 1908 Boston Marathon. Sullivan himself came to observe from the comfort of an automobile. It was spitting tiny snowflakes in the runners' faces at the start as Hayes, wary of the harsh hills that lurked at the tail end of the course, allowed the others to push for the early lead. Roy Welton, a local kid from Lawrence, surprised the pack by establishing a pace that, well past the halfway point, surpassed Longboat's in 1907.

With Coach Hjertberg accompanying him, Hayes waited to pounce. He was thirtieth in Natick, surged to nineteenth in Wellesley, and was fifth at Coolidge Corner. He made up nearly five minutes in the last three miles, passing the laggards "like a torpedo boat running by a ferry,"[6] according to the *Globe*.

But he had "stayed in the rear of the field too long,"[7] he later admitted, and he could only watch from second place as Thomas Morrissey of the Mercury Athletic Club in Yonkers held on for the victory. Hayes was twenty seconds behind, with teammate Mike Ryan fourth and Welton fading to ninth.

Johnny was disappointed, figuring that a victory after his Yonkers performance would cement his place on the Olympic team. He settled for a personal best on the course, in 2:26:04, and then a wait-and-see approach as Sullivan told reporters that "it will be at least a couple of months before a selection will be made"[8] for the marathon. Less than two weeks after Boston, the Missouri Athletic Club staged the second marathon tryout. Chicago's Sidney Hatch took this twenty-five-miler, outsprinting Joe Forshaw, the 1906 Olympian, by a scant four seconds.

In early June, Alonzo Stagg and nineteen other coaches and administrators met at Sullivan's offices on 21 Warren Street in lower Manhattan to select the U.S. Olympic team. On June 8, at the Astor House, Sullivan named the seventy-six athletes on the squad.

For the marathon, the first two finishers in both Boston and St. Louis were selected: Morrissey and Hayes, Hatch and Forshaw. Johnny's doubts gave way to relief and then excitement, and he probably could have skipped across the Atlantic. Hjertberg counseled caution, and the two resumed workouts in and around Celtic Park, joining the many other I-AAC men named to the team. All were fitted for national uniforms and given physical exams. Johnny made one purchase for himself: an autograph book with a red leather cover. Inside was stated: THE RACE IS TO THE SWIFT. He vowed to get the signature of every U.S. Olympian.

Sullivan picked several athletes for a supplemental list, including

Welton and Ryan, based on their times in Boston. These men had to pay their own expenses to London (estimated at $325). To round out the marathon corps, Sullivan added Louis Tewanima, a Hopi Indian from Shungopovi in northeast Arizona. Born and raised in the rarified air of Second Mesa, where the altitude approaches 5,700 feet, Tewanima had been brought against his will, in the company of fellow Native Americans considered prisoners of war, to the Carlisle Indian School in Pennsylvania, an institution similar to the one that Tom Longboat had fled from in Brantford.

He arrived "thin, emaciated, and beligerent [sic],"[9] according to the War Department, of indeterminate age and not knowing how to read, write, or speak English. Unknowingly, they had delivered to Carlisle an athletic prodigy, someone who liked to run sixty miles, to the town of Winslow, Arizona, just to watch the trains roll by. Not long after Tewanima was enrolled at Carlisle and began his apprenticeship as a tailor, he approached Glenn "Pop" Warner about joining the school's track team. The storied coach initially dismissed the 110-pounder, whose rejoinder, according to Warner, was curt: "Me run fast good. All Hopi run fast good."[10]

Tewanima had never previously worn running shoes, but his inexhaustible endurance was a revelation. Carlisle teammate Jim Thorpe liked to boast (with only some exaggeration) how he, Tewanima, and a third student-athlete took on and defeated a thirty-man track team from Lafayette College, with Tewanima dominating the distance races, Thorpe cleaning up everything else, and Warner chortling on the sidelines.[11]

Murphy and Sullivan bypassed several veterans—Sam Mellor, Mike Spring, Bill Frank—in favor of Tewanima, even though he had never entered a marathon. Privately, they thought that, in the raw and untested Hopi, they might have found their own Native Indian to take down Tom Longboat.

. . .

Dorando Pietri did not compete in any major races in the winter of 1907. He was pointing toward Italy's national championships in June, which also served as the Olympic team trials.[12] He concentrated on training until late April, when he reemerged and won a 10K race in Pistoia. He followed that with victories in Verona and Bologna in late May.

He arrived in Rome as the heavy favorite and entered two races on successive days—the 20K on June 2 and the marathon on June 3. Why Italian officials scheduled the half-marathon on the day before the marathon has never been explained. Why Dorando thought it would be smart to compete in both races, back-to-back, has also never been explained.

He won the 20K on June 2, clocking 1:10:54 to beat his rival Pagliani. The following afternoon, with the marathon title on the line, Dorando vied against Umberto Blasi and Augusto Cocca. He knew the Rome course well, and he didn't fear Blasi or Cocca. But neither of his opponents had run the 20K the day before, and Dorando was clearly tired. At the 33K mark, he dropped out because of heatstroke, as Blasi coasted to victory.

Pietri had now failed to finish the last three marathons he entered, a pattern that did little for his confidence. He needed to prove to himself—as well as to La Patria and the Italian Olympic committee—that he was capable of contending in the upcoming Games. A 40K solo run was planned for Carpi on July 7.

Dorando trained hard in the interim and, on the day of the exhibition, powered to a fast start. He churned out the first 20K in an impressive 1:14:20. Now came the second half, as much a mental challenge as a physical one, especially in a showcase without opponents to push him. But Dorando slowed only slightly to finish in 2:38. It was the fastest time ever recorded for that distance, according to marathon historians David Martin and Roger Gynn.

After three consecutive failures, a relieved Dorando had finally conquered his second marathon. But the cost was steep. His body had just seventeen days to recover before the Olympic marathon in London.

C anada's Olympic committee organized two marathon trials. The first was held over fifteen miles in Montreal. The second, a twenty-five-miler in Toronto in early June, was the main event, with the top five finishers qualifying for the team: Harry Lawson, of the West End YMCA, finished first in 2:38:11, followed by William Wood, William Goldsboro, Fred Simpson, and George Lister.

Tom Longboat did not run in either race because of a medical excuse. He had cramps, bad boils, and carbuncles. His remedy was to take a curative soak at the Preston baths. He was selected to the Olympic team based on his brilliant record since 1906 but, because he had missed the tryouts, he was asked to prove his fitness. On June 12, over the fifteen-mile Montreal loop, he faced five runners who each covered three miles. Longboat clipped nearly three minutes off his own record, despite holding a handkerchief to his face because of the dust. "I could have gone faster," he said, "but Flanagan would not let me."

The *Montreal Star* concluded that he "effectively silenced all who since the beginning of the year have busied themselves spreading all sorts of rumors about his physical decline." Longboat was more succinct: "I knocked the knockers."[13]

Undoubtedly, he received special treatment, but Canada badly wanted to defend Billy Sherring's 1906 Olympic marathon title. They were not about to leave their star home. In fact, of the twenty-seven Canadian track-and-field athletes who competed in London, twelve were marathoners, the maximum allowed in the event. Sherring himself was appointed track coach.

The Canadian team left for London on June 11. Tom Flanagan had other plans for his prized runner. He and Longboat departed separately, on the *Empress of Britain* steamer, and their destination was the Flanagan family farm in Ireland. Such a setting, the promoter figured, would allow Longboat to prepare without distraction for the most important race of his career.

One looming obstacle remained. James Sullivan had formally protested Longboat's inclusion on the Canadian team to Lord Desborough in London, sending a nonrefundable £1 deposit with his objection that Longboat was a professional. Longboat's fate was now in the hands of the British Olympic committee.

Early on the morning of June 27, Johnny Hayes and the rest of the U.S. Olympic team descended on the American Line pier at the foot of Vesey Street in lower Manhattan. There, they boarded the SS *Philadelphia*, a two-funnel ocean liner. Johnny stashed his gear in the cabin, then stood at the rail with his brother, Willie, marveling at the huge crowd that had gathered to see them off.

The horn blew and Willie wished Godspeed to his brother. He returned to shore and joined the throngs waving farewell as the steamer slowly maneuvered through the water. Two tugboats decorated in red, white, and blue escorted the *Philadelphia* out of New York harbor, tooting their whistles until the big ship dipped into the open ocean for the journey to England.

Almost immediately, Coach "Silent" Mike Murphy assembled the team. Hard of hearing and slight of build, Murphy had been a crack runner in his own right. He had a reputation as a brilliant, innovative trainer. He was said to have invented the "crouch start" for sprinters, and to have whipped the great heavyweight champ, John L. Sullivan, into shape (no easy task). His track teams, first at Yale and then at Penn, were among the most successful in the collegiate ranks, and James Sullivan had enlisted Silent Mike and his ubiquitous derby hat to supervise the U.S. Olympic effort.

Murphy, from County Limerick, was not silent in appealing to national pride—American national pride, that is. "You're not ordinary men," he declared, looking directly at each athlete. "You're America's best men. It's up to you to see that you're in good condition to do justice for your country and yourselves when the time comes at Shepherd's Bush. You have the pure red blood in your veins of men that are men."[14]

Training commenced the next day. Johnny and the other marathoners logged miles on a cork track laid out along the promenade deck. Baths and vigorous rubdowns followed, then a meal and a nap. A vigorous walk constituted the afternoon workout. At night, they marveled at the amount of food inhaled by the Irish Whales. Martin Sheridan tallied the damage wrought by hammer thrower Matt McGrath at one sitting: "Five plates of soup, four orders of fish, three broiled chickens, two steaks, six English plover, seven cups of custard, three pieces of apple pie, four cups of coffee and two pounds of cheese."[15]

Johnny already knew many of the fellows—twenty members of the Irish-American Athletic Club were onboard—but the college lads dressed smarter and spoke a different language. Giant Ralph Rose and John Garrels came from the University of Michigan, the latter known for his stint on Fielding Yost's undefeated "point-a-minute" Wolverine football team of 1904. Murphy brought along several athletes from Penn, including ace sprinters Nate Cartmell and John Baxter Taylor, a veterinarian student and one of two African-Americans on the squad. Yale pole-vaulter A. C. Gilbert boasted a

Tom Longboat in a posed studio portrait, circa 1907. *Canada Archives*

Tom Longboat, manager-promoter Tom Flanagan (seated), and heavyweight boxer Jack Johnson. The caption reads: "Red, White & Black." *Flanagan Family Archive*

A panoramic view of the Olympic Stadium at Shepherd's Bush. The swimming pool extends along the straightaway (right), opposite the Royal Box. *LA84 Foundation*

At the Opening Ceremony, shot-putter Ralph Rose refuses to dip the American flag as he leads the U.S. team past the Royal Box. *LA84 Foundation*

The Liverpool Police tug-of-war team (left) defeats the American squad amid charges that the British team wore illegal shoes. *LA84 Foundation*

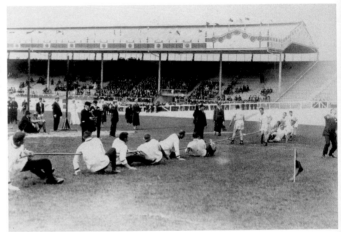

A HARD LOSER!

OLYMPIC TEAM

Newspapers on both sides of the Atlantic were transfixed by the American-British rivalry during the "Battle of Shepherd's Bush." An illustration from the *Brooklyn Eagle* newspaper shows Uncle Sam getting the better of John Bull. *Private collection*

Before the start of the marathon, the runners walk past the statue of Queen Victoria in Windsor. Johnny Hayes is at the front of the pack (far right, front row), while Dorando Pietri is in the middle of the second row (dark shorts). *LA84 Foundation*

Tom Longboat is the center of attention just before the start of the race. Behind his left shoulder is Fred Simpson, who finished sixth. *LA84 Foundation*

Tom Longboat (#72) leads Dorando Pietri (#19) as the marathoners leave Windsor Castle behind. *Kenneth Cook, Society of Olympic Collectors*

Dorando Pietri, on the road to Shepherd's Bush.
LA84 Foundation

Johnny Hayes runs through Willesden, trailed by his bicycle attendants. *LA84 Foundation*

Officials surround an exhausted Dorando Pietri, who has entered the Stadium in first place.
LA84 Foundation

Dorando Pietri, after collapsing to the track during the final lap. Dr. Michael Bulger cradles his body; Jack Andrew (pointing) attempts to keep order. *LA84 Foundation*

Dorando finally reaches the finish line, bracketed by Jack Andrew (left) and Dr. Bulger.
LA84 Foundation

Trailing Dorando in the Stadium, Johnny Hayes churns toward the finish line.
LA84 Foundation

A dejected Johnny Hayes is consoled immediately after the race.
LA84 Foundation

The day after the race, the Queen of England presents Dorando with a gold cup in commemoration of his performance. Next to the Queen is Lord Desborough, the chief organizer of the 1908 Olympics. Applauding behind the Queen (at right) is Pierre de Coubertin, credited with reviving the ancient Olympics. *LA84 Foundation*

After receiving the Olympic gold medal and marathon trophy (atop table), Johnny Hayes is escorted by teammates (from left) Roy Welton, Louis Tewanima, Mike Ryan (hidden), Tom Morrissey, and Joe Forshaw. *LA84 Foundation*

President Theodore Roosevelt (center, white suit) hosts the 1908 U.S. Olympic team at Sag Harbor. To Roosevelt's immediate left is James E. Sullivan, the head of the team, while Johnny Hayes, in cap, stands to Roosevelt's right. *Theodore Roosevelt Birthplace/ National Parks Service*

Dorando Pietri and Johnny Hayes square off before their first professional marathon race at Madison Square Garden, with "Boss" Croker as the starter. *Dr. Edward Kozloff*

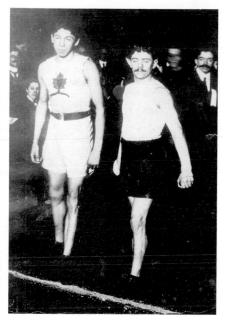

Tom Longboat and Dorando Pietri before their second professional marathon duel, in Buffalo, 1909. Dorando's brother, Ulpiano, stands far right. *Private collection*

Cigarette cards of Johnny Hayes and Tom Longboat, circa 1909. *Private collection*

Before the start of the first Marathon Derby, held at the Polo Grounds in New York, with (from left) Alf Shrubb, Dorando Pietri, Henri St. Yves, Tom Longboat, Johnny Hayes, and Matthew Maloney. *Library of Congress*

Song sheet of "Dorando," the first hit song written by Irving Berlin. *Music Division, The New York Public Library for the Performing Arts, Astor, Lenox and Tilden Foundations*

Tom Longboat (right) buys a newspaper while serving in France during World War I. *Canada Archives*

The bronze statue of Johnny Hayes that stands today in Nenagh, the town in Ireland from which his father emigrated to America.

superb pair of arms honed from farmwork in Oregon. He had introduced the spikeless bamboo pole, which was lighter and more pliant than the clunky hickory and spruce models and allowed him to accelerate faster down the runway. He had soared past the world record to 12 feet, 7¾ inches at the Olympic trials.

The men relieved the monotony with rope-climbing contests, tether tennis, cards and checkers, and a shuffleboard tourney. At night, Carlisle's Frank Mt. Pleasant entertained passengers with popular operas on the piano, while Gilbert wowed with sleight-of-hand magic and his club swinging turn. Everyone joined together to sing "The Star-Spangled Banner" and "America" on July 4.

The steamer reached Southampton the next morning, and British journalists came onboard in search of Louis Tewanima, the Hopi marathoner. Gilbert, who was "brown as a berry from the sun," decided to play another trick. "I mussed up [my hair], grabbed a fire-axe off the wall, and raced up on deck letting out war whoops and dancing around the reporter and photographers with wild brandishings of my axe," he recalled. "The reporter couldn't say anything but 'My word!'"[16]

The team was supposed to stay at the Morton Hotel at Russell Square, but complaints about the accommodations, as well as the crowded practice conditions at the Stadium, forced an abrupt change. The marathoners were taken to Brighton, some fifty miles south of London, which meant that Johnny and the others would have to skip the upcoming Opening Ceremonies. But Murphy figured that the seaside resort would eliminate the distractions of London-town, where dancer Isadora Duncan and temptress Maud Allen, appearing as Salome, were performing nightly. The Brighton bunch ensconced at the Hotel Metropole, a stately presence fronting the English Channel, and prepared, under Murphy's watchful direction, on the grounds of the cricket club at nearby Preston Park.

Johnny filled his autograph book and made arrangements to visit his father's hometown in Ireland, Nenagh, after the Games. On one train ride in London, he shared a compartment with a stranger he later described as a "patriotic Irishman." Suddenly, the man pointed to a graveyard and said, "That's the finest sight I have seen since I struck England."[17] When Johnny asked him to explain, he replied that he had not seen so many dead Englishmen in a long while.

This sort of comment—and this anti-British attitude—wasn't foreign to Johnny. The setting raised the stakes. With the U.S. team led by Sullivan and Murphy and dominated by Sheridan, McGrath, and Flanagan on the field—all either Irish born or Irish by blood—they wanted nothing more than to kick the English arse on their home turf.

The Canadian squad stayed at the Sussex Hotel in London under Coach Billy Sherring's leadership. But its most famous team member was not with them. Tom Longboat arrived in Ireland in late June and decamped to the family farm of his coach-promoter, Tom Flanagan, in County Limerick. They stayed in a stout stone home that overlooked a splendid 100-acre spread in Kilbreedy, complete with a cow barn and a 50-foot-deep well, tucked in rolling farmland that was not dissimilar to the Six Nations Reserve. Flanagan's mother, Ellen, provided mountains of hearty food.

Longboat had rested on the trip across the Atlantic save for an exhibition to aid the Seamen's Home. Flanagan soon put Longboat through his paces along the dusty, rutty roads around Kilbreedy. A fifteen-mile loop took him past the Ballinvana creamery to Kilfinane, then toward Kilmallock, where the Run O'Luck tavern displayed an American flag, and back to the starting point.

If Flanagan thought that Ireland would offer tranquil sanctuary for Longboat, he was dead wrong. Every workout was dissected, with daily dispatches printed in newspapers throughout Ireland, Canada, England, and America. Hundreds lined the roads to watch his workouts; dozens attempted to keep pace on bicycles. On a twenty-mile run that started in front of Cruises Royal Hotel in the city of Limerick, one reporter wrote that Longboat accelerated so fast that "swift cyclists [were left] far behind, tired and discomfited."[18]

The crowd roared with applause when he concluded with a rousing sprint in Kilmallock. "The people formed into groups and discussed what they had seen—for a fact nothing else is discussed by the man in the street, or the man in the fields, or as for that, the fair sex—it is Tom Longboat everywhere, and wherever athletics are spoken of, Tom Longboat's name will find an honoured place," the local newspaper reported.[19]

Another journalist felt compelled to touch Longboat's body: "His biceps are not mighty but of that springy, firm feel that tells of splendid quality. The muscles of his thighs and calves are soft and velvety as a glove when in repose, but when the runner tensed them—why they were hard as steel!"[20]

About ten days before the London Olympic marathon, Longboat was running a fourteen-mile tune-up when a trotting pony pulled alongside him. "The reins were thrown loose on the back of the animal, which the driver forced with every means to increase speed," the writer noted. But it was in vain. "On went Longboat with extraordinary power and speed, his head erect, his chest extended, while his stride and agility were marvelous to behold. He had considerably increased the distance between himself and the pony, and the animal that had never known defeat had now for the first time to taste it."[21]

But the victory proved costly. Rains had left the track muddy and, while turning toward Kilbreedy amid the large crowd, Longboat apparently collided with a wagon and fell. He emerged with scrapes on his arms and legs and a sore right knee. "It will knock him off his training for three or four days, perhaps a week," Flanagan said, "in fact, he may not do any more work as the running might interfere with his knee."

He remained confident that Longboat would prevail in London. "I am almost positive that if this has not hurt him he must win," he said. "He is in a class by himself no matter what they may say about the other men."[22]

The injury, and Flanagan's attempt to downplay the incident, was only partly successful. Inevitably, rumors began to spread that Flanagan had lost control of his charge. Longboat was said to be sampling the fare at the local pubs and allegedly bribing dairymaids to spike his milk with whiskey. One reporter noted that he "smoked a cigar nearly all the time," with Longboat affirming, "A good cigar is no harm. I smoke up to the day of the race."[23]

"How do you like Ireland?" he was asked.

"I like Ireland well—especially your Irish girls."

"When do you go to bed in training?"

"Eleven."

"And you get up?"

"Nine, ten—maybe half-past ten—I'm fond of sleeping."

His body weary but his spirit willing, Dorando Pietri joined the rest of the Italian team in Turin. Their budget was meager. They brought just twelve track-and-field competitors, with only Dorando and Umberto Blasi in the marathon. *La Patria* had to borrow money to support Dorando and fund his trip. The sixty-six-man squad traveled third class, with money for one meal a day. After stopping in Paris to change trains, they crossed the English Channel and arrived in London on July 11, two days before the Opening Ceremonies.

Dorando was welcomed by his older brother, Ulpiano, who was a waiter in London and spoke some English. He directed Dorando to stay at Wedde's Hotel and Restaurant,[24] near Leicester Square in Soho, a place managed by two Italians. The next day, in a sixty-horsepower Fiat owned by Italy's IOC member Brunetta d'Usseaux, Dorando toured the marathon course with Primo Bongrani of the *Gazzetta dello Sport* newspaper. He raved about the roads to his brother. There was never a moment of monotony, he said.

No coach supervised Dorando's training. English-language reporters did not come to Soho to interview him. The small contingent of Italian fans in London concentrated their rooting support for the thirty-two-man gymnastics squad, led by Alberto Braglia, from Modena. Dorando had to purchase his own supplies—ice, medicine, a vial of salts, camphor oil—and rent bicycles for his attendants to use during the race.

He drew inspiration from an unlikely source. A month before the Games, a filly from Italy named Signorinetta had lined up for the Epsom Derby against a stellar field of male horses. But the 100:1 long shot had shocked the punters by winning England's most prestigious race. Two days later, she returned to capture the all-filly Oaks, a near-unprecedented double. Perhaps, Dorando thought, he himself would spring the upset and prance away with the title, just like Signorinetta.

ELEVEN

With the world's best athletes converging on London, Imre Kiralfy had turned Shepherd's Bush into a sprawling pleasure ground that resembled an enormous wedding cake. The structures of the Franco–British Exhibition—twenty palaces, seven enormous pavilions, a 300,000-square-foot machine hall—were clad in white plaster, with a billowy architectural flare that one critic described as "Mohamedan-Hindoo."[1] The 8.5 million visitors to the fairgrounds navigated miles of artificial waterways in swan-shaped gondolas and walked through "Ballymaclinton," a faux Irish village, complete with a replica Blarney Stone. From France came the brothers Pathé, showing off moving pictures, the latest technology, at the Cinematograph Hall. (Pathé held the exclusive right to film the Olympic Games.)

Kiralfy the showman also created "Merryland," an amusement-park area that his acolytes consider to be a forerunner to Disneyland, with submarine and toboggan rides and a mountain railway reminiscent of the Matterhorn. Overhead soared the Flip-Flap, a towering metal structure that scissored two counterpoised viewing carriages 200 feet in the air. From the apex of the Flip-Flap, just beyond the Palace of Music and the Fine Art Building, one could glimpse the grandeur of the Stadium, what one observer called "the great achievement of the Franco–British Exhibition and of the engineering profession."[2]

In less than one year's time, Kiralfy had built only the second concrete-and-steel sports stadium, following Harvard University's football stadium in 1903. The budget for the London oval had climbed almost as high as the Flip-Flap—reportedly as much as £85,000. Financial and time constraints had compromised Kiralfy's original vision. The boulevard-like pedestrian entryway was discarded, as was the sportsman's promenade underneath the seating area. The British Olympic Association's request to obtain G. F. Watts's bronze statue, "Physical Energy," for the entrance of the Stadium went unfulfilled. (Kiralfy did manage to build the Imperial Sports Club, an exclusive clubhouse for gentlemen and their guests located next door to the Stadium.)

The exterior of the Stadium was an unfinished, utilitarian shell of exposed steel stanchions and girders, punctuated by billboard advertisements for Schweppes and the *Pall Mall Gazette*. But the Stadium's vast interior dwarfed Harvard's—or any other arena for that matter. There was seating and standing room for as many as 80,000 spectators, including areas for royalty and the media. Underneath the grandstands were thirty-six dressing rooms and a press room with telephones and a direct cable to the United States. The grassy infield, which measured 700 feet by 300 feet, was for the jumping, hurdling, and throwing events, as well as gymnastics and wrestling. A 110-yard swimming tank stretched along one side of the infield, closest to the royal box, complete with a retractable diving tower.

Two concentric tracks circled the infield: a running track that measured a third of a mile (or 586 yards, 2 feet) and a cycling oval of 640 yards. The banked concrete cycling track was built to the specifications of the fastest ovals in Europe, and Charles Perry, the pioneering groundskeeper at the London Athletic Club's facility at Stamford Bridge, had produced a wondrous running track. Perry meticulously handcrafted a spongy but solid surface comprised of three layers: 6 inches of ashes, 1 foot of well-rolled pieces of broken brick, topped off by another 6 inches of engine and house ash, screened and rolled so as to bind together. One expert called it the "fastest cinder-path in the world."[3]

The paint was still drying, and the athletic facilities were untested, but Kiralfy's masterpiece was ready. "It was not just a stadium," wrote historian Rebecca Jenkins. "It was a statement."[4] In anticipation, some 2 million tickets were offered for sale for the two weeks of the Olympic Games, with the Opening Ceremonies expected to be a sellout.

L ord Desborough and the British Olympic Council delegated the planning of the marathon to the Amateur Athletic Association (AAA), England's governing body of track and field. But the AAA had no previous experience with such a race. No marathon had been held in the country since its invention in 1896. The last amateur footrace of twenty miles or longer in Britain had taken place in 1894. By October 1907, a course had not yet been selected or laid out.

The AAA handed off responsibility for the marathon to the Polytechnic Harriers. The London-based track club was part of the Polytechnic Institute, a young men's Christian school started by education reformer Quintin Hogg and moved to its Regent Street location in the early 1880s. (Its motto: "The Lord Is Our Strength.") The Harriers were a preeminent club and had organized long-distance road competitions in the past, including a London-to-Brighton walking race of about fifty miles.

Charged with coordinating the Olympic marathon, as well as Britain's main trials race in April, was the Harriers' honorable secretary, Jack Andrew.[5] He was given two parameters for the course: It must avoid, as much as possible, the busiest roadways of central London, and it must end on the track at the Stadium, which Kiralfy was furiously erecting. A specific distance was not fixed. According to the agreement struck between the British Olympic Council and the IOC, the course was to measure twenty-five miles.

Andrew's first chore was to determine the starting point. What attracted Andrew's attention was the town of Windsor, practically due west of Shepherd's Bush. Specifically, he was drawn to Windsor Castle, home to the royal family since William the Conqueror completed the first stone edifice in the eleventh century. There was no more appropriate place for the start of the Olympics' most prestigious race than the symbolic power seat of the British Empire, with its iconic Round Tower standing sentry along the River Thames. It would be the equivalent of beginning the marathon in, well, Marathon.

The permission of King Edward VII was necessary to use the private grounds of the Castle; the Poly's director of education, Robert Mitchell, delivered the written request to Windsor. Meanwhile, Andrew consulted ordnance survey maps of the area and plotted out a point-to-point course, as was used in Greece and in Boston. By November 1907, using a measuring wheel and a pedometer, he had sketched out a rough version that began in Windsor and then meandered northeast through the suburban market towns of Slough, Uxbridge, Ruislip, and Pinner before veering south past Harrow, Wembley, and Willesden and then arriving at the Stadium. That measured about twenty-five miles. After tinkering with the route to circumvent hard cobbled streets and tramlines, Andrew reckoned the distance to be twenty-six miles.

No task was too small for "the indefatigable Jack."[6] He negotiated with local police superintendents and traffic officials about safety and crowd control along the public roads. He arranged for mileage distance tablets to be designed, forged, and posted along the route (complete with the Polytechnic Harriers' logo). Hotels were enlisted to accommodate the runners, and Andrew commandeered a special train to transport the competitors to Windsor on race day. An endorsement deal was struck with OXO to be the official caterers for the marathon and supply the runners with a flask of OXO beef stock (hot and cold), rice pudding, raisins, bananas, soda, eau de cologne, and sponges at four stages of the race. OXO also promised to have stimulants on hand "in cases of collapse."[7]

Rules for the marathon allowed for two bicycle attendants per runner and required that each contestant "undergo a medical examination previous to the start." Another read: "No competitor either at the start or during the progress of the race may take or receive any drug. The breach of this rule will operate as an absolute disqualification."[8] These conditions were distributed to each team. A program, complete with advertisements and a map of the course, was printed and sold to the public for 6d.

Most of the proposed course was used at Britain's main trials marathon in April, although the entire route was not accessible because the Stadium was unfinished. Nasty weather narrowed the field to sixty-eight, with two runners from the Polytechnic Harriers, James Beale (finishing second) and Harry Barrett (fifth), qualifying for the British team. The route, all agreed, was a fair test. It narrowed at certain places, but it was not particularly hilly, at least compared to Athens and Boston.

The details remained in flux as Andrew dealt with numerous natural and man-made obstacles. A last-minute adjustment to the entrances leading to the Stadium caused him to shift the tunnel that the marathoners used to access the venue. In turn, he switched the direction the runners traveled on the track to clockwise ("right hand inside"), as opposed to counterclockwise. These changes reduced the circuit on the cinder oval to two-thirds of a lap.

Finally, the royal family greenlighted access to the Castle grounds. Andrew was able to locate the starting point on the East

Lawn, some 700 yards from the mammoth statue of Queen Victoria. The Windsor-to-Shepherd's Bush route was now fixed. From the Castle grounds to the winning post opposite the royal box inside the Stadium, the course measured exactly 26 miles, 385 yards, or 42.195 kilometers.

The implications were extraordinary. Andrew had created the longest marathon course in Olympic history, for a group of runners who were expecting a race of about twenty-five miles. And, somewhat haphazardly, even randomly, Jack Andrew had established the abstruse distance that would become the standard for the marathon.

Later, long after the race achieved mythic status, the facts about how Andrew decided on the 1908 marathon route and its unique distance would become twisted. Even today, journalists state that the Princess of Wales demanded that the start of the race take place on the East Terrace of Windsor Castle so that her children could witness the event from the nursery windows. And the ending at the Stadium was reportedly changed so that the race would conclude in front of the royal box.

Newspaper articles from 1907–1908 and papers from the British Olympic Association tell a different story. "No evidence has been found to support"[9] that the Princess requested the location of the start, according to marathon scholar Bob Wilcock. Simply put, when King Edward VII gave his "gracious consent" for the marathon to begin at the Castle, Andrew selected the East Terrace as the most suitable spot, both for its privacy and its access to the road leading to the town of Windsor.

At the finish, the competitors were originally slated to enter the Stadium through the tunnel under the royal box, and then complete a full lap (one-third of a mile) in the counterclockwise direction. This entry became inaccessible due to last-minute construction in and around the Stadium, and so Andrew shifted the entrance to a different point. According to Wilcock, "the direction of running was altered to clockwise, so that the runners would pass in front of both stands, to arrive at the planned finishing line in front of the Royal Box. This meant 385 yards on the track. There was no royal influence on the determination of the distance."[10]

TWELVE

There was no sunshine on the morning of July 13, the opening day of the Fourth Olympic Games, as Londoners woke to heavy rains. Gloomy skies persisted throughout the day and dampened expectations for a glorious beginning. Only 30,000 spectators showed up for the Opening Ceremonies at the Stadium. Most huddled in the cheap seats, which offered no protection from the rain. Instead of "dainty dresses, by which the ladies would have given brightness and colour to a spectacle, umbrellas and raincoats figured everywhere," the *Evening News* reported.[1]

Following a leisurely lunch at the Imperial Sports Club, Lord Desborough, Baron Pierre de Coubertin, and Imre Kiralfy strolled next door to the Stadium in frock coats and black silk top hats to await the arrival of King Edward VII and Queen Alexandra. Other dignitaries filed in: the Crown Prince and Princess of Greece, the Crown Prince and Princess of Sweden, the prime minister of Nepal, the royal children, and Whitelaw Reid, the former editor of the *New York Tribune* and the current U.S. Ambassador to the Court of St. James.

James E. Sullivan kept his distance from Coubertin. He inspected the rain-soaked track with groundskeeper Perry, schmoozed the press, and visited the U.S. athletes gathered in their dressing room beneath the grandstands. The Americans had noticed a curious feature atop the Stadium, where the flags of each nation competing at the Olympics were flying. The American and the Swedish flags were missing, while those of China and Japan (neither of which fielded a team in

London) were on display. The athletes couldn't help but wonder: Was this an oversight or a deliberate insult?

In the afternoon, the rains paused as King Edward VII and Queen Alexandra were driven from Buckingham Palace in an open landau drawn by four horses. They entered the Stadium via a carpeted passageway, which was covered with an awning, and were greeted by Lord Desborough. He presented the King and the Queen to Baron de Coubertin, who in turn introduced them to the other IOC members.

The King stepped toward the front of the royal box, and the National Anthem was struck. Facing his enclosure was a lettered inscription that read: EDWARD VII, REX, IMPERATOR. Across from him, on the grass infield behind the swimming pool, stood approximately 2,000 athletes representing eighteen national teams, what one observer described as "young men and maidens, in the prime of life and the pink of condition."

Shortly after 3:50 p.m., Lord Desborough approached the King: "Will your Majesty be pleased to declare the Fourth Olympiad open?"

In ringing tones replied Edward VII: "I declare the Olympic Games of London open."

The Grenadier Guards played the National Anthem again as each nation dipped its flag in respect. Then, as the band swung into "Entry of the Gladiators," each team took to the track to march past the royal box. The most vociferous greeting was reserved for Denmark, Queen Alexandra's homeland. When the twenty-strong ladies gymnastics team pranced along the track, coquettishly attired in white frocks and creamy yellow stockings, the crowd exploded. The host country, with by far the largest contingent, was led by J. E. K. Studd, a former cricket star. Tom Longboat, still in Ireland, did not take part in the Opening Ceremonies[2] with the rest of the Canadian team, clad in all-white suits.

The sixty-odd athletes from Italy presented a tidy uniformity in black and white: white straw hats with a black band, black jackets, white knickerbockers, black stockings, and white shoes. Dorando Pietri breathed in the heady atmosphere. The feeling was different from two years ago, when the historic aura of Athens and Marathon gave the Games a classical feel. The new stadium was modern, contemporary. He walked along the cinder track, feeling the slight give beneath his feet.

With Johnny Hayes and other Americans left behind in Brighton, it was left to a small contingent of athletes, mostly the throwers and those who were to compete later that day, to represent the United States. The men did not dress in their athletic uniforms; most wore everyday suits. John Garrels, the Michigan hurdler, held the UNITED STATES placard, while shot-putter Ralph Rose was the flag-bearer.

When the team passed the royal box, Rose was supposed to lower the flag, as every nation seemingly had done, in a show of respect to the King. The Stars and Stripes did not dip.

The incident has been the subject of debate ever since. Some observers believed it was inadvertent. Teammate Wilbur Burroughs commented that Rose "had not noticed what the other nations did when they passed the box of the king, and it was just a case of stage fright with him."[3]

Marathoner Sidney Hatch blamed it on the flag—or lack thereof. "At the top of the stadium they had the flags of all the nations, excepting the American," he recalled. "Rose saw this and took it for granted that an attempt was being made to slight the Americans, so in turn he refused to dip the flag to the King when he passed."[4]

With Imre Kiralfy in charge of every detail at the Stadium, it's doubtful that the omission was deliberate. The impresario had lived in the United States for years and made his reputation (and much money) there. His own son, Edgar, was on the U.S. team as a sprinter.

Others have speculated that Rose wanted to make a political statement, citing the controversial quote attributed to Martin Sheridan, who reportedly thundered, "This flag dips for no earthly king."[5] The Irish-American star almost certainly did not say this in 1908. No newspaper in America or England reported such an utterance at the time. According to historian Bill Mallon, *New York Times* columnist Arthur Daley first credited these words to Sheridan in 1952, years after Sheridan's death in 1918, and then kept embellishing the story.

Whatever Rose's motives, and whatever Sheridan did or did not say, the absence of an American flag atop the Stadium rankled the U.S. team. A complaint was registered, Lord Desborough apologized, and the oversight was corrected. But an acrimonious tone lingered over the Stadium long after King Edward VII had departed the Franco–British Exhibition grounds.

The Battle of Shepherd's Bush was officially on.

T he first week of the 1908 Olympics did not go well for England. The weather was "base beyond description,"[6] according to one observer, with "Aquarius [holding] high revel."[7] The heavy rains, in turn, prevented the anticipated crowds from flocking to the Stadium. DESERTED STADIUM,[8] read the *Daily Chronicle* headline, after only 4,000 spectators showed up on July 16.

"No such opportunity will ever come in the lifetime of most of us to see the finest sport with the minimum of expense and trouble," grumbled Arthur Conan Doyle. "The present apathy of the public is very little to our credit as a sporting nation."[9]

Most agreed that the tickets were too expensive. The cheap seats, costing one shilling per session, were selling briskly, but these were located at the rounded, uncovered extremities of the Stadium, "whence the swimming and gymnastic displays and contests and most of the athletic field events are hardly visible," *The Field* noted.[10] The more expensive areas, wrote another, are "practically empty, a howling wilderness, crying out for patronage."[11] The outcry forced Kiralfy and the Olympic organizers to reduce ticket prices during the second week of the Games.

One part of the Stadium was always packed: Section K in the covered part of the western grandstand. Through his Spalding company connections, Sullivan had arranged for this spot to be reserved for U.S. supporters. In the so-called "American Cheering Section," collegiate-like war whoops and chants prevailed, accompanied by rattles and penny trumpets:

> *Rah! Rah! Rah! Our men are on the field,*
> *Rah! Rah! Rah! They will never, never yield,*
> *And we'll swing and shout till they have swept the field,*
> *There'll be a hot time in the old town tonight, Oh! London.*

> *America, America, U. Rah! Rah! America!*
> *Hail to thee we sing, Hail to thee, our native soil,*
> *U. Rah! Rah! America!*[12]

At first amused, and then dismayed, the home supporters soon were answering, "shouting themselves hoarse when the Union Jack is in the ascendant."[13] But those moments were infrequent as, with much teeth gnashing, the British watched their chief rival, "Uncle Sam's Argonauts," romp on the track.

Mel Sheppard, the Irish-American club's brilliant middle-distance man, captured the 1,500 meters over the local favorite, Harold Wilson, then returned days later to take the 800 over Italy's Emilio Lunghi. The Irish Whales grunted and powered to glory, with Sheridan leading an American sweep of the discus and mighty John Flanagan surpassing Matt McGrath on the final toss to earn his third Olympic gold in the hammer. Rose defeated Irishman Denis Horgan in the shot (with Garrels third), and buoyant Ray Ewry completed another "double" with victories in the standing high jump and broad jump.

The British won their fair share of medals, but Sullivan was quick to point out that the majority of those came in events the Americans ignored or discounted. The hosts swept yachting, polo, and rowing against no U.S. competitors. Their tennis triumphs at Wimbledon were accomplished without an American opponent. Their twenty-eight-strong swim team and thirty-seven-man cycling squad far outnumbered the eight swimmers and two cyclists for the Americans.

On July 17, four days after the Opening Ceremonies, the tug-of-war provoked another U.S.–Britain contretemps. The first round pitted a makeshift American squad, including strongmen Rose, Flanagan, McGrath, and Burroughs, against a well-trained team of Liverpool policemen, in a best-of-three match. With a hearty "pull," the cops yanked the Americans over in "the shortest time on record." Sullivan charged that the Liverpudlians had donned illegal shoes, with spikes and cleats that allowed them to dig their heels in the turf, and should be disqualified. British judges rejected the protest on the grounds that the cops were using standard boots, and so Sullivan withdrew the U.S. team from the competition.

BIG SHOES STIR WRATH,[14] screamed the headline in the *Chicago News*. Hearst newspapers charged that the hosts "brazenly violated Olympic rules" by wearing "monstrously heavy boots with great pieces of iron."[15] (A team of London cops ended up winning the gold medal, with Liverpool second.)

Sullivan also challenged the pole-vaulting conditions, after A. C. Gilbert and other U.S. jumpers were banned from their customary practice of digging holes underneath the bar into which they inserted their poles. This protest was rejected, and the Americans were forced to use unfamiliar equipment and techniques.

Another complaint came after Sullivan noticed that the U.S. runners kept being drawn into the same preliminary heats, thereby lessening their chances of advancing to the medal round. Thus, after eight heats in the 1,500-meter race, only two Americans survived to take on five Brits in the finals (won by Peerless Mel Sheppard). "It seems hardly just that the lots should have been drawn not upon the basis of the team we actually brought over but upon the entries," Sullivan barked. "Had our best men not been bunched in the first two heats I think we should have captured four [heats]."[16]

Sullivan's daily harangues about the hosts and their officiating methods fed a voracious press that delighted in every angle of the trans-Atlantic rivalry. BOLD YANKEE BOYS TWIST LION'S TAIL, read the headline from the *Boston Herald*, while the *Long Branch Record* proclaimed, EAGLE'S CLAWS ROUT THE LION. The *Brooklyn Citizen* newspaper mocked the British for "making a vaudeville show of the Olympiad. The Americans [are] afraid that England will yet count Ping-Pong [in the scoring]."[17] Cartoons depicting Uncle Sam grappling with John Bull accompanied the articles.

On the Sunday after the first week of the Games, a special service was held for competitors and officials at St. Paul's Cathedral. The Bishop of Central Pennsylvania, Ethelbert Talbot, who was attending the Lambeth Conference of Anglican bishops, was invited to give the address. In his sermon, Talbot addressed the discord at the Olympics:

We have just been contemplating the great Olympic Games. What does it mean? It means that young men of robust physical life have come from all parts of the world. It does mean, I think, as someone has said, that this era of internationalism as seen in the Stadium has an element of danger. Of course, it is very true, as he says, that each athlete strives not only for the sake of sport, but for the sake of his country. Thus a new rivalry is invented. If England be beaten on the river, or America outdistanced on the racing path, or that American has lost the strength that she once possessed. Well, what of it? The only safety after all lies in the lesson of the real Olympia—that the Games themselves are better than the race and the prize. St. Paul tells us how insignificant is the prize. Our prize is not corruptible, but incorruptible, and though only one may wear the laurel wreath, all may share the equal joy of the contest.[18]

Heads nodded at Talbot's underlining message: It doesn't matter whether you win or lose. What's important is to take part.

Sullivan, for one, refused to heed Talbot's words. The 400 meters, contested at the Stadium on the day before the marathon, was the most controversial and argued-about event of the Games to that point. The finale pitted Scotsman Wyndham Halswelle, a local favorite and Boer War veteran, against three Americans: John Carpenter, John Taylor, and William Robbins. Halswelle was the fastest qualifier, having set an Olympic record of 48.4 in the second round, and he was seeking redemption following his defeat at the 1906 Athens Games by American Paul Pilgrim.

Robbins took an early advantage, only to be passed by Carpenter and Halswelle. As they turned toward home, Carpenter on the inside began to bore away from the rail, forcing Halswelle to the outside of the track. The *Daily Mail* charged that the American "gave the Englishman two distinct 'elbow jabs' in the chest," with Halswelle "thrown out of his course and his stride."[19]

Halswelle slowed as Carpenter continued sprinting. But before the American had even crossed the finish, track officials signaled for the worsted finish line to be broken. The race was rendered void, and photographs of the runners' footprints in the cinder track were taken as evidence.

British newspapers claimed collusion among the American three-some, alleging that Carpenter committed "the foulest and dirtiest piece of running that has ever been seen on an athletic track in these islands amongst amateurs or professionals. The black work was not the work of him who was not white,"[20] a reference to Taylor being African-American.

U.S. team manager Matt Halpin retorted that, "It was a case of being Halswelle's day, and as Halswelle did not win, it was no race. We came to win on our merits, which we did in this race."[21]

Officials conferred into the evening before releasing their ruling. Carpenter was disqualified, and the 400-meter final was ordered to be rerun without him. The United States protested the verdict and refused to allow Taylor and Robbins to take part in the runoff, leaving Halswelle with the gold medal in a walkover.

The crux of Sullivan's objections was with the governance of the Games. In 1907, the IOC had agreed to let the hosts draw up the regulations for each event and to select the officials to oversee them. In effect, the English not only made up the rules, they were in charge of enforcing them. This gave them an inherent advantage, Sullivan claimed, and sullied their well-polished reputation as upstanding sportsmen.

As he well understood, this was the worst possible insult he could muster about Englishmen in the Edwardian Age. Establishing a proper code of conduct and observing the rules of fair play were surely embedded in their DNA. "England is, by common consent, the hub of the world of sport," the Pall Mall Gazette sniffed. "It is, perhaps, no exaggeration to say that in no language in the world but the English are there any words possessing quite the same connotation as our 'sport,' 'sportsman,' 'sportsmanlike.' They have a moral as well as a physical signification: only in English is it possible to describe an action that savours of dishonour as being 'not cricket.'"[22]

Still to come, on the final full day of competition, was the marathon. And, if the British thought that James E. Sullivan was "not cricket" to this point, they had not seen anything yet.

THIRTEEN

Daily reports from Ireland kept Tom Longboat's name in the news, but the international press corps did not require his presence in London to breathlessly hype the marathon. It was "the great event of the 1908 Olympiad,"[1] "the *Ultima Thule* of the hopes of all countries who are supporters of the Games,"[2] and "the blue riband of the Olympic Games."[3]

"Every competition in the Games is important, but the Marathon race is the event around which clusters the most sentiment," the *Sporting Life* opined. "It seizes hold of the imagination, and has been elevated to the highest plane of athletic glory. To win the Marathon race even in these degenerate days ensures international and undying fame."[4]

Longboat remained the overwhelming favorite among London's degenerate bookmakers handicapping the most international field ever assembled for a marathon, with fifty-five starters from sixteen nations. "There is a lot of money being bet on the result of the Marathon," the *New York Press* reported, "the Englishmen freely backing [Alex] Duncan of the Salford Harriers . . . while the Canadians are ready to support [Longboat] almost to any amount."[5]

Of the eleven other Canadians, Harry Lawson, the winner of the Toronto Trials race (and a native of Leeds), was made a solid pick. Veteran Jack Caffery, the double winner at Boston in 1900–01, was considered too old, while Willie Wood from Brantford, near the Six Nations Reserve, was considered too young. Team manager J. Howard

Crocker mentioned Fred Simpson as the insider's choice. The unheralded Simpson was the "other" Native Indian, overshadowed by Longboat's considerable achievements (and often mistaken for him by newspaper caption writers). A Mississauga of the Ojibwa tribe, from the Alderville Reserve in south-central Ontario, the rangy Simpson had impressed with his training runs and low-key demeanor.

South Africa, then a British colony, was allowed to enter its own team, but its top runner, Charles Hefferon, was considered one of the family. He had been born in England and raised due west of London before emigrating, first to Canada and then to southern Africa to fight for the Empire during the Boer War. He settled there and worked in the prisons department; the rugged conditions had sharpened his training. Hefferon attracted smart money. But he had dropped out of the qualifying trials in Africa; he was also entered in the five-mile event at the Stadium, six days before the Marathon, leaving many to wonder whether the thirty-four-year-old would have anything in reserve.

Several journalists hopped on the Scandinavian bandwagon, well aware that the region was blossoming into a distance-running stronghold (thanks to altitude training and, some said, the wintertime rigors of cross-country skiing). Sweden returned Johan Svanberg, the silver medalist in 1906, as well as his diminutive rival, Gustaf Törnros, the fourth-place finisher, while Finland's Kaale Nieminen had won the Trials race in Helsinki.

From the two Italians, Dorando and Blasi, little was expected. One journalist identified Dorando as "a well-known stayer, who will probably stand the warm weather better than some of the men from Northern climates."[6] More typical was that he was misidentified in the newspapers. He was, variously, "Pietri Dorando" and "P. Docando."

Johnny Hayes and the six other U.S. marathoners were seen as practice fodder. According to *The Sportsman*, "Little is known of the

American representatives, but we may say, without disparagement, that they are not seriously feared."[7] Coach Murphy seemed to agree—despite overseeing the team's training in Brighton. He regarded their chances of success as "practically nothing. . . . We [have] but one man in the lot, all the others being immature boys, and small ones at that."[8]

Only Morrissey, on the basis of his Boston Marathon win, and Tewanima were touted as possible contenders. One team member told a reporter that, in Brighton, Tewanima was "running like a streak of greased lightning. The bunch covered 18 miles of the course the other day and the Indian lost them. Hayes was the only one of the bunch that stayed anywhere near him after the tenth mile."[9]

England had held four selection races, the first being a twenty-five-miler won by Jack Price, a muscular steelworker from the coal-rich Black Country of the Midlands. He skipped the main trial on April 25, on the Windsor–London course that mimicked the Olympic layout (albeit several miles shorter). In miserable conditions, Alex Duncan came home first, followed by James Beale, Fred Lord, Tom Jack, and Harry Barrett. Fred Appleby, a South London dentist who had twice beaten the great Alf Shrubb, and Billy Clarke, winner of the Liverpool trial, were among those added to the team.

With twelve solid entrants and home-turf advantage, the British were the consensus favorites—and, after all, a runner from the host country had won three of the four Olympic marathons (with Sherring's victory in Athens being the exception). "Among sound judges today there are no fears that we shall fail," promised the *Star* on the morning of the race.[10]

The American press agreed. "One event stands out in which the rivals of the United States appear to have a better chance of winning than the Americans. This is the twenty-six mile Marathon road race," commented the *New York Evening Sun*. "It cannot be truthfully said that the chances of the Americans overshadow those of the English and Canadians. . . . A victory in this great Olympic feature event would be the athletic surprise of the meet."[11]

Britain's confidence came from a deep-seated belief that their cross-country tradition would carry the day. "The Briton has, I am convinced, a far greater stamina, as has been proved over and over again by our superiority in long-distance races, a superiority which our American cousins even will readily admit, once they are seriously challenged on the point," professional runner Alf Shrubb boasted. "The Marathon race, which we have hitherto allowed to go to one or other of our rivals, should be regarded as a British preserve, as it is just the sort of race at which our men commonly excel."[12]

What Shrubb and the experts on both sides of the Atlantic downplayed, or ignored, was the one significant disadvantage faced by the British. England had never staged a marathon before the Trials. Their longest races tended to be fifteen-milers, and these often occurred on the track, not on the open road. A total of five Englishmen had competed in the four previous Olympic marathons (and one of those runners, John Daly, was actually Irish). Joseph Cormack's fourteenth place in 1906 was their best showing in the Olympics.

Compared to the Americans and the Canadians, weened on the well-established Boston Marathon and the various marathons throughout the Midwest and in Canada, the British were marathon novices, with little understanding of the delicate balance between pace and endurance required for the *Ultima Thule*.

Tom Longboat arrived in London three days before the marathon. With Tom Flanagan and Lou Marsh, he checked into the White Hart Hotel in Windsor, to be near the start of the race. Longboat visited the state apartments at the Castle and took a spin over the course in a motorcar provided by the *Star* newspaper. Flanagan left Marsh to supervise Longboat as he chatted up the bookies in London's pubs.

The morning before the race, Tom loosened up with a three-mile jog. "I have not trained until recently," he admitted, but he was optimistic about his chances. "I don't care what sort of day it is, but I think if it rains it will suit me best. I can tell you that the man that beats me will know that he is in a race."

He didn't attempt to hide the injuries he suffered from the collision in Ireland. The *Evening News* reported that he had "a nasty bruise on his right leg and his feet were blistered," and that Marsh was "attending to Longboat's feet."

His sense of humor remained intact. Marsh commented that a guest had approached Longboat at the hotel bar, apparently without recognizing him, and asked, "Do you think Longboat will win the big race?"

"No, I am sure he can't," Longboat replied with a straight face. "He's been drinking something awful lately. I am Fred Simpson, and I can beat his head off."[13]

Longboat could not laugh off the wrath of James Sullivan, who had continued to pursue his protest about Tom's amateur eligibility and, in the process, reignited the Athletic War of Canada. The day before the marathon, he co-opted Montreal's Amateur Athletic Federation of Canada to split from their alliance with the Toronto-based CAAU and join with him in petitioning British Olympic administrators to bar Longboat. It was a desperate act, but one Sullivan knew would stir dissension. One observer called it "the most Judas-like action I ever encountered in athletics."[14]

Facing betrayal by his own country on the eve of the most

important race in his career, Tom conferred with Flanagan, Marsh, and Sherring. They agreed to leave the decision in the hands of the British Olympic committee.

In this they were rewarded. No doubt sick of Sullivan's shenanigans, the British dismissed his Hail Mary with one sentence: "Longboat runs in the Marathon race under protest from the committee of the U.S.A. and also the A.A. Federation of Canada, who desire to protect their own registered athletes in America."[15]

His body sore, Longboat rested. The rains, he noticed, had halted.

One day after the Opening Ceremonies, Dorando Pietri competed in a preliminary heat for the three-mile team race at the Stadium. The Italians performed poorly, with Dorando recording a DNF, as the British handily took the event. He then angered national officials by refusing to run in the five-mile event on July 15. For once, it seemed, Dorando was opting not to dissipate his strength before the marathon.

He tested parts of the course on four occasions,[16] running for about an hour and twenty minutes without stopping each time. On the days in between he rested and walked, then he finalized arrangements with his bicycle attendants.

Forty-eight hours before the race, he ceased all activity. He retreated to his room, relaxing his body and his mind and steeling himself for the agony ahead. He visualized approaching the stadium at the front of the pack.

He dozed.

The workouts in Brighton had sharpened Johnny Hayes. He tapered training once he and the rest of the American team moved to the hotel in Uxbridge, although they scouted sections of the course. Joe Forshaw led them to a nearby fishing hole a couple of days before the race, which angered the taskmaster in Coach Murphy. He thought they were too loose. Maybe they were; no one gave them a chance to win.

Johnny went to bed two days before the race. He rose only to eat and talk strategy with Murphy and his teammates. He reminded Cameron, his bicycle attendant, that he would follow his usual strategy of starting slowly before surging at the end. He read countless stories in the newspapers predicting a rout by the British team.

Only one runner concerned Johnny: Tom Longboat.

He slept.

Friday dawned. The last full day of Olympic events at the Stadium. Marathon day.

It was hot, a sticky cauldron with "hardly a breath of wind, ideal for a bathe or a game of cricket perhaps, but terrible for a feat of endurance of mind, stamina, muscle, and feet," according to the *London Times*.[17] Race director Andrew directed crews to water and sweep the roads in an effort to reduce the dust. Policemen lined the course hours before the scheduled 2:30 p.m. start time. By then, it was nearing 80 degrees.

Except for donning hats to block the sun, none of the fifty-five marathoners prepared any differently for the temperature. The runners left the cool of Windsor railway station shortly after 2 p.m. and felt the full impact of the heat as they walked slowly up the hill toward the grounds of the Castle. Dozens of bobbies restrained the crowd, seven deep, from the cobblestone streets. Spectators held up umbrellas to ward off the sun and yelled out to Price, Duncan, Appleby, and Lord, the favored British runners, decked out in pristine, all-white outfits with a circular logo on their chests.

The Princess of Wales and her children had just arrived on the East Terrace of the Castle from Frogmore House, a private retreat near the Castle. She stood under the shade of a luxurious hawthorn tree, in a blue-flowered muslin dress and a hat trimmed with forget-me-nots, with her children—Mary and the four princes, Albert, Henry, George, and John. A ring of scarlet-upholstered gilt chairs encircled a table on which were a bowl of red roses and a telegraph box with an electric button.

The Princess peered at her program to match the runners with the numbers on their chests as the youngsters took photographs. Tom Longboat walked by swinging his arms. Johnny Hayes followed alongside teammates Morrissey, the youngster Roy Welton, the towering Ryan. Behind them was Dorando Pietri, eyes alive, his mustache gleaming with sweat. In his right hand was a handkerchief; he gripped a wedge of cork in both hands. Trailing the pack was lean Charles Hefferon, a white handkerchief tied around his neck, the dark green uniform of South Africa emblazoned with the figure of a springbok, and Johan Svanberg, in the blue shorts of Sweden.

Jack Andrew briskly assembled them into four rows, in an order determined at the Stadium the day before, when Swedish Olympic official Fred Lowenadler drew the runners' names from a hat. Longboat stood in the middle of the front row with Welton, Morrissey, Ryan, and fellow Canadian Indian Fred Simpson. Hayes was placed in the third row next to Joe Forshaw and Louis Tewanima. Dorando and Hefferon stared at their backs from the rear.

Andrew retreated to an open automobile. He joined Lord Desborough, who was holding a pistol. Standing on the grass next to the runners was the Crown Prince of Sweden. Ahead of them was positioned a motion picture cameraman.

There was, suddenly, silence.

At 2:33 p.m., Princess Mary pressed the button on the table. An electric cable transmitted a signal to Lord Desborough. He shouted "Get ready!" and the runners tensed. Then he fired the gun into the air.

Some twenty-six miles distant, the red-cloaked master of ceremonies walked onto the track at the Stadium in Shepherd's Bush, raised a gigantic megaphone to his mouth, and announced to the vast assemblage that the runners had departed from Windsor Castle.

The 1908 Olympic marathon had begun.

FOURTEEN

Billy Clarke of Britain and Arthur Burn of Canada spring ahead at the sound of the gunshot.[1] Through Sovereign's Gate, they leave the emerald lawns behind and begin to navigate the steep cobblestone path of Castle Hill, Tom Longboat and Dorando Pietri trailing in third and fourth. They pinwheel past Queen Victoria's statue as a roar from the crowd rattles the centuries-old fortifications of the Castle. Following close behind the runners are the officials' cars ferrying, among others, Lord Desborough and Jack Andrew.

The pack begins to separate as they tear along High Street, with Britain's Thomas Jack and Jack Price now in front. They cross the River Thames and then the first mile marker, at Barnespool Bridge, the roadway leveling out and heading north. The Scotsman Jack churns out the opening mile in a tick over five minutes. Fast, especially when accounting for the precipitous slope in Windsor.

The Brits dominate the front ranks, almost as if they are working as a team, with Jack trailed by Price, Fred Lord, and Duncan, with Dorando and Hefferon attached. They pass the venerable walls of Eton College, and the "playing fields" immortalized therein, greeted by a throng of schoolboys in silk hats and black coats.

Jack maintains his edge as the dusty road straightens toward Slough, his time an exceptionally swift 10:11 after two miles. They head into the countryside. Beneath his pith hat, Jack steadily builds his advantage after crossing the canal bridge, clocking 15:42 after three miles and 21:18 after four miles. That's a 5:20 pace. Still speedy.

Inside the Stadium, the numbers worn by the top three runners are displayed on a leaderboard. London's own toastmaster, Albert William Knightsmith, resplendent in scarlet evening attire, delivers the update to 80,000 people via a gigantic megaphone: "Four miles: T. Jack, Great Britain, leads by forty yards. J. Price, Great Britain, and A. Duncan, Great Britain, close up."

Arthur Conan Doyle nods his approval in the press zone. The Englishmen are pulling together.

Lurking are Hefferon, wearing number 8 and showing no ill effects from his fourth-place finish in the five-mile race less than a week ago, and Dorando, whose bright-red shorts make him easy to spot. Longboat seems content to allow them to set the early tempo. There is no sign of Johnny Hayes.

The route to Uxbridge offers temporary but welcome shade from lofty elms. Hayfields stretch into the distance. The runners encounter a slight rise at Langley as Jack powers through mile five in 27:01. The officials' car kicks up a haze of dust.

They approach the six-mile mark. In front of the Crooked Billet Inn, the bicycle attendants join the proceedings. Lou Marsh and William "Doc" Morton, a bronze medalist in the team cycling pursuit, shadow Longboat. Emilio Lunghi, Italy's 800-meter silver medalist, and Giuseppe Brocca trail Dorando. George Cameron and Percy Henry await Hayes.

Near Iver Heath, spectators stand outside their motorcars and carriages to cheer on the field. F. S. Kelly, the gold-medal rower and composer, notices that "the wretched competitors" trailing the officials' caravan are "inhaling a delicious mixture of smoke and dust."[2]

Jack fades, the needlessly rapid pace too taxing, and countryman

Lord, the Yorkshire coal stoker from Wibsey Park, takes over first. He goes by the six-mile mark in 33:09. Price and Duncan hold steady in second and third, the race still all-England to the delight of the onlookers. Hefferon, Dorando, and Longboat linger right behind.

Sunshine withers the flattened road as Lord zips through mile seven at 38:57, reaches mile eight at the Long Bridge on Uxbridge Moor in 44:52, and makes mile nine, at The Lodge on High Street, in 50:50. The steamy conditions produce casualties. Jack, the early leader, falls to the side of the road at seven miles. Blasi quits at mile eight, leaving Dorando as the lone Italian.

Marsh and Morton pedal with Longboat, about 200 yards behind the leaders. Morton rides ahead to observe the front-runners and breathlessly reports, "They are running as if the devil himself were behind." The devilish pace catches Duncan as the runners encounter a series of three hills. The long-striding winner of April's trials marathon slows to a walk, his sturdy chest heaving in disappointment. He drops out, disconsolate, at ten miles.

The road extends toward Ickenham and patches of shade from weeping willows, the meadows abloom with fragrant flowers. Price, the gritty steelworker from the Midlands and the Small Heath Harriers, takes the torch from Lord, reaching mile ten in 56:53, with Hefferon chugging comfortably into third, trailing by 100 yards.

Then comes Dorando, moving well, followed by Tom Longboat, smiling grimly. Pietri complains to his cyclists when an automobile moves in front of him and blocks his sight. Brocca speaks to the driver and asks him to leave them in peace.

Johnny Hayes is sitting twelfth by mile ten. He cannot see the leaders, but he has settled into his steady, rhythmic plodding. He gargles water. Murphy's words echo in his head: "Run your race."

He loses contact with Morrissey, Hatch, and Ryan, who have fallen out of contention. But the raw Welton forges on, as do Tewanima and a game Forshaw, who is following instructions from Murphy to guide the Hopi through the first half of the race.

An hour has passed. Price clings to the lead past Ickenham. At mile eleven, he clocks 1:02:44, then 1:08:56 at mile twelve just outside of Ruislip. He cruises past Ye Olde Swan pub in Ruislip and reaches mile thirteen in a time of 1:15:13, as Hefferon surges into second past Lord.

At the halfway point of the race is the first of the four OXO refreshment stops, stationed outside The Poplars hotel. Motion picture operators have set up cameras here, and a plague of cyclists jams the intersection.[3] The mob of spectators urges Price on even as Hefferon closes the gap. At mile fourteen, near the Eastcote Post Office, Price's advantage over the South African is seven seconds.

Price slows, then he sits down to catch his breath. Hefferon leaves him and, for the first time since the start of the marathon, Britain is out of the lead. Lord is second, with Longboat and Dorando vying for third.

At the Stadium, where every quarter hour white-suited men carry out placards that give the numbers of the leaders, the crowd stirs impatiently as Britain's gold-medal hopes melt away in the afternoon heat. An English victory in the swimming relay diverts their attention only momentarily.

The veteran South African now controls the race as he approaches the Pinner Gas Works, the first sign of urban life. Hefferon runs with an ungainly style, his body thrown far forward and his elbows held wide of his sides, but he seems sturdy enough to handle the ten-plus remaining miles. His time at mile sixteen is 1:35. Just under 6 minutes per mile.

In second is Lord, then Dorando, and, with renewed vigor, Longboat, whose time in the sixteenth mile is some thirty seconds faster than Hefferon's. He overtakes Dorando, but the Italian answers back. The two swap positions several times, the Canadian dwarfing the Italian, as the course begins to dip south toward the Stadium.

Ahead, Lord veers off the course into the arms of a spectator. Dorando is now in second, with Longboat third. Britain is down to one medal contender: Fred Appleby, underneath a floppy hat, motoring in fourth.

Hayes pushes into the top five. His cyclist companion, Cameron, pedals ahead and reports back: "Easy now, Johnny. Take your time. You'll get 'em all right."

Hefferon holds his edge as he passes the seventeenth mile in 1:41:17. He runs by the second refreshment booth, near the Roxborough Hotel, as the road narrows and skirts the famous hill at Harrow. The crowds are especially deep here, with only just enough space for the officials' cars to pass. The students of Eton's longtime rival are out in force, waving their canes and yelling for Hefferon.

His time is 1:48:51 at mile eighteen, good enough for a 3-plus minute advantage over runner-up Dorando, with Longboat now walking occasionally. Near the Harrow Nursery, at mile nineteen, Hefferon is at 1:55:29.

T wo hours into the race, the sun hangs like a bronze disc. Hefferon plods relentlessly, his dark green jersey heavy with sweat. Dorando stares vacantly, mouth open, his trot a study in tireless efficiency. Longboat is taking liquids from Marsh.

From back in the pack, the Americans trudge forward. Hayes, patient for nearly twenty miles, enters the fray as if dropped from above onto the macadam. His breath coming in gasps, he no longer hears anything but the rustling sound of his feet and Cameron's entreaties. The vast crowds form a vague, moving wall.

"Now's the time, Johnny," Cameron urges. "Now's the time to get on it."

He passes Longboat into third. Sherring yells: "Come on you, Tom, get the kid. You got him once before."

Longboat mounts another effort, his strides lengthening. Doc Morton senses that he is about to assert himself: "It's all over but the shouting," he tells Marsh.

Suddenly Longboat staggers, throws up his hands, and falls against Marsh's bicycle wheel. The two attendants quickly remove him from the roadway. His eyes flutter. Marsh and Morton administer more liquids. A race official walks over and examines Tom. He shakes his head and mutters, "He's dead beat. He's out."

Marsh protests, but it's no use. Dazed, Longboat is helped into a trailing automobile. He slumps beneath a blanket that is wrapped around his body. His legs feel as heavy as pianos.

The news hits the Stadium like a shot. Longboat, the favorite, is out! The Indian is done! And then, quickly, another bulletin: Appleby has followed Longboat to the sidelines. The last medal contender for Britain is finished. At around the same time, the coach bearing the Queen of England approaches the canopied entrance to the Stadium.

At mile twenty, in a time of 2:02:26, Hefferon maintains a comfortable edge over Dorando. Hayes's surge now has him third, but he trails Dorando by several minutes. Forshaw, after a nip of brandy, and Welton are rallying into medal contention, as is the band of resolute Canadians taking up the slack from Longboat—Wood, Lawson, and Simpson. Tewanima continues to grind, his knees balky from the hard surface. Trailing far behind, American Mike Ryan hits the wall at nineteen miles. Boxer Jack Johnson, driving on the course in his automobile, comes to Ryan's aid and scoops him into the car.

Hefferon strides on to Wembley and the first of several rises. Five miles from home, his time is 2:08:58. At the third refreshment stand, outside the Swan Hotel at Sudbury, he pauses. When he resumes, it's clear that he is slowing, perhaps because the runners have to navigate the tramlines, which make for uneasy footing. It takes him nearly eight minutes to reach mile twenty-two, near Stonebridge Park, as Dorando continues to stalk.

The conditions toughen as the exhausted front-runners prod onward. Another mile, another eight minutes for Hefferon. The crowd, ten deep on either side, screams encouragement as he reaches the last refreshment station, just past the Jubilee Clock Tower at Harlesden. Here, Jack Andrew and Lord Desborough abandon the course and head directly to the Stadium.

Dorando grabs for a sponge at Harlesden and splashes his face, the water soaking the front of his dust-splattered white shirt. His legs keep twitching, his motion uninterrupted. He has cut a minute off Hefferon's advantage. Just over two miles remaining.

Hayes, four minutes behind Dorando, gargles with brandy and splashes water on his face. He swallows some of the whiskey and feels sick. He can't spot either Hefferon and Dorando: Is there enough time to overtake them?

Cameron urges him on from his bicycle: "Don't give up, Johnny. You can catch 'em. Steady on."

Hefferon labors beneath the Great Western Railway lines. He's been at or near the front since the first mile, and he's carried the pace for the entire second half of the race. He stops to swig champagne, hoping this will provide him enough lift to make it home.

He slows further, his depleted body cramping and in distress. He requires over eight minutes to reach mile twenty-five, at the entrance to Wormwood Scrubs and its gloomy prison. On plows Dorando, equally drained and fatigued, but he can see that he's reeling in Hefferon.

There sounds a double-boom of cannons, alerting the crowd in the Stadium that the runners are approaching. The megaphonist Knightsmith reemerges on the track: "Clear the course for the Marathon race!"

Dorando advances on Hefferon. The South African gives him a long, sad look as Dorando steams past and plunges across the open space of Wormwood Scrubs, a black ball of muscle and grit accented with red.

Knightsmith informs the crowd: "The leading runner, an Italian, is in sight!"

Dorando canters along the cow paths between the Hammersmith Infirmary and the walls of the prison, the gleaming domes and turrets of the Exhibition ahead appearing like a tall-masted ship. He turns into the lane that leads to Ducane Road and, beyond, the Stadium.

The first marathoner to enter the Stadium is not Dorando but Tom Longboat, who has arrived by automobile. He is helped in by two attendants and sinks to the grass.

Dorando is stretching toward the Exhibition grounds. Hefferon, staggering, holds second, but Hayes is coming hard, trailed by Forshaw and then Welton.

"Rip it, Johnny," Cameron yells. "You'll get second yet. Go it, old boy."

Dorando Pietri is three minutes ahead, the gold medal all but his. But his last rally to overtake Hefferon, after nearly three hours and twenty-six miles of exertion in sultry heat, after having run the fastest 40K in history just seventeen days previous, is now proving too much. He slows and doubles over, overheated and underhydrated.

Attendants rush to his quivering body. He cannot move. Stimulants are delivered. His legs tremble to life.

"*Vincerò o morirò.*"

He pushes forward, his face a shade of pale gray. Hands push him toward an opening. It is the entrance to the Stadium. He navigates the passageway leading to the track. Sunlight beckons in the distance. He is somewhere between exhaustion and hallucination.

I will win or I will die.

He comes to the end of the tunnel. He passes beneath an advertising sign—J. LYONS REFRESHMENTS—and emerges into the vast arena. A deafening roar from 80,000 spectators greets him as he lurches onto the cement cycling oval like a drunk at last call.

Jack Andrew, Dr. Michael Bulger, and a phalanx of officials and police converge and await his next step. He sways. His feet dither. His eyes are spacey.

The crowd gazes down at a sallow little man in droopy red breeches and a sweat-and-water-soaked white zephyr. From tier to tier across the expanse of the Stadium, the multitude falls silent.

The Queen of England peers down from the royal box.

Sir Arthur Conan Doyle rises from his seat in the press area.

Baron Pierre de Coubertin and Lord Desborough stare from their perch.

James E. Sullivan and Mike Murphy squint in disbelief.

Tom Longboat, groggy, collects himself.

Just outside, Johnny Hayes has vanquished Charles Hefferon and is churning toward the entrance of the Stadium.

FIFTEEN

Two-thirds of a lap separates Dorando Pietri from the winning post opposite the royal box.[1] About 385 yards.

On instinct, he reels to his right so that he can circle the track counterclockwise, the direction he ran when he competed in the three-mile team race at the Stadium ten days ago.

Today, it is the wrong way. In his addled state he's forgotten—or perhaps he was never directly told in Italian—that the marathoners must run this final stretch clockwise.

Officials yell at him in a language that he doesn't comprehend. Their voices sound as if they're underwater. They shoo him to the left, and he pinballs in that direction. His head droops to his chest, arms at his side as he wobbles forward, trailed by Jack Andrew, Dr. Bulger, groundskeeper Perry.

He stumbles onto the cinder track. Another few steps, and then he swoons to the ground, a collection of useless limbs. Has he fainted? Is he dead?

Officials gather around him. Andrew waves his megaphone and tries to keep order as Dorando's teammates yell encouragement from the infield.

A cry from the stands: "Let him alone!"

Seconds pass. Somehow, Dorando totters to his feet, still clutching his handkerchief and cork grips. He pitches forward into a slow dogtrot. The crowd breathes again.

"Go, Italy!"

"Run! Run!"

He falls again. Precious seconds tick away. Water is thrown in his face. His breath comes in a sputter, his pulse stammers. Dr. Bulger, a large Irishman with a Dublin accent, rubs Dorando's chest and yells instructions to Andrew. Dorando's feet move and he is stood up and pushed on, wobbling forward like a top.

The band plays "Conquering Hero."

Andrew looks back to the entrance. No other runner has entered the Stadium. Less than 200 yards to go, just beyond the far curve, Dorando steps once and twice, momentum building, then sinks to the track for the third time. Something stronger is needed—brandy, smelling salts, some sort of stimulant.

"That's not sport!"

Dorando coughs. His body quickens to life. A step forward, balance regained, and then his legs give way yet again.

From the portal beneath the J. Lyons Refreshments sign emerges Johnny Hayes. The number on his chest, 26, matches the number of miles he's covered. Dusty, sweaty, and parched but churning under his own power, he is oblivious to what is going on in front of him. His stride eats up the yardage on the track between him and Dorando.

Pietri regains his feet. He sees nothing clearly, the 80,000 spectators and the gigantic Stadium fading into a kaleidoscopic haze. He draws breath and totters to the last bend, now 100 yards left, now 75, and then down once more. Bulger cradles him and massages his lifeless limbs, slaps his face.

"They have killed him!"

Hayes chugs on, his strides short, his feet aching. Blasts of sounds come from above.

"Go! Come on!"

"Get up, Italy!"

Cameron, from the infield, urges on Hayes. He is closing.

Dorando regains his breath. Is he done? No, he is yanked to his feet, floundering and swaying, the white cloth atop his head askew, the worsted rope of the finish line just ahead.

I will win or I will die.

He waddles forward and breasts the tape, escorted by Andrew on his right, Bulger to his left, photographers and camera operators massed around the finish line to document this moment forever.

He collapses to the ground, senseless, and disappears from view beneath a small army of medical attendants, bobbies, and Olympic officials. A litter is found.

Hayes approaches the final stretch, his legs trembling, scarcely aware of the commotion ahead. Andrew watches him to the end as Johnny angrily strides past, his surge coming too late, just like in Boston in April, when he fell short chasing Morrissey.

Dorando is carried off to a dressing room beneath the stands. Hayes, his breath coming in bursts from deep within him, is led from the track by Cameron.

Dorando's time is 2:54:46. Hayes is clocked at 2:55:18.

Nearly a minute later Hefferon appears, weak and faltering, followed by Forshaw, who makes a detour and jumps into the swimming pool to cool off. Then come Welton and three of the Canadians—Wood, Simpson, and Lawson—with the Swede, Svanberg, and Tewanima rounding out the top ten. Still, no Englishman.

The Italian flag is run up the pole beyond the swimming bath. Underneath is the Stars and Stripes.

Telegraph operators transmit the news around the globe: DO-RANDO WINS.

The *Brooklyn Citizen* rushes to press with a special edition: ITALIAN IS WINNER OF MARATHON, reads the headline.

SPLENDID VICTORY FOR ITALY, announces the *Westminster Gazette*.

Finally, the first British runner arrives: Billy Clarke in thirteenth, in 3:16:08.

The Stadium is in an uproar long after Dorando is carried away. Conan Doyle scribbles notes for his *Daily Mail* story. Another journalist, James Connolly, the same man who won the first-ever modern Olympic gold medal in 1896, is yelling at anyone with an official's badge that Dorando must be disqualified.[2]

James E. Sullivan and Matt Halpin, the U.S. team manager, approach Lord Desborough and demand that the Italian flag be removed and replaced by the American banner. Jack Andrew grips his megaphone and maintains that no rules were broken. The South Africans get into the act, charging that Johnny Hayes received aid.

The other events go unnoticed. Americans A. C. Gilbert and Edward Cook tie for first in the pole vault, setting a new Olympic record at 12-2, despite the fact that they're barred from digging holes in the dirt for their poles.

The arguments about the marathon continue. The officials insist that Dorando is the legitimate winner. Halpin files a formal protest.

The Queen departs for Buckingham Palace. The crowd begins to disperse.

In the dressing room, Johnny Hayes gets a rubdown and vomits up the whiskey in his stomach. He changes into street clothes and takes a taxicab to St. Ermin's Hotel in Westminster, complaining only that his feet are sore. He replays the race in his head: Should he have picked up the pace sooner? Did the added distance, from twenty-five miles to twenty-six, throw off his timing? If he'd known how bad the Italian was doing, could he have overtaken him in the Stadium?

Tom Flanagan and Lou Marsh ferry a woozy Tom Longboat to their hotel. His right leg is cramping. He says little before turning in. Flanagan and Marsh drink away the night and discuss what went wrong on the course.

British Olympic committee members agree to investigate the end of the marathon and invite Sullivan to attend the meeting. He declines, and the committee decamps to the Imperial Sports Club.

Minutes pass, then an hour. An official who examines Dorando in the dressing room reports that the runner's heart has shifted half an inch, although how he could possibly determine this is never explained.

Dehydrated and muddled, Dorando slips out of the Stadium with his brother. He returns to Soho in a taximeter motor cab and takes to bed.

Another hour's wait. Rumors circulate that the Italian has died. In the near-empty Stadium, Canada's George Lister, the last of the twenty-eight marathoners to finish, staggers home in 4:22:45.

Oblivious to Dorando's recovery, the *Boston Globe* publishes "the sad news" that "Dorando had failed to rally from the exhaustion and strain and was dead."

The British Olympic committee rehashes the ending in the Stadium. Jack Andrew and Dr. Bulger are questioned about two issues: Could Dorando Pietri have won the race unassisted? And, have any of the printed rules been broken?

The answer to the first question is obvious. Dorando entered the Stadium out on his feet and, during the last lap, collapsed five times. It's extremely unlikely that he would have been able to finish, let alone win, if not for the doctor and the chief clerk massaging his legs and chest, supporting him, and helping him to his feet.

All 80,000 spectators, including the Queen, saw this. The eye-witness accounts will soon be buttressed by black-and-white evidence from the photographers and the motion picture camera operators who captured the scenes in the Stadium, including the final stage, when Dorando was practically cradled across the finish by Andrew and Bulger.

That film is hastily being developed even as the British Olympic Council members consider the ten written rules for the marathon. None expressly prohibits giving assistance to a competitor, although as Gustavus Kirby of the American Olympic Committee later points out, "To state such a rule would be as absurd as to say that in a 100-yard dash the runners must not use an automobile."[3]

Still, there is sentiment in the room to deny Sullivan's latest complaint, not so much to deprive the Americans of the gold medal (although that would be satisfying), but to reward the Italian. Such verve! Such perseverance in front of the Queen! And what about the unwritten rules, the ones that concern sportsmanship? A gentleman would no sooner protest this enormous show of courage than insult his mother.

It is the tack taken by Charles Hefferon. "Such a race as this I will either win by being first past the post, or I will not win at all," the South African says. "Dorando has won; he deserves the great victory, and I will not do anything to rob him of it, nor will I seek to gain second place on a protest. Dorando is the best man; let him have the honour. No protests for me."[4]

For two hours they deliberate. The Stadium empties.

Finally, the committee emerges to issue its verdict: "That, in the opinion of the judges, M. P. Dorando [sic] would have been unable to finish the race without the assistance rendered on the track, and so, therefore, the protest of the U.S.A. is upheld, and the second man,

Mr. J. Hayes, is the winner, the protest being made by the South African team being withdrawn."[5]

The Italian flag is taken down, replaced by the American.

Johnny Hayes is eating dinner with Mike Ryan and George Cameron when an American official rushes in to inform him that Dorando has been disqualified and that he is the champ. At first skeptical and then jubilant, he accepts congratulations from his teammates.

Reporters scurry to the hotel to get his reaction. "The only part of the race that worried me was when I was three or four miles off the end and I had to run on the hot asphalt," he says. "We American boys are not used to running on asphalt and it worried me a bit, I can tell you. My feet felt as though they were sticking, and I could not get along well."

He gives full credit to Cameron and Henry and to Coach Murphy, and jabs at the pundits who favored the British marathoners. "I always knew that I had a chance, and I felt pretty certain that whoever beat me would have to run," he says. "You see, all our team were much better than anybody here imagined. We didn't do any bragging. We left that to the Englishmen. But we felt confident we wouldn't be so far out of it at the finish."[6]

He downs ginger ale after ginger ale, nineteen bottles in all, and goes to bed in the early morning hours. His feet feel as if they've been lashed, but his heart is singing. Little Johnny Hayes, the Irish-American kid from the tenements of New York, has won the Olympic marathon in a tale that even Horatio Alger would find unbelievable.

. . .

All of Fleet Street is in search of Dorando. The *Daily Mail's* G. Ward Price locates him at 8 Church Street, off Shaftesbury Avenue, where police are guarding the front door of a small house. Price sneaks inside when Italy's IOC member Count Brunetta d'Usseaux, the same man who helped arrange the transfer of the 1908 Olympics to London from Rome, arrives to inform Dorando that he has been disqualified.

"On an iron bedstead lay the now famous Dorando, pale and haggard, but definitely not dead," according to Price. Told of the decision, "Dorando almost wept, rolling dark eyes in his pallid face. . . . He was evidently protesting, while the members of the Embassy staff were proferring explanations and sympathy."

Dorando tells Price through a translator: "I was all right till I entered the Stadium. When I heard the people cheering and knew that I had nearly won, a thrill of emotion passed through me and I felt my strength going. Then I fell. I tried to struggle to the tape, but fell again. I never lost consciousness of what was going on. Even if the attendant had not picked me up, I believe I could have finished unaided."[7]

Exhausted and heartbroken, the gold medal now a dream taken from his grasp, he sleeps.

That evening, the British government hosts a dinner reception at the Grafton Galleries attended by Pierre de Coubertin. The baron has kept a low profile during the Games, watching with alarm and then disgust as Sullivan turned Shepherd's Bush into a British–American battleground.

When he rises to speak, Coubertin invokes the words from Bishop Talbot's sermon at St. Paul's Cathedral from the previous Sunday. "The important thing at these Olympiads is not so much to win as to take part," he says, jabbing at Sullivan's win-at-all-cost mentality. "The important thing in life is not the victory but the struggle. The essential thing is not to have won but to have fought well."[8]

With the memory of Dorando's faltering yet determined footsteps fresh in everyone's mind, his speech is received with an ovation. Lord Desborough then announces that Queen Alexandra, so moved by the runner's efforts, will personally present Dorando with a special gift at tomorrow's medal ceremony at the Stadium. A rousing chorus of "Hear, Hear!" follows before the evening concludes with cigars and rounds of claret and champagne.

The 1908 Olympics are wobbling to a close.

SIXTEEN

On Saturday morning, the world woke to the outrageous news from the Stadium:

MARATHON IS OURS, proclaimed the *Washington Post*.

LONGBOAT FELL SENSELESS, FORBIDDEN TO GO ON, reported the *Toronto Daily Star*.

DYING MAN NEARLY WON GREAT RACE, according to the *Boston Post*.

IRELAND WINS MARATHON, declared the *Weekly Freeman* in Dublin.

BRITISH COMPETITOR MAKES A POOR SHOW, read London's *News of the World*.[1]

On its front page, the *New York Times* neatly conflated the ancient Olympic Games with the mythic run after the Battle of Marathon: "It would be no exaggeration in the minds of any of the 100,000 spectators who witnessed the finishing struggle of the Marathon race, won by John J. Hayes of New York, at the Olympian arena today to say that it was the most thrilling event that has occurred since that Marathon race in ancient Greece, where the victor fell at the goal and, with a wave of triumph, died."[2]

The *New York Tribune* called the proceedings barbaric: "The distressing ending of the Marathon race today has caused a revulsion of public feeling respecting the classic sport. . . . The Marathon race is condemned tonight by those who witnessed it as a contest which ought never to be repeated in any civilized country."[3]

For his story in the *Daily Mail*, Conan Doyle spun a suspenseful tale that brought readers inside the Stadium during Dorando's dramatics:

Out of the dark archway there staggered a little man, with red running-drawers, a tiny, boy-like creature. He reeled as he entered and faced the roar of the applause. Then he feebly turned to the left and wearily trotted around the track. Friends and entourages were pressing round him.

Suddenly the whole group stopped. There were wild gesticulations. Men stooped and rose again. Good Heavens, he had fainted; is it possible that even at this last moment the prize may skip from his fingers? Every eye slides round to that dark archway. No second man has yet appeared. Then a great sigh of relief goes up. I do not think in all that great assembly any man would have victory to be torn at the last instant from this plucky little Italian. He has won it. He should have it.

Thank God, he is on his feet again, the little red legs going incoherently, but drumming hard, driven by a supreme will within. There is a groan as he falls again to his feet. It is horrible, and yet fascinating, this struggle between a set purpose and an utterly exhausted frame. Again, for a hundred yards, he ran in the same furious and yet uncertain gait. Then again he collapsed, kind hands saving him from a heavy fall.

He was within a few yards from my seat. Amid stooping figures and grasping hands I caught a glimpse of the haggard, yellow face, the glazed, expressionless eyes, the lank, black hair streaked across the brow. Surely he is done now. He cannot rise again.

From under the archway has darted the second runner, Hayes, Stars and Stripes on his breast, going gallantly well within his strength. There is only twenty yards to go if the Italian can do it. He staggered up, no trace of intelligence upon his set face, and again the red legs broke into their strange automatic amble.

Will he fall again? No, he sways, he balances, and then he is through the tape and into a score of friendly arms. He has gone to the extreme of human endurance. No Roman of the prime ever bore himself better than Dorando of the Olympic of 1908. The great breed is not yet extinct.[4]

Later, as years passed and memories grew dim, Conan Doyle's role at the Olympics would become exaggerated. As one of his biographers falsely wrote, "At the 1908 Games, [some] spectators, Conan Doyle amongst their number, guided and helped the exhausted and confused runner [Dorando] to the finishing line. . . . There are those who believed that Conan Doyle felt guilty for having steered the runner in the direction of the finishing tape and that his fundraising efforts [on behalf of Dorando] were aimed at assuaging his guilt."[5]

In a column that appeared in the *British Journal of Sports Medicine* in 1999, authors A. J. Wood and R. J. Maughan wrote that Conan Doyle was "on the field in the dual capacity of *Daily Mail* correspondent and marathon medical officer. . . . What is not so well known to sports historians is that the medical officer attending to Pietri . . . is none other than Sir Arthur Conan Doyle."[6]

Alas, while Conan Doyle may have had a passing resemblance to Dr. Bulger, he was simply another journalist working under a tight deadline.[7] But portions of Conan Doyle's enthralling game story were reprinted and translated in countless newspapers around the world, helping to give the story legs, as it were.

The photograph of Dorando at the finish line, framed by Andrew and Bulger, was reproduced everywhere. The haunting black-and-white image gave the public immediate visual corroboration of the race that everybody was talking about. Credited to the Topical Press Agency of Fleet Street, it is now regarded as the first great sports-action photograph ever published, as well as the first to capture the climactic moment of a major sporting event.

One person remained upset. James E. Sullivan insisted that the officials' interference with Dorando, and their reluctance to disqualify him at the first moment they rendered assistance, prevented Johnny Hayes from being properly recognized as the actual winner. According to Sullivan, the fans were screaming "'Hurry! Hurry! Here comes an American!' It was then the attending physicians and prejudiced officials seized the gasping, senseless form [of Dorando] from the ground and literally bore it across the finish line. . . . Then, after Dorando had been disqualified and Hayes declared the winner, the British refused to displace the Italian flag with Old Glory for some hours."

The marathon incident, charged Sullivan, showed the "warped trend of British sportsmanship."[8]

With his stunning defeat in the marathon, Tom Longboat was shunned. All of the prerace hype now was turned against him. He was derided as "the greatest newspaper runner of the lot."[9]

Billy Sherring and Howard Crocker of Team Canada were determined to prove that the result was a fluke. Immediately after the race they announced that Longboat, Wood, Simpson, and Cotter would run the Windsor–Shepherd's Bush course again. This would prove, they maintained, that the Canadians were faster than Hayes. The trial was called off when the weather in London remained too sultry.

Dorando Pietri realized that his life was forever changed when he awoke on Saturday. A horde of adoring fans was stationed outside the front door of his Soho flat. Flowers arrived, sent by Lord and Lady Desborough, filling the small room with color.

Acting astonishingly chipper for someone so close to death just hours ago, he and Ulpiano met again with Count Brunetta d'Usseaux. They decided to lodge a counter-protest with the British Olympic Association on the grounds that Dorando had not asked for the help rendered inside the Stadium. The BOA summarily dismissed the protest: Hayes was the official winner. Resigned to his fate, Dorando agreed to go to the Stadium to accept the gift from the Queen.

Johnny Hayes and several teammates were fêted at the House of Commons in Westminster. He posed for a series of photographs taken by politician-portraitist Sir Benjamin Stone and filled his autograph book with signatures. Members of Parliament, especially those representing Ireland, like Michael Flavin, John O'Connor, and William O'Malley, wanted his John Hancock, too.

Back at the Stadium, he changed into his running togs for more photos and watched the American team end its stay in London on a triumphant note as Mel Sheppard earned his third gold medal in leading the medley relay team to victory, with Penn's John Taylor becoming the first African American to win Olympic gold. An American sweep of the 110-meter hurdles capped the day as Forrest Smithson outdueled Garrels and set a world record.

The final medal tally vindicated Sullivan. The United States hauled in sixteen gold medals and thirty-four total in track and field versus seven gold and seventeen total for the British. Counting Hayes's win, Irish-American Athletic Club members claimed ten firsts. The countries of Canada and Italy managed just one gold combined.

The medals ceremony followed,[10] with the band of the Grenadier Guards playing the national anthems of all the participating countries. Queen Alexandra distributed the Sir Bertram MacKennal–designed gold medals, which were tucked inside a square red leather case. Lord Desborough helped with the honors, with Pierre de Coubertin and the ambassadors from the United States and Italy observing the proceedings. The King declined to appear, apparently because he was upset at the Americans' antics. He sent along oak leaves from Windsor Forest for the winners.

The athletes were lining up to receive their medals when the crowd of 60,000 stirred. At about the same hour that he had staggered into view twenty-four hours previously, Dorando Pietri appeared at the entrance to the arena.

"It's Dorando!" a cry went up.

"Viva Italia!" yelled another.

He stood alone, a dark speck on the green expanse, dressed in knickerbockers, a Norfolk jacket, green stockings, and a tiny bow tie. His black hair gleamed in the late afternoon sun as he doffed his cloth cap, his mustache neat and upswept. He walked briskly, a modest smile on his face.

A man ran onto the track with Italy's banner. Dorando graciously took the honor.

"Bravo! Bravo!" came from every row.

He stood by the railing, scribbling autograph after autograph and accepting congratulations. Finally, the Queen of England beckoned.

Just opposite from the spot where he had collapsed for the final time, Dorando climbed carpeted steps. Queen Alexandra extended her sympathy and proffered a polished gold trophy.

"I am glad to give you this for your splendid race," Her Majesty said. "I hope you are none the worse now after the terrible strain of the race."[11]

Dorando stiffly bowed, his body bent double, then stood at attention before accepting the cup and stepping down from the platform. The trophy was not engraved—there had not been time for that—so a handwritten note was included: "FOR P. DORANDO. In Remembrance of the Marathon Race from Windsor to the Stadium. FROM QUEEN ALEXANDRA."

He nodded to the crowd and hugged the trophy to his heart as he circled the track for one final time, waves of applause preceding his every footstep. As he ducked into the passageway, a well-dressed woman unfastened a bracelet from around her wrist and passed it to him. "Wear this for me, you brave little man," she whispered.

The parade of American winners was greeted politely, with Johnny Hayes given a warm cheer when he received his gold medal from Queen Alexandra. He also was awarded a special trophy for the marathon—an enormous statue called "Dying Pheidippides."

Six teammates, anchored by Ryan, Forshaw, Tewanima, and Welton, lifted Johnny and the bronze statue onto a table and carried him on a circuit of the Stadium. The American section roared as the pint-sized gold medalist waved the Stars and Stripes and, finally, was given his crowning moment in London.

Dorando had stolen the spotlight again, the press agreed. He was FIRST, NOT FIRST, MORE THAN FIRST! He was "the man who won, but lost, and then won." He was the toast of London and beyond.

He was offered 12,500 francs for the cup from the Queen. He turned it down. A woman whose "heart is free" made him a proposal, but Dorando replied that his heart wasn't. He dined with Enrico Caruso and composer Luigi Denza ("Funiculì, Funiculà") at the Italian Club. The great tenor from Naples praised Dorando's courage and sketched his caricature.

With his brother advising him, he signed to appear at music halls in London, including the Oxford, the Tivoli, the Hammersmith. His "act," such as it was, involved coming onstage in his running gear, giving a demonstration of his athletic stylings, and showing off the cup given to him by the Queen. Ulpiano did the translating, and the crowds lapped up every moment.

Conan Doyle followed his story by starting a subscription for the runner. "I am sure that no petty personal recompense can in the least console Dorando for the national loss which follows from his disqualification," he commented. "Yet I am certain that many who saw his splendid effort in the Stadium—an effort which ran him within an inch of his life—would like to feel that he carries away some souvenir from his admirers in England."

He pledged £5 and, a few days later, he and his second wife, Jean, presented Dorando with a check for £308 in a gold cigarette case at the *Daily Mail* offices in Carmelite House. "My wife made the presentation in English, which he could not understand; he answered in Italian, which we could not understand," Conan Doyle wrote. "But I think we really did understand each other all the same." Later that summer, he paid further tribute by giving the (slightly misspelled) surname of "Durando" to a character in a Sherlock Holmes short story entitled "The Adventure of Wisteria Lodge."[12]

Finally, Dorando left London. He had arrived and competed as a virtual unknown, at least to the English-language press, until the moment he entered the Stadium. Now, as he boarded the train for Italy in August, his name and face were famous the world over. He had amassed a small fortune—more money than he had dreamed of earning—and intended to use his stake to open his own bakeshop, something that a gold medal could never have made happen.

On the express train to Turin, with the Queen's gold cup in a brown leather satchel, Dorando relaxed and enjoyed a large bowl of pasta. "If only I had had a dish of macaroni before the marathon race," he said to a reporter, decades before the concept of carboloading was introduced. "I am sure I should have arrived a quarter of an hour before anyone else."[13]

An immense crowd greeted Dorando at the train station in Carpi.[14] He and Italy's other Olympic hero, all-around gymnastics gold medalist Alberto Braglia, were carried to a brougham and escorted to City Hall. The route was lined with people screaming their names and throwing thousands of little squares of paper, the words "*Evviva Dorando*" written on them. A procession of long-winded speakers followed before Dorando could finally escape to his parents' home on Corso Alberto Pio.

His father's stern visage was beaming, and his mother's wrinkled face creased into a joyous smile when he arrived. She threw her arms around her son, murmuring softly and sobbing with delight. She was, everyone agreed, the happiest woman in all of Italy.

The most celebrated and disgraced athlete of the 1908 Olympics arrived in New York on the *Kronprinz Wilhelm*. A humbled Tom Longboat met the press with praise for Johnny Hayes. "When he passed me I declared that he would surely win the race," he told the *New York American*. "I never saw anyone running more freely after having covered close to twenty miles. The way he ran the last seven miles was truly remarkable."

Longboat blamed his defeat on the conditions. "It was terribly warm, or it surely did feel that way, as it was the first bright sunshiny day succeeding a long spell of damp, chilly weather. And the roads were fierce. Asphalt and cobblestones that simply pounded to pieces the feet of one used to running on dirt roads."[15]

Reporters who had built up Longboat as invincible searched to explain his failing. "It would seem that the Canadians were 'tired' and 'worn' before the real test began," wrote the *Toronto Daily Star*. "It would seem that the strenuous 20-mile trial and the numerous exhibitions in Ireland by Tom Longboat reflect seriously on Tom Flanagan's judgment."[16]

The muttering grew vicious. Longboat was said to have been

drinking heavily the night before the marathon, a charge that team manager Howard Crocker said was "without foundation" because Crocker personally "saw him in his room at 10:45 in perfect condition."[17]

Longboat weighed retirement. The $500 that the city of Toronto had raised for him after his Boston Marathon victory would provide him with a decent stake. He had also met the woman who would soon become his wife, Lauretta Maracle, a Mohawk from a reserve east of Toronto, and harbored thoughts about settling down.

But Longboat had held no job since his "ownership" of the ill-fated cigar shop. He had no serious prospects. He was not ready to give up competitive racing, not while he was in his prime and not with the bitter experience from London fresh in his memory. Flanagan held out the promise that Longboat could test the professional circuit against, among others, Alf Shrubb, who had challenged the Canadian while he was an amateur and was now toiling in North America. As soon as Tom reestablished his racing stripes, Flanagan said, there was money to be made.

SEVENTEEN

Directly after the Olympics, Johnny Hayes made a pilgrimage to his ancestral land. He and fellow Irish-American Athletic Club members first went to Dublin and, personally chauffeured by John Dunlop—the tire inventor and manufacturer—visited Richard "Boss" Croker,[1] the former head of the Tammany Hall political machine, who was now living at his Glencairn estate eight miles outside of the city. Croker showed off his prize possession, the stallion Orby, who shocked the sporting press in 1907 by becoming the first Irish-trained horse to capture the English Derby.

Croker drew Hayes aside as the team was leaving. "Johnny, my boy," he said proudly, "you went over to England and did to them much the same as I did there."

Johnny was introduced to another Irish-American power broker, John Fitzgerald, the former mayor of Boston, who was escorting his daughters to boarding school in Europe. In his book Johnny collected the signature of "Honey Fitz" as well as that of his eighteen-year-old daughter, Rose, who would become the mother of John F. Kennedy, the thirty-fifth president of the United States.[2]

He visited Belfast and the Blarney Stone and drew tremendous crowds for cameo appearances at athletic carnivals. He'd jog for a mile, enough to sate the fans. At a meet at Ballsbridge, the *Limerick Leader* described him as "a regular pocket Hercules" with "a storehouse of grit and doggedness secreted somewhere away in his diminutive physique. . . . We cheered him and cheered him. If the volume of sound were corked up in a barrel, they'd weigh more than J. J. Hayes. They rolled in tons across the arena. And little Hayes smiled."[3]

In the success of Hayes and the other Irish-American athletes, the press in Ireland delighted in taunting the English. The *Cork Examiner* noted the "inadequate recognition" that the British accorded to Hayes and added, "It is strange they should be so sparing of their praise for the man who won the Marathon fairly and squarely without being helped. Is it because he is an Irishman and ran for America instead of Great Britain? The fact that the Americans, with the aid of Irishmen, have carried off all the greater honours of the Olympiad is indeed a bitter pill for them to swallow."[4]

"The Englishman thinks all these nations wrong and himself right," *Sinn Fein* newspaper concluded. "But everyone else thinks the Englishman wrong and the world right. The officials who were guilty of breaches of duty in helping the Italian home in the Marathon Race, because an Irish-American was following close behind instead of a British favourite, admit they did wrong. There was no other alternative open to them."[5]

The highlight for Johnny was his journey to Nenagh,[6] the town in County Tipperary that his father, Michael, had left in 1880. Seemingly every villager turned out to greet him, all 4,000 of them, when the train from Dublin pulled into the station. The mob mistook his stocky friend, Mike Ryan, for Johnny and rushed toward him. Ryan shouted, "I'm not Hayes," and made his escape.

Johnny was borne shoulder high to a waiting carriage amid fireworks and, with the horses unhitched, pulled through the streets to the cottage of the aged, beaming man he was named after, John Hayes, his grandfather, on Silver Street. A brass band and a fife and drum corps played outside the residence until late into the night.

It was an emotional, often overwhelming, reunion to "the island surrounded by water on the outside, and whiskey and soda on the inside." He heard the familiar sound of his late father's lilt whenever his grandfather spoke to him. He saw Michael Hayes's features in the faces of aunts and uncles and distant cousins he met. He ate the bread his grandfather baked and toured the bountiful countryside of the Golden Vale. Neighbors lined up to introduce him to their daughters; everyone asked to touch his gold medal. His only lament was that his parents weren't alive to hear of his good fortune.

In Cork, the Lee Rowing Club honored him with a dinner at Flanagan's Hotel and presented him with a gold medal. Johnny was handed a poem, entitled "Exit Longboat," that honored his victory and jibed at his erstwhile rival for dropping out of the race:

> He could jump like a deer!
>   He could run like a goat!
> A Canadian Red Indian,
>   His name was Longboat.
>
> They brought him to Ireland
>   To add to his fame;
> He ran very well—
>   Give him credit for same.
>
> Yes, he ran very well,
>   He bate horses galore!
> When it came to the men,
>   He was on the ice shore.
>
> They forgot poor old Ireland—
>   Those that joined the Red men,
> And the brave doughty Hayes
>   Had passed out of their ken.

> When they entered the straight,
>   'Twas a bit of a jar;
> Longboat finished first—
>   In a swell motor car![7]

Tickled, Johnny brought home several copies when he left Queenstown for America on the White Star Line steamship *Oceanic*. He came bearing a gift for his younger sisters: six Irish goldfinches.

The warm welcome he experienced in Ireland was mere prelude to the reception he and the U.S. Olympic team received in New York City in August. A float bearing his marathon trophy led the parade, followed by motorcars carrying the athletes. More than half a million people, a solid mass of banked humanity, cheered them on along Fifth Avenue and Broadway, the biggest celebration in the city, all agreed, since that accorded to Admiral George Dewey after the Spanish-American War.

A gloating James E. Sullivan appeared with a pasteboard lion cub in chains, a visual reminder that the Americans had vanquished the British Lion. At City Hall, acting mayor Patrick McGowan presented Hayes and John Carpenter, "robbed" of the 400-meter triumph, with special silver cups. The band started playing "The Star-Spangled Banner," accompanied by a group of school children, and the refrain "was taken up by the multitude until Hayes stepped down from the table," the *New York Times* reported. "There were tears in the eyes of the little runner as he realized that the outburst had all been for him."[8]

As Johnny stood with the other athletes, "a smartly-dressed woman rushed forward, flung both arms around his neck and kissed him several times," one reporter noted.[9] Hayes blushed furiously, but before he could escape he was surrounded by other women, who fought for the chance to kiss him. Five succeeded before he managed to free himself.

"They seem to think I am a remnant sale," he muttered.

Following the parade, the athletes returned to Celtic Park for a meet to raise money for a firemen's memorial fund. Johnny was again mobbed and had to rush to the dressing room to escape the crowd's clutches. Entertainer George M. Cohan provided the team with front-row tickets to his latest musical, *The Yankee Prince*, followed by a banquet at Keen's Chop House, where the tables sagged with food. Every dish on the menu was named after an athlete: "The Stuffed Baked Potato: John Flanagan." For Johnny Hayes it was "The Cake"—as in, "he takes the cake."[10]

Finally, they cruised on a steamer to the summer White House in Oyster Bay to meet Theodore Roosevelt. He greeted them dressed in a white duck suit, accompanied by his second wife, Edith; daughter Ethel; and sons Kermit and Quentin.

The President's enthusiasm was infectious, and he had a comment for every athlete. "Here's the top-notcher boy!" he said, shaking hands with Johnny Hayes. "I'm bully proud of you. Awfully pleased to have you out here. I'm proud of the fact that you are a New York boy, too."

Roosevelt said he was surprised at the Americans' phenomenal showing in the marathon. "You know, the English always said that while we had speed we had no endurance," he commented. "But we showed them, I guess, that we had both!"

Johnny gave the President a blackthorn shillelagh that he brought back from Ireland, and the team gathered around them for photographs. Roosevelt offered some advice, the same words, he said, that he gave his crew of Rough Riders after the action in Cuba. "Remember you're heroes for ten days," he said. "When time's up drop the hero business and go to work."[11] Before leaving Sagamore Hill, the team unloosed three mighty cheers for the President.

Later, Roosevelt sent Johnny a gushing thank-you note for the "big stick," adding, "All good Americans sincerely rejoice in your victory. I felt that it reflected credit upon our people; and we were particularly glad that it should be won by a man who had been emphatically a good citizen, a man who had worked hard and done his duty and yet had found time for the healthy play which is so excellent a help to work. Let me see you whenever you are in my neighborhood."[12]

Little Johnny Hayes was now a star attraction. Perhaps it was his diminutive size. Perhaps the public appreciated his humility after the victory; in every interview he credited Coach Murphy for being "white as aces" in whipping the team into shape in Brighton. Or, perhaps, his rags-to-gold-medal tale was so compelling.

He is "all nerve, pluck, never-say-die," according to one newspaper. "Three-fourths of his opponents were bigger, stronger, lustier than he. But he won—on nerve."[13] In answer to the question, "Who are the five greatest living Americans?" journalist Grantland Rice replied:

> Take a look at these, old scout—Melvin Sheppard—Johnny Hayes—
> Martin Sheridan—there's three worthy of the spotlight's rays;
> Picking up another pair just to finish up the job,
> Get down with a bet on these—Honus Wagner—Tyrus Cobb.[14]

Wrote Joseph Clarke, in a poem reprinted in the *Gaelic American* newspaper:

> Of Hayes, who is Gael every inch of him.
> His is the fame that loud rings.
> Better than winning in Athens, he won it
> In England. From Windsor, the home of their kings,

> To London, he ran with the heart of the heroes
> Of Ireland, the legs and the fire of them.
> If America gave him a birthplace, he carried
> Her flag to the front, nor stumbled nor tarried
> A step on the way.
> For his fathers were sons of Tipp'rary. . . . [15]

Every newspaper repeated the story that Johnny worked in the dry-goods department at Bloomingdale's, "in a confidential position as assistant to John J. Reilly, the superintendent."[16] Supposedly, he trained for the Olympics on a rooftop track built by Samuel Bloomingdale himself. Photographs of Johnny dressed in a suit and writing at a desk appeared in many publications after the Olympics. Posters of him in his track gear hung in the windows of Bloomingdale's. It was mentioned that he had earned a promotion.

That was bunk, Johnny later admitted. The Irish-American Athletic Club had arranged the "job" so he could train full time. It's unclear whether he actually reported to work. But Samuel Bloomingdale happily reaped the post-London publicity. (One of his department store rivals, John Wanamaker, was starting his own track team, which would lead to the establishment of the annual Millrose Games.)

The fact was, Johnny did not have a profession to return to. He needed income to support himself and his siblings, familial responsibilities that went unreported at the time. Indeed, while hundreds of newspapers breathlessly parsed the Olympic marathon and Johnny's grit and courage, none described that he had been parentless since his teens and that his siblings had been placed in an orphanage.

What had changed since London was that, like Dorando, Hayes was now famous. He had, in effect, won the lottery. He received several offers to train other runners, and vaudeville impresario Joseph Hart approached him to put together a sketch about the marathon.

The work was easy, and the money was a reported $10,000 over six months—a tidy fortune in those times. He made extra cash by selling an illustrated pamphlet with details of his running career, and he moved into rooms in the Vanderbilt Hotel at 42nd Street, a sportsmen's hangout that long served as boxing champ John L. Sullivan's headquarters. He was spotted squiring an attractive young lady.

Coaching and performing onstage meant that Johnny was profiting from his athletic feats. He was forced to renounce his amateur status. James E. Sullivan accepted his resignation with regret. "I believe the great runner has made a mistake," he said before adding: "What I admire about Hayes is the very honorable way in which he withdrew from the amateur ranks. He did not go about it surreptitiously and do things in violation of the rules of the governing body."[17]

Hayes's abrupt exit from amateur competition left some observers uneasy. "It arouses the feeling that there was something more in his striving than the love of sport," the *New York Tribune* commented. "The keen pleasure that the victory brought to all true sportsmen in this country is nullified to a large extent by the introduction even at this late day of the breath of commercialism."[18]

The 1908 Olympics quietly drew to a close on the afternoon of October 31, when Britain defeated Ireland in field hockey, 8–1, at the Stadium. At the same time, the Franco–British Exhibition concluded, having drawn 8.4 million visitors to Shepherd's Bush and made a nice profit for Imre Kiralfy.

In the official tally, the British claimed 146 total Olympic medals, with 56 gold. The runner-up Americans won 47 total and 23 gold. It was a Pyrrhic victory. Just as the United States ignored the nontrack events during June and July, it bypassed the "winter" segment of the 1908 Games, which featured competition in soccer, rugby, lacrosse, and, for the first time at the Olympics, figure skating (with Sweden's Ulrich Salchow dominating the men's division).

The controversies from the summer, however, refused to die. English and American sports officials and journalists continued to trade vitriolic accusations, countercharges, recriminations, and retorts on topics ranging from the tug-of-war to the officiating. Gustavus Kirby wrote one such screed, entitled "An Answer to Statements of the Amateur Athletic Association of Great Britain Concerning the Olympic Games of 1908," only to be countered by Theodore Cook's exhaustive "The Olympic Games of 1908 in London: A Reply to Certain Criticisms."

In the *London Illustrated News*, G. K. Chesterton wrote, "The American is a bad sportsman because he is a good Jingo. . . . One American phrase constantly recurred: 'Our boys were in to win.' Which means: 'This is sport to you, but death to us—death or immortality.' For them the game is really worth the candle—because the game is not really a game. The real problem, I admit, remains with us. How are we to deal with this gigantic daughter who, in her youthful innocence, supposes that we mean what we say? We said that football was the foundation of English ethics and philosophy; but we never imagined that anybody would believe us."[19]

Pierre de Coubertin blamed the chaos on his archrival. "I just could not understand Sullivan's attitude here," he wrote. "He shared the team's frenzy and did nothing to try and calm them down. This was followed on his return by a new betrayal: he persuaded the Amateur Athletic Union to appoint a commission for the purpose of forming a new International Olympic Committee and drawing up the statutes of future games."[20]

Coubertin's longtime IOC confidant, Columbia University history professor William Milligan Sloane, concurred, calling Sullivan "a ghetto-poor Irish-American, a man whose great faults are those of his birth and breeding."[21]

Caspar Whitney, the *Outing* publisher and former U.S. member of the IOC, scolded Sullivan for his behavior. But he also blamed Coubertin, whom he called "a well-meaning, fussy and incompetent little Frenchman," for the problems in London. Whitney called for new leadership "for international meetings of this character. [T]here should be international rulings and a real international committee. . . . It is idiotic that England and America, who supply seven-eighths of the athletes of the world, should be at the pleasure of such a foolish organization as this present International Committee."[22]

The exchanges grew so nasty that the White House intervened. Roosevelt advised Sullivan to tone down the rhetoric, lest the Games turn into an international incident. "We won a remarkable victory anyhow, and for us to make complaints of unfair treatment does us no good," Roosevelt wrote. "The dignified and wise thing for us to do is to make no public comment of any kind."[23]

The marathon remained the number-one topic of debate, with every angle dissected. Many in Britain remained upset that the Americans had protested the verdict. "It is a very unfortunate thing that the man who came in second at the Marathon race last week happened to be an American," one writer lamented. "If he had been an Englishman it may be safely assumed that he would have brought no objection to Dorando. Of course, Hayes was rightly given the race as soon as he had made his protest, but by making this protest he lost the opportunity of his life. If he had been a sufficiently good sportsman to allow Dorando to retain the prize he would have been the most popular man in England, and he would have done much to wipe out the feeling of disgust which had been generated by the conduct of the American athletes and their rowdy supporters."[24]

Notwithstanding the fact that Johnny Hayes could not have cared less about being "the most popular man in England," more serious charges emerged. The U.S. camp accused Dorando of being given drugs after he collapsed for the first time just outside the Stadium. If true, it would explain Dorando's actions inside the Stadium. In other words, he wasn't suffering just from exhaustion, dehydration, and sunstroke; he was staggering and near unconscious because of being doped.

This would also have meant that he had violated the fourth rule of the marathon, which stated: "No competitor either at the start or during the progress of the race may take or receive any drug. The breach of this rule will operate as an automatic disqualification."

Reporters never directly questioned Dorando about drug use. However, Jack Andrew later confirmed this. "Dr. Bulger told me that Dorando had taken a dope of strychnine and atropia, and only his attention both on the track and in the dressing room saved his life," he confessed. "One of my cycling stewards saw [Dorando] take the dope on the far side of Wormwood Scrubs."[25]

Left unmentioned was why, if Andrew and Bulger were aware of the Italian's doping, they did not immediately remove him from the race.

But Dorando was not the only marathoner connected with drugs. In August, team manager Howard Crocker submitted a comprehensive report about the Canadians' showing in London, including Longboat's performance. "My experience in racing leads me to believe that Longboat should have won his race," Crocker wrote. "His sudden collapse and the symptoms shown seem to me to indicate that some form of stimulant was used contrary to the rules of the games. I think that any medical man knowing the facts of the case will assure you that the presence of a drug in an overdose was the cause of the runner's failure."

When he examined Longboat at the Stadium, Crocker noted, "I found a weak pulse—the respiration very slow—a 'pin point' pupil of the eye and an unconscious condition which was not sleep. To all appearance some one had got anxious and thinking to help the Indian by giving a stimulant, had given an overdose. I feel sure he had a narrow escape from death."

Crocker felt compelled to report this publicly, he said, because "the Indian is credited with selling the race by some parties, and by others of being 'yellow' and quitting. This does a good runner like Longboat, uneducated as he may be, a great injustice."[26]

Also accused of "selling the race" was Tom Flanagan. He was rumored to have ordered Longboat doped to collect on bets made against the Native Indian. Flanagan denied these charges, saying that stimulants were resorted to only after Longboat had fallen and was bleeding from the nose and mouth.

Said Flanagan: "We lost honestly."[27]

The uproar about the 1908 marathon brought the race from the shadows of sport into the mainstream. The word itself entered the vernacular. Marathon was a place in Greece, but "marathon" was used to describe anything that lasted a long time or was exceedingly difficult: a "marathon debate in Congress," a "marathon journey to the North Pole."

In a letter responding to criticism from his pal William Carlos Williams, Ezra Pound argued that his poetry career was "only at the quater [sic] post in a marathon." Pound added, riffing on the theme, "I wonder just where you think the tape is stretched for Mr. Hays [sic], 'vittore ufficiale' ['official winner'] and Dorando Pietri, hero of Italy. That was by the way delightful to get in Italy & to get here—one of the men who arranged the events, one of the trainer sort . . . said Pietri would have never got there if he hadn't been helped."[28]

Writer Finley Peter Dunne's sagacious invention, Mr. Dooley, the Irish immigrant saloonkeeper, explicated the results of the Olympic marathon in the pages of *American Magazine*:

> Th' concludin' event in th' meetin' was th' famous Marathon race, which was conceded to be a gift f'r th' English team. But they magnanimously declined, preferring a sound position in th' fifth division. Th' race was won by a son of our old impeeryal ally, Italy. He ran a superb race, doin' th' last mile in an autymobile in two minyits. Arriving in th' Stajum with superb pluck, he was carri'd acrost th' line be th' judges an' revived in about half an hour. Owin' to some stupid misconstruction iv th' rules, th' race was given to a Yankee who resorted to what we must call th' very unspoortsmanlike device iv runnin' th' entire distance. Th' decision was greeted by th' spectators with cries iv "Shame!" an' "Foul!" showin' that Englishmen, however much they admire their cousins acrost th' sea, love th' spirit iv fair play more. . . .
>
> "Do you think th' English are good losers?" asked Mr. Hennessy.
>
> "Good losers, says ye? Good losers? I'll back thim to lose anny time they start."[29]

Interest mushroomed, with the number of marathons and the quantity of entrants markedly increasing. Marathons debuted in San Francisco, Los Angeles, New Orleans, and Pittsburgh. In the New York City area alone, seventeen amateur and professional marathons[30] took place between November 1908 and May 1909, including two on one day, according to historian Pamela Cooper. The *New York Journal*–sponsored marathon, which started in Rye, in Westchester County, and ended at Columbus Circle, drew over 700 applicants. The 1908 Boston Marathon had 120 entrants; the 1909 version attracted 164.

Hayes sparked a miniboom among fellow Irish-American marathoners. Matthew Maloney won two marathons within a two-week span in 1908–09, and the I-AAC's James Crowley triumphed in the 1908 Yonkers marathon. Longboat, Tewanima, and Simpson brought other Native distance runners to the fore, with Paul Acoose and Albert Smoke emerging in Canada, and Andrew Sockalexis, Albert Ray, and Philip Zeyouma in the United States.

After its lackluster showing at the Olympics, England got into the act with several marathons (including one for professionals) in 1908. Jack Andrew and his Polytechnic Harriers club hosted the inaugural Poly Marathon the following year, with the start again at Windsor Castle. *Sporting Life* sponsored the event and donated an enormous silver trophy.

In 1909, in a sign of its arrival as a popular, legitimate event, the Spalding company published *Marathon Running*, the first-ever training guide for the race. Authored by none other than James E. Sullivan, it offered fitness tips ("Don't let anyone give you 'dope' in a race."), hints for novices, rules for the road, advice for event organizers, and, not so incidentally, advertisements for "the new Spalding Marathon Long-Distance Running Shoes," offered at $8 per pair.

Still others continued to argue that the marathon was unsafe. It is "worse than prize fighting or bullfighting," groused one columnist. Another noted: "Sport is sport, but this is another thing. The day of human sacrifice is past—gone with the Roman amphitheater and the downward turning thumb."[31]

Former Olympian James Connolly baldly stated, "A man cannot pursue the practice of 25-mile running without permanent nervous and muscular deterioration."[32] This was seconded by the *Journal of the American Medical Association,* which concluded that physical damage to the so-called "athlete's heart" was an "unquestionable" by-product of marathoning.

"Chances are," the *New York Times* editorialized, "that every [marathon runner] weakens his heart and shortens his life, not only by the terrible strain of the race itself, but by the preliminary training which produces muscular and vascular developments that become perilous instead of advantageous the moment a return to ordinary pursuits and habits puts an end to the need for them. For the great majority of adults, particularly in an urban population, to take part in a Marathon race is to risk serious and permanent injury to health, with immediate death a danger not very remote."[33]

Doctors would soon learn to diagnose "athlete's heart," which is often enlarged and with murmurs, as a normal physiological feature after strenuous exercise. Indeed, doctors found "no evidence of permanent injury"[34] from runners competing in marathons, provided they had trained diligently and underwent regular medical exams.

The story of the courier who ran from Marathon to Athens and then perished—the myth that begot the marathon—was itself dying, albeit slowly.

EIGHTEEN

I n 1908, controversy was becoming a valued currency in professional sports as savvy promoters saw how the notorious attracted the public's attention. Dorando was an international sensation because of how he won, then lost, the marathon in London. In boxing, Jack Johnson caused outrage among fans who wanted the heavyweight title to be held exclusively by white men; they stormed the box office to root against Johnson. The New York Giants and Chicago Cubs staged a pennant race for the ages that turned on a mistake by the Giants' first baseman Fred Merkle, a play that fans from both cities endlessly debated.

So it was that Patrick Powers, from his office inside the Flatiron Building in Manhattan, took notice of marathoning.[1] Powers was a baseball lifer who had been a major league manager during the 1890s before becoming president of the Eastern League. He ran the National Association of Professional Baseball Leagues, the organization that, essentially, presided over the Minor Leagues. Powers was also a serial entrepreneur who staged prize fights and organized the popular six-day cycling extravaganzas (reflecting the fact that everyone rested on Sundays).

The rotund promoter recognized that, in the marathon, he had a built-in audience. Between the 80,000 people who watched the ending of the race inside the Stadium in London, the hundreds of thousands of spectators who saw parts of it on the road from Windsor Castle to Shepherd's Bush, and the millions who viewed film clips of

the Games in nickelodeons and vaudeville halls for months afterward, the 1908 Olympic marathon was the most-watched sporting
event in history up to that time.

The notoriety of the race, combined with the macabre but titil-
lating possibility that a runner might actually keel over and die, appealed to the promoter in Powers. Surely, he thought, the public would
pay to watch the top marathoners in action. Surely, the press would
cover every angle. Surely, interest among sportsmen and their bookies would be as high as the skyscraping Flatiron.

Powers envisioned a different kind of format than, say, the Boston Marathon, which featured its competitors running along a course
open to the public. There was no way to sell tickets and thus profit
from that type of event. However, if Powers were to bring the marathon indoors, he would control the gate and be able to charge top
dollar for tickets. He also thought to arrange it as a one-on-one contest, like a boxing tilt, which would enable fans to better follow the
action.

With manager Harry Pollok, Powers went to work to sign the biggest name in marathoning. They contacted Armando Cougnet, the
director of the *Gazzetta dello Sport* newspaper in Italy, who in turn
telegraphed Dorando Pietri in Carpi. They negotiated terms for a
promotional contract and, by late October, had agreed to pay all of
Dorando's expenses to come and race in the States.[2]

Powers and Pollok reserved Madison Square Garden for the evening of November 25, the night before Thanksgiving, and scurried
to line up an opponent. They contacted Tom Flanagan in Toronto
about Tom Longboat's availability. Despite James Sullivan's protestations to the contrary, Longboat was technically an amateur and unable
to sign with Powers immediately. They also considered Alf Shrubb,
who was now coaching at Harvard University, but he was not in racing
form.

Their main target was New York's own Johnny Hayes. The American had fallen out of shape, thanks to the demands of the vaudeville and banquet circuits, and he initially told Powers that he would not be ready by Thanksgiving. Powers preyed on Johnny's ego, telling him that experts were whispering that he had not earned the gold medal, that he had won because of Dorando's last-lap collapse. If Johnny were to beat Dorando again, Powers argued, he would silence the critics. Hayes agreed to the race, even though he would have less than a month of serious training to prepare.

That hardly mattered to Powers. He had lined up the dream race: Johnny Hayes versus Dorando Pietri. The Olympic gold medalist pitted against the man who had the race won and then lost it in front of the Queen of England. The Irish-American lad from New York City against the Italian dynamo from Carpi, at the full "London distance" of 26 miles, 385 yards. The grudge match, the revenge match, the rematch: live from the mecca of entertainment, Madison Square Garden.

The first marathon boom was about to hit the United States, and it was going to be as big as the waistline of William Howard Taft, America's newly elected president.

Dorando Pietri made a quick stopover in London to collect his brother, then set sail from Liverpool on November 11 on the *Kronprinzessin Cecilie*. He arrived in Hoboken eight days before his race against Johnny Hayes wearing a brilliant green hat and a matching necktie. A mob of media and countrymen rushed to greet him, ignoring fellow passenger Thomas Fortune Ryan, the tobacco industrialist and one of the nation's wealthiest men.

With Ulpiano by his side, Dorando felt at ease in New York City. The previous year, some 285,000 of his countrymen had entered the

United States, about one-quarter of new arrivals, with more than two million Italians pouring into America during the first decade of the twentieth century.[3] Many settled in lower Manhattan, often in the dejected tenements formerly occupied by the earlier wave of Irish immigrants, finding enough work to send home money and enough compatriots to speak with in their mother tongue.

The brothers stayed at the Bartholdi Hotel, next to Madison Square Garden, and took meals at a friend's flat on Hudson Street. In an interview with *La Stampa,* one of several Italian-language publications in New York, Dorando addressed his famous collapse in England. Near the Stadium, he told the reporter, "I feel free, strong, ready. Then, my chest swells and it feels like vertigo. It feels like I'm being lifted and dragged, all the energy draining from my body. A last gasp and I am into the Stadium. I am the first . . . and then I fall and then I don't remember anything anymore."[4]

He had done few drills on the boat and was shocked to discover that the race was going to be held inside. He muttered that it was a trap to give Hayes an advantage. He began training at the Columbia University gymnasium, paced by the cross-country team, to get accustomed to the tight turns required for indoor running. But when word leaked out that a professional athlete was running alongside college amateurs, university officials ordered him off the campus. He resumed workouts at the Pastime Athletic Club.

His opponent was also rusty. But Johnny Hayes had signed a contract for big money and, with his cyclist from London, George Cameron, at his side, started running on the familiar roads of Westchester County. He also logged miles on the track at William Vanderbilt's American Horse Exchange, at 50th Street and Broadway, and tested the indoor facilities at the 8th Regiment Armory.

Their concern about the conditions was well-founded. No one had ever devised an indoor marathon, much less raced one, and the pounding their legs would take was bound to be severe. Former distance star "Sparrow" Robinson started crafting a cinder track on the floor of the Garden two days before the race, building a slightly banking incline along the curves. A fence surrounded the oval, which measured 10 laps per mile, meaning Dorando and Hayes would have to make 262 dizzying circuits (plus an extra 33 yards) to complete the marathon. The finish was at the customary point: in the middle of the arena, on the 27th Street side of the building.

Dorando and Hayes saw each other for the first time since London five days before the race.[5] They met at the Hoffman House Hotel at Madison Square Park. The two shook hands and, speaking through translators, exchanged polite pleasantries. They sized each other up, each about 5 foot 4 and 125 pounds, Dorando black-haired and olive-skinned, his face decorated with a black mustache; Hayes brown-haired and fair with a poker face. They resembled two actors who would soon be famous: Charlie Chaplin and Buster Keaton.

As Powers had predicted, tickets sold briskly. Box seats went for $10, as the New York City tabloids and the Irish-American and Italian-language newspapers hyped the contest like a heavyweight fight. One measured the different strides of the two runners, with Hayes's averaging 5.5 feet and Dorando's 4 feet. The publisher of *Il Progresso Italo-Americano*, Carlo Barsotti, offered a special cup to the winner.

GREATEST INTEREST OF ANY ATHLETIC EVENT IN YEARS, was the *Evening World*'s headline on the eve of the race.

M adison Square Garden was not just a building, but a state of mind. Every act worth the price of admission played the palace of pleasure on 26th Street and Madison Avenue, from Buffalo Bill to John L. Sullivan to William Jennings Bryan to the Westminster

Dog Show. The chronicler of New York City, O. Henry, called it, "the center of the universe."[6]

Designed by noted architect Stanford White and opened in 1890, the Garden anchored the entertainment district around Madison Square Park. The Moorish-styled arena featured an auditorium, with seating for 8,000 and room on the floor for thousands more, a 1,200-seat theater, a 1,500-seat concert hall, the biggest restaurant in town, and a roof-garden cabaret. Rising 320 feet into the air was a tower topped by a statue of the naked goddess Diana.

On the evening of November 25, Pat Powers watched with glee and then concern as swarms of people, with and without tickets, jammed the Garden's entrance. Upward of 15,000 partisan fans squeezed into the main amphitheater, filling the balconies, the sky gallery, and the floor area, brandishing Irish, Italian, and American flags and puffing excitedly on cigarettes and cigars. A dense haze of smoke settled above the tan bark track as Bayne's 69th Regiment Armory band dueled with Professor Volta's Italian band. A score-board stood at the ready to tally the runners' laps.

The combatants made their entrance at just past 9 p.m. The Irish contingent stomped their feet as Johnny Hayes walked in with a bull-dog covered in a blanket that spelled "H-A-Y-E-S." He wore a white bathrobe over the Olympic uniform from London. He was seconded by Cameron, with Mike Murphy and Ernie Hjertberg giving support.

The Italian section greeted Dorando with whistles and chanting as their man came onto the track in a lurid, cardinal-colored robe trimmed with fur. He sported his trademark flame-colored trunks and a sleeveless white jersey across which was printed the red-white-and-green-striped logo of Prospero De Nobili, a cigar and tobacco manufacturer on Long Island. He held cork in both hands, with a handkerchief in his right hand.

The bands played the Italian and American national anthems to ringing applause. At just after 9:15 p.m., Richard Croker, back from Ireland to cheer on Hayes, stood behind the runners—in his dinner coat with a fresh flower in his lapel—and fired the starter's pistol toward the rafters.

The crowd erupted as Dorando dashed to the inside and took the lead. Hayes was content to settle two feet behind him. They passed through the first mile in a brisk 5:27, their legs adjusting to the unfamiliar surface.

The one-on-one format in an enclosed space offered a very different marathon experience, both for the competitors and the spectators. Hayes did not dare allow Dorando to gain much separation; the fans were able to follow every step and, not so discreetly, place bets on the action.

Every cheer of "Go, you, Johnny!" was parried by "Viva Dorando! Viva Italia!" The bands played on.

The pair clocked 29:24 for the first five miles, or fifty laps. They ran as if hitched together, slogging in a monotonous rhythm, the Italian grim-faced in front, the American tenaciously trailing, lap after endless lap. Occasionally, Johnny spurted by Dorando, his supporters roaring, only to have Pietri snatch back the advantage.

They passed the ten-mile mark in 1:00:06; Hayes stuck on Dorando like a leech. At fifteen miles, in 1:31:43, they maintained the same position, their clothes clinging to their sweaty bodies. Every mile, Ulpiano handed Dorando a brown bottle and he took a swig. Hayes did the same from a tin flask.

The pace slowed, Dorando's stride shortening. The American probed, only to have the Italian answer. Hayes passed him during the twenty-third mile, but Pietri responded. Ulpiano began to shower him with seltzer water. Cameron urged on the Olympic champ.

Through the twenty-fourth and twenty-fifth miles, they ran together, their breaths coming in short bursts, their eyes glazed, the tension building throughout the Garden, Dorando glancing backward to measure his opponent

The gun sounded. One mile to go. Johnny hung back, harnessing his reserves for a final burst. Two laps left. He gathered for his push but, in a flash, it was Dorando surging, distancing himself, taking the turns in full stride and approaching the tape in a furious lather, Johnny broken and fairly beaten as Dorando crossed in a time of 2:44:20, a third of a lap ahead.

The crowd spilled onto the track in a delirium of enthusiasm. Dorando was grinning as his brother hugged him, and everybody in the arena who spoke Italian clamored to hoist him onto their shoulders.

A scream suddenly came from Box 58, by the finish line, where a woman had fallen over in a faint. She was later identified as Florence Mason, Johnny Hayes's "sweetheart and fiancée."

It was "the most spectacular foot race that New York ever has witnessed," commented the *Times*.

Ulpiano immediately sent cables to Carpi, letting their parents know the result, while Dorando basked in the sweetness of the moment, having in one stroke avenged the defeat at the Olympics, beaten Hayes on his own turf, and earned an excellent payday for his efforts. He received $2,000, plus another 1,000 lire (about $200) and the silver cup from *Il Progresso*. Hayes was paid $4,500. Powers and Pollok split $6,000 in profits.

"I so much wanted to see Hayes at the finish," Dorando said afterward. "I wanted to kiss him for he gave me such a great race."

Johnny was downcast as he left the arena with his brother and Cameron. His hometown was suddenly a desolate place. Everything that he had gained after London—the flattering words from the President of the United States, the adoration from the public, the respect from the press and the Irish-American community—was of little consolation. He felt like Tom Longboat did after the Olympics: He had let down an entire following.

He blamed the lack of preparation time for the defeat, but vowed to get back into "London shape." He asked anyone who would listen for another chance to meet Dorando. Several days later, there was more sad news: John Taylor, his Olympic and Irish-American club teammate, had died suddenly from typhoid pneumonia. Johnny immediately departed for Philadelphia for Taylor's funeral.

The brothers Pietri and the Italian community in New York celebrated deep into the night. At Café Martin, patrons shouted the now-familiar "Viva Dorando!" and "Viva Italia!" and ordered bottles of champagne. Then, everybody stood for Italy's national anthem.

The money started rolling in. Oscar and Willie Hammerstein signed Dorando as an act for the Victoria Theater vaudeville house at 42nd Street and Seventh Avenue. Dorando appeared onstage in his suit and trotted around the stage while emcee Loney Haskell described how many miles he ran and what foods he ate during training.[7] He later played Keith & Proctor's theater in Harlem to give the Italian community in uptown Manhattan a chance to see him.

The following week, Barsotti and Il Progresso hosted a lavish banquet in Dorando's honor at the Hotel del Campidoglio on Bleecker Street. He was presented with gifts, floral bouquets, and cash, and then everybody (including Count Massiglia, the Italian Consul General) feasted: antipasto (olives, salami, radish, anchovies, celery), vegetable soup, fish with mayonnaise sauce, ravioli alla Genovese, lamb with peas, punch, roast chicken, ice cream, cheese, fruit, coffee, Chianti, and spumante. Later that night, Dorando returned to Madison Square Garden as the honorary starter for Pat Powers's latest six-day bicycle race. His appearance provoked a deafening ovation.

The press dissected every detail of his running style—including the rumor that he downed Chianti while training and during races.

With Dorando and the marathon white hot, Powers wasted no time in announcing the next contest in the series. Dorando's opponent would be none other than Tom Longboat. The date: December 15, or less than three weeks away.

Since his return from London, Tom Longboat had allowed his body to heal. Then, he got back into racing. He showed his mettle by defeating fellow Olympian Fred Simpson in a five-miler in Hamilton. He set a Canadian record for the five-mile run against Percy Sellen and took the fifteen-mile Montreal Marathon in October. He capped the comeback with his third consecutive victory in the nineteen-mile Ward Marathon, romping over a quality field by more than one mile.[8]

"Longboat is Longboat again," the *Toronto Globe* reported.

"He has since his return [from London] proven himself the greatest long distance runner of the century," said CAAU president William Stark.[9]

Under Tom Flanagan's charge, he officially turned pro. Veteran trainer Tom Eck, along with Mike Flanagan, Tom's younger brother, took charge of Longboat's workouts before his match against Dorando. Tom ran in Clifton, New Jersey, before switching to the Berkeley Oval at Morris Dock, near to their rooms on Jerome and Burnside Avenues. A tune-up 10-miler against Percy Smallwood in Philadelphia, designed to give him indoors experience, appeared to backfire when the Welshman whipped Tom by 1.5 laps. Eck claimed that Longboat performed poorly because the new brogans he was wearing caused his feet to slip and then blister.

Flanagan and Marsh were not certain Longboat would last the full distance and downplayed his chances, but pundits wondered whether the Canadians were setting up Dorando and the Italians. "It looks fishy," *Evening World* columnist Robert Edgren wrote. "Must be something in that betting proposition."[10]

Longboat penned an odd column for the *Evening World* (probably ghostwritten by Lou Marsh) and pleaded his case: "Some will say the only good Indian is a dead Indian. I am not a good Indian, but I want to be known as an honest Indian. I have never taken any money for my races until a few weeks ago when I turned a professional."[11]

One week before the race, Longboat turned in a brisk clocking of 54:57 over ten miles, including a head-turning last mile in 5:15. The odds turned in his favor, especially as trainloads of Canadian backers chugged south. Flanagan and Marsh, believing Longboat wasn't ready, refused all bets.

ALL NEW YORK HAS CAUGHT THE MARATHON BUG, read the *Evening World* headline.[12]

The prospect of another victory by the indefatigable runner from Carpi brought out torrents of Italian flags and fans on the evening of the race. The jammed sidewalks outside Madison Square Garden "made the Brooklyn Bridge in rush hour look like a deserted mining camp,"[13] according to Edgren. Many spectators discovered that the tickets they'd purchased from unscrupulous speculators were worthless pieces of cardboard when they were refused entrance to the arena. The police and the fire departments were summoned to restore order. Across town in Times Square, the streets were clogged with people waiting for bulletins to be posted at the newspaper's offices.

The Garden was filled from floor to roof.[14] The infield space inside the cinder track was jammed. Dorando came out of his dressing room at 9 p.m. He stood underneath an *Il Progresso* banner, and supporters threw flowers at his feet as he bowed and shook the hands of his friends. Underneath his coat he displayed his lucky red shorts.

Longboat emerged minutes later in a black vest, seconded by the Flanagan brothers, Marsh, and Eck. He wore an old shirt with the green maple leaf and orange harp of the Irish Canadian Athletic Club. He tested the soft track surface and smiled at a number of Native Indians in war paint seated by the rail. In box seats sat Johnny Hayes and Richard Croker.

The lanky, sinewy Longboat towered over the muscular Dorando as the two shook hands and posed for photographers. Floyd MacFarland, the winner of the just-concluded six-day bicycle race, did the starting honors amid a deafening chorus of chants, Indian cries, and foot stomping. Again, Dorando sped to the front, his elastic legs churning in a ceaseless rhythm. Longboat eased behind him in an ungainly lope, his stride chopping slightly as he adjusted to the tight turns.

Dorando set the pace, but it was Longboat who set the tone. He didn't allow Pietri to find a consistent tempo. Several times, he sprinted past Dorando and kept the advantage for several laps before slackening and allowing Dorando to regain the lead. They resembled Alphonse and Gaston, one reporter noted, referencing the popular comic strip characters and their "After you, my dear Alphonse" exchange.

Together they toiled, lap after lap, the crowd a noisy backdrop, alternately tense and celebratory. Dorando struggled manfully to withstand Longboat's surges, but by the twentieth mile his face was alabaster white and his eyes a glazy stare.

Ulpiano pleaded for more from Dorando, dousing his brother's legs with mineral water and passing him coffee. Dorando slowed considerably. Longboat pressured and probed, now taking the lead for longer stretches.

During the twenty-second mile, Tom Flanagan fetched Tom's fiancée, Lauretta Maracle, from the stands and positioned her at the edge of the running surface. She waved her handkerchief as Longboat ran past. He seemed to draw strength from her presence, but the outcome would be decided by his opponent. As Dorando gathered himself to chase down Longboat, he seemed to strike the wooden edge of the track. He fell, his supporters crying out and then falling silent as he writhed in pain. Longboat pushed on, attacking the last mile alone, floating home in 2:45:05.

Dorando lay exhausted, his mustache wilting, done in by the exacting toll of two indoor marathons in twenty days and a never-ending series of banquets, toasts, and vaudeville appearances. It was the Olympic marathon redux, but without Jack Andrew and Dr. Bulger to give assistance, and without the Queen of England in attendance.

Doctors removed him, unconscious, to the dressing room, as Ulpiano explained to anyone who would listen that Longboat had tripped his brother. Olympian Martin Sheridan, who witnessed Dorando's fall, commented, "He wobbled and stepped on the curb and fell on his haunches. He got up and fell again, all in. Longboat never touched him at all."

The winner wore a huge grin and credited Flanagan for being "on the job faithfully. When he thought I needed encouragement he brought my sweetheart to the trackside. I looked at her once and then went to the front. I felt like stopping to tell her how confident I felt, but didn't dare take the chance.

"I had to use my head to beat Dorando," Longboat continued. "I had to worry him. I think I did this by passing him every once in a while and then stepping aside to let him make the pace."

Neither man argued about the payday. Each share was worth a reported $4,000. Longboat also won a diamond medal, offered by *Il Progresso* publisher Barsotti and worth $500.

Longboat, Flanagan, Marsh, and Irish Canadian club members hit the town to celebrate. They mocked James E. Sullivan for disparaging Longboat's reputation, and then drank to Longboat's health. At some point, Tom disappeared from the party. They figured he was sleeping, but he was discovered at the Seville Hotel at Dorando's bedside. He consoled Ulpiano as Dorando rested from what one doctor called "a strained heart."

"I'm going to give him another chance," Longboat said. "He is a game runner."

R edemption.
Just as Dorando Pietri had regained his reputation by defeating Johnny Hayes in a head-to-head race, Longboat had redeemed himself after his galling disaster in London. His triumph silenced more than a few critics. TOM LONGBOAT RETRIEVES HIS OLYMPIC DEFEAT, proclaimed the front page of the *Toronto Globe*, adding he "is undoubtedly the finest and fastest long distance man in the world."

Tom had little time to celebrate. He and Lauretta rushed back to Ontario; they were due to marry. The newspapers approved of his bride-to-be, a schoolteacher at the Mohawk Reserve near the town of Deseronto, seeing her as a "civilizing" force for the marathoner. "The Indian traits are well covered [in Lauretta]," opined the *Globe*. "Few would imagine that she had been born and raised on an Indian reservation and was of Indian blood. In every way she is a winsome little girl who has, as she says, been educated away from many of the traditions of her race. She does not like to talk of feathers, war paint or other Indian paraphernalia. She is ambitious for Tom and if anybody can make a reliable man and good citizen of that elusive being, Tom Longboat, it will be his wife."[15]

There was one catch: Lauretta was a Christian. She insisted that Tom get baptized before their wedding. He was not keen on doing this. He identified himself with the Longhouse spiritual traditions of the Six Nations Reserve, and his memory of his stay at the Mohawk

Institute was not a fond one. But, dutifully, he was baptized in Ontario days before the marriage ceremony.

In Toronto, Archbishop Sweatman caught wind of the conversion. He banned Anglican ministers from performing the wedding, alleging that Longboat's hasty conversion "from heathendom to Christianity was not sincere."[16] Tom Flanagan intervened, and the archbishop withdrew his opposition. On December 28, with Longboat admitting he was more nervous than before a big race, the couple was married at St. John's Anglican Church in Toronto, with Lauretta dressed in white satin. None of Tom's family attended; no one from the Six Nations Reserve came. Longboat invited Dorando Pietri to the reception, but Dorando was unable to make it.

Flanagan served as best man, although he forgot the marriage license at the hotel. The ceremony was delayed for thirty minutes while Flanagan hurried to retrieve it and Longboat sweated in his tuxedo jacket. A public reception followed at Massey Hall, with Hugh Graham, the publisher of the *Montreal Star,* sending the newlyweds a $500 check.

The year 1908 was coming to a close. It had indeed been "one hell of a ride around the sun."

NINETEEN

I n little more than a month, Dorando Pietri had crossed the Atlantic Ocean, raced two indoor marathons, appeared regularly on a vaudeville stage, gorged nightly, done many interviews, acquired a spiffy and expensive wardrobe, and made more money than his father had earned in his lifetime.

His weary body craved rest. His blistered feet needed time to heal, and his legs were sore. His lungs could have used a breather. But he was both protagonist and hostage to marathon mania; his legs and lungs brought in revenue while his overall health suffered. Just eighteen days after their meeting in Madison Square Garden, he traveled to upstate New York to take on the just-married Tom Longboat.

This time they clashed in Buffalo, on January 2, 1909, a wintry night that didn't discourage 10,000 spectators from packing the 74th Regiment Armory.[1] Many came from Toronto to cheer on Longboat, including Mayor Joseph Oliver, taking advantage of a special excursion train provided by the Irish Canadian Athletic Club. Unnoticed, Alf Shrubb slipped into the arena to scout the contestants.

The early going on the nine-laps-per-mile clay track was punishing, with the first mile in 5:07, Dorando charging ahead as if to run the newlywed aground. In the first lap of the third mile, Tom stumbled on the uneven footing and sprawled to the dirt, his knee striking the stout timber that held the track in place. Dorando opened a twenty-five-yard advantage, but Tom jumped up and gave chase, his leg bleeding, as the Armory denizens applauded his gameness.

They covered five miles in 27:32, and ten in 56:30, the pace wickedly fast. The race was playing out like their first one. Longboat allowed Dorando to have the lead, all the while controlling the tempo. He toyed with the Italian, running abreast of him and flashing a smile, then falling back.

They passed the fifteen-mile mark in 1:26:34. Dorando looked winded and called on Ulpiano for liquids. He sprinted furiously at the start of the nineteenth mile, but when he couldn't shake the tenacious Indian, his body seemed to wither. Five laps later he stopped running and clutched his heart. He slipped off the track on queasy legs into his brother's arms. He had nothing left to give.

Even the Canadian contingent fell silent as Ulpiano escorted Dorando away to the dressing room. Longboat continued on, walking the remaining six miles without opposition, kibitzing with fans and chatting with Flanagan and Lou Marsh. A grin played across his face as he contemplated returning to his Lauretta with another victory and a check for several thousand dollars. The band played "The Maple Leaf Forever" over and over.

Pat Powers immediately announced the next race: Tom Longboat against Alf Shrubb, Canada versus England, in the ultimate grudge match, scheduled for January 26 at Madison Square Garden.

Dorando's twin defeats to Longboat did not diminish his draw at the gate. If anything, the results reinforced his image from London as the plucky competitor who ran till he dropped. And, indeed, he ran on. With Powers and Pollok fielding offers from cities across the nation and handling the local press, Dorando hit the road and raced in Pittsburgh, Louisville, St. Paul, Indianapolis, and Toronto. He won ten-milers in Rochester and Syracuse, then gritted through two more marathons to close out the month of January: a victory over Percy Smallwood in St. Louis, where Italian immigrants from the neighborhood they called *La Montagna*—known not so affectionately as "Dago Hill"—came out to cheer him on,[2] and a win over Frenchman Albert Corey in Chicago, presided over by White Sox owner Charles Comiskey.

Powers and Pollok added other runners to their stable, including Patrick White from Ireland, and persuaded Matthew Maloney, who had set the amateur marathon record of 2:36:26 in the Rye-to-New York City race, to turn pro. Sweden's Johan Svanberg and England's Fred Appleby, veterans from the London Olympics, decided to cash in in the States, as did a young Frenchman named Henri St. Yves, winner of the Edinburgh Marathon. In Canada, Fred Simpson declared his intention to leave the amateur ranks.

Marathon mania was now in full swing. At the heart of the boom, in New York, a singing waiter at Jimmy Kelly's saloon in Union Square took notice. Israel Baline had written the lyrics to his first published song in 1907, around the time his name changed to Irving Berlin. The attention given to the races at Madison Square Garden inspired him to come up with "Dorando," a ditty about an Italian-American barber who places a big bet on his running hero. The first verse went:

> I feel-a much-a bad like anything
> All the night I nunga canna sleep
> It's a my pizon Pasquale
> He say we take da car
> And see Dorando race a-"Long-a-ship"
> Just like the sport, I sell da barbershop
> And make da bet Dorando he's a win
> Then to Madees-a Square
> Pasquale and me go there
> And just-a like-a dat, da race begin.

And then the refrain:

> *Dorando! Dorando!*
> *He run-a, run-a, run-a, run like anything*
> *One-a, two-a hundred times around da ring*
> *I cry, "Please-a nunga stop!"*
> *Just then, Dorando he's a drop!*
> *Goodbye poor old barber shop*
> *It's no fun to lose da mon*
> *When de son-of-a-gun no run*
> *Dorando*
> *He's a good for not!*

And then the second verse:

> *Dorando, he's a come around next day,*
> *Say, "Gentlemen, I wanna tell-a you,*
> *It's a one-a bigga shame,*
> *I forgot da man's a-name,*
> *Who madke me eat da Irish beef-a stew;*
> *I ask-a him to give me da spagett,*
> *I know it make me run a-quick-a-quick,*
> *But I eat da beef-a stew, And now I tell-a you,*
> *Just like da pipps it make me very sick."*[3]

Berlin sold the song for $25, and vaudeville singer Amy Butler helped turn it into a modest hit. With his first taste of commercial success, Berlin left Jimmy Kelly's to try his hand at songwriting full time.

In *Collier's*, Charles Dana Gibson sketched "Effect of the Marathon Craze," which showed ordinary citizens of all ages and occupations rushing to join the mania. Below Gibson's illustration the caption read:

> Once Johnny Hayes worked in a store, Dorando once made pies,
> But now they're known from pole to pole, and everybody cries,
> "There goes the man who won the Marathon!" So how can you
> Tell what, if we should train and drink Chianti, we might do?
>
> Each man should be his motor-car, and each his Arab steed,
> And have within himself six cylinders or more of speed.
> The crowd may shout: "Aw, get a horse!" or grin and call us freaks;
> They simply do not understand that we're the modern Greeks![4]

Companies eager to link their products to the marathoners signed them to endorsement deals. Hayes and Dorando plugged Bovril, while Johnny appeared in advertisements for O'Sullivan's Live Rubber Heels, promising "the easy, graceful stride in running or walking." A boardgame from Owbridge's Lung Tonic ("for coughs or colds") used Dorando and Hayes on the cover. Finally, in a move that would be unheard of today, images of Hayes and Longboat appeared on cigarette cards for the tobacco brands Pet, Mecca, and Kopek.

The Postum cereal company took a different approach in its marketing campaign. Its ads began with this copy: "Dorando had a cup of coffee the morning he didn't win the marathon." Concluded the company: "The ones with strong heart and nerves win in the race of life. When coffee hurts, try Postum. There's a reason."[5]

Putting the craze into perspective was Finley Peter Dunne's infallible Mr. Dooley. If, a few thousand years in the future, someone were to write the history of "th' state iv America in nineteen hundherd an' nine," Mr. Dooley commented, "th' principal occupations iv th' people were murdher, divoorce, prize-fightin', lynching, Marathon racin', abduction, burglary, an' Salomying. . . . Th' most prominent citizens iv th' decayin' raypublic besides [boxer] James J. Jeffries were T. Longboat, [women's health advocate] Lydia Pinkham."[6]

Teddy Roosevelt, now living full time in Oyster Bay as a private citizen, wrote that the recent experiences of "the pastry cook, the floorwalker, and the Indian have tended to make the thing a screaming farce. The fact is that the three men are all exceptionally good long-distance runners and exceptionally close together, so that one might win at one time and the other at another, and no one could be sure of the result on a given occasion. . . . They are all three of the professional type pure and simple, and to have all the yell and trouble concerning them as amateurs at the Olympic games does seem a little absurd."[7]

Johnny Hayes was now the odd man out. His defeat by Dorando, in his hometown, had crushed him. The press turned on him and reported that he had not trained hard or long enough, then whispered that his Olympic victory was a fluke. Powers and Pollok complained that Johnny had been difficult during the negotiations, and they dropped him from their marathon series after Dorando's victory.

Worse, Johnny's reputation as the flesh-and-blood embodiment of a Horatio Alger tale was under attack. His decision to turn pro, appear onstage, and sign endorsement deals was seen as a betrayal of the amateur ideal. "So the mighty fall," the *Washington Post* reported. "There stands out the pathetic story of the passing of a world-famed hero. In his bare little room in the Vanderbilt Hotel, Johnny Hayes sits these days, alone and almost friendless, all his glory gone, many friends estranged, and little hope or prospect in the future. For all of which he can thank himself."[8]

"Too many athletes have been feted out of their prowess to believe that one who accepts attention as readily as Hayes will come out any better in the end," wrote another. "Too many others have been made useless blowhards, or walking advertisements for some candy store that needs to sell its chocolate creams, to make any one hope that that is the way Hayes will go."[9]

Johnny did not regret turning pro. The money was excellent, and he needed every cent to support the family. But the competitor in him burned for a rubber match against Dorando, and there was only one way to accomplish that: Get back in the good graces of Powers and Pollok. He called in his coach from the Irish-American Athletic Club, Ernie Hjertberg, and focused on rebuilding his endurance. He hired a new manager, Charles Harvey, to negotiate with the promoters.

When Dorando raced Corey in Chicago, Hayes followed as if obsessed. "My one ambition in life is to meet Dorando Pietro [sic] again and wipe out the defeat he handed me in New York when he caught me out of condition," Johnny told one reporter.[10]

Alf Shrubb had been goading Tom Longboat for two years. The spindly Englishman, who had moved to Canada after losing his amateur eligibility, wanted to race Tom at any distance, from two to fifteen miles, to determine who was the best distance runner in North America. Shrubb had tried negotiating with Tom Flanagan, and he had tried to provoke Longboat by belittling him to the newspapers. But until Longboat turned professional, his lobbying was for naught.

As wiry as a piece of rope, Shrubb was 5 foot 6 and 125 pounds. At twenty-nine, he was considerably older than Longboat. He wore his slicked-back hair parted in the middle, with a dapper black mustache set off against a pale face. He sometimes competed in dark socks pulled up over his calves.

He approached running as a craft and trained with a scientific efficiency that set him apart from his peers. He was one of the first athletes to keep a diary of his regimen, and he wrote two of the earliest, most comprehensive training manuals on running. "The principal item is walking," he advised. "Get out for a sixteen-mile walk three or four times a week, and walk at a good steady four-and-a-half miles an hour pace."[11]

The Englishman's first love was cross-country, but he had taught himself how to race on the track and held almost every national record, from two miles to the distance covered in one hour (nearly twelve miles). He was a front-runner who liked to push the pace and was virtually unbeatable up to fifteen miles. Sadly, he did not get a chance to compete at the 1904 Olympics, during his prime, because Britain did not send a team to St. Louis. The following year, he was banned from amateur sports after officials ruled that he had accepted excessive expense money. He came to North America to make a living as a professional, sometimes running against (and defeating) horses. He had just taken a coaching job at Harvard when, finally, he was matched against Longboat.

Shrubb had never run a marathon. In fact, he seldom raced past twenty miles. But the self-confidence of "The Little Wonder" was high. "I shall run Longboat off his legs," he said. "He will either have to follow me or let me go. If he follows me I will kill him in ten miles. If he lets me go, I shall have such a big lead on him that I shall win."[12]

Longboat no sooner had signed the contract to race Shrubb than his relationship with Tom Flanagan ruptured.[13] Longboat had just competed in, and won, two indoor marathons in a short span. His body was sore, and he wanted rest. He also wanted to spend time with his new wife. Instead, he found himself training and racing almost nonstop, with a reported 50 percent of his earnings going to his manager.

Flanagan thought that Longboat was relaxing just when he was positioned to take home big-money purses. Flanagan's younger brother, Mike, quit as Longboat's trainer, saying, "I wouldn't take $200 a day and handle that fellow. He's the most contrary piece of furniture I ever had anything to do with."

Mere weeks after performing as best man at Longboat's wedding, Tom Flanagan sold the runner's contract to Pat Powers for $2,000. He told the press, "I would give a finger to have him beat Shrubb for Canada's sake, but I'll not be on the track or have anything to do with him personally. He can win if he is right and I know it, but I am out of the Indian's game for good."

Longboat was upset at Flanagan's action. He told Lauretta, "He sold me just like a race horse to make money."[14]

Tom left home to take on Shrubb under the care of trainer Jimmy De Forrest. He worked out on the boardwalk at Asbury Park, and even did some ice-skating when the roads were covered with snow. He also helped collar a thief in Manhattan, a feat that drew headlines.

With race day approaching, Shrubb sustained a blister on his left big toe and pulled out of the contest. Longboat suspected that this was a bit of gamesmanship, but Powers dutifully rescheduled the match for February 5. The bettors made Shrubb the slight favorite at 8:5 odds.

Longboat wallowed in New York, writing friends that "I am not in shape for this race. I am just thinking of quitting the race before it gets too late . . . I wouldn't bet a cent if I were you. I'm good for nothing now."[15]

He received another shock when, despite his disavowal, Tom Flanagan showed up in New York. With the professional marathon championship at stake, Flanagan couldn't stay away. He promised to help Longboat defeat Shrubb.

Madison Square Garden was again sold out for the fourth edition of Powers's marathon series.[16] Shrubb appeared on the track with the Union Jack on his red jersey and a bandage around his ankle. Longboat was in white, with the Irish-Canadian emblem on his chest. At least three prominent Sullivans were in the house—John L., James E., and "Big Tim," the notorious Tammany Hall power broker, who handled the starting honors.

Cigar smoke created wispy wreaths beneath the skylights as the frisky Shrubb, as promised, snapped through the first mile in 4:52. He lapped Longboat during the second mile and, by the fifth mile, had lapped him twice more. His five-mile time was 27:54. By ten miles, he was fully one-half mile ahead, in 57:32, and looking to break Longboat.

"Why, that man's as strong as a bull," remarked Billy Sherring, Canada's Olympic coach.

"Hey, Tom, take a taxi," wisecracked one spectator.

Longboat chuckled, but he refused to run Shrubb's race. Inexorably, the Englishman padded his lead. Longboat pottered along. At the fifteen-mark, he was three-quarters of a mile behind. As they passed the twenty-mile mark, Shrubb clocking 2:01:25, eight laps separated the two.

Nearly a mile behind, Longboat was all but beaten. But Shrubb's inexperience at the marathon showed. He stopped to change his shoes after twenty miles, and Longboat cut into the margin by a lap. By the time Lauretta made another cameo appearance, jumping up and down and waving a white fur scarf, Longboat surged again.

Exhausted, Shrubb slowed to a walk, his face the color of tallow. The crowd roared for Longboat to catch him. In violation of the rules, Flanagan and Jimmy De Forrest came onto the track and began pacing and yelling instructions to Longboat.

By mile twenty-three, the deficit was cut in half. By mile twenty-four, Shrubb was ahead by just two laps and doing more walking than running. The Canadians raised a din as Longboat, at long last, caught Shrubb early in mile twenty-five.

The end came quickly after that, with Shrubb staggering off the track. Longboat watched him exit, then kept to business and jogged to the finish. The tortoise had beaten the hare.

Tom and Lauretta celebrated the victory together. By the time they returned to Toronto, where thousands had gathered in front of the *Star*'s offices to follow the progress of the race through telegraph bulletins, he was hailed as the "Undisputed Long Distance Champion Runner of the World."[17] Even the poets paid tribute:

> O Tommy, Tommy Longboat
> You're a whirlwind on your feet
> You're the idol of your country—
> Hear 'em cheering in the street!
> And you're game right through and through;
> God bless you, Tommy Longboat
> For the nation's proud of you.[18]

Shrubb admitted that he was beaten fairly and conceded that the marathon distance was "too far." He challenged Tom to another race, this time at fifteen miles. "I came to Longboat at his distance," he said. "Now I want him to come to me at mine."

Longboat demurred, wanting to enjoy the moment. But he found that, even in victory, he couldn't escape Flanagan's shadow. "Flanagan's brains won the big race," Lou Marsh wrote, and he "came to the rescue for the honor of Canada . . . forgetting his personal grievance against the Indian for throwing him down three weeks ago."[19]

Marsh conveniently omitted that Flanagan had sold out Longboat, not the other way around. Longboat was incensed, telling one reporter, "I do not like the idea of doing all the work and somebody else getting all the credit for winning my victories. Do you think that Flanagan could make me run if I do not want to? I can get along without assistance and if any of these runners want to race me they will have to make arrangements with me, and no one else."[20]

With that, Tom settled in with Lauretta in Toronto and took a well-earned vacation.

Johnny Hayes yearned to race Dorando again and turned to his latest manager, Charles Harvey, to negotiate with Pat Powers. Harvey argued that the ban against Hayes was hurting both parties. After all, Johnny was still a major draw, especially in New York City. True, he had lost to Dorando, but unlike in the Longboat–Dorando and Longboat–Shrubb contests, he hadn't quit before the finish. Powers agreed to match Hayes against Dorando again, so long as Hayes posted a $1,000 forfeit. The date was set: March 15, at Madison Square Garden.

Dorando's whirlwind schedule had not ceased. He even substituted for Longboat after Tom refused to take on Shrubb in Buffalo. At the Englishman's preferred distance of fifteen miles, Shrubb easily defeated Dorando.

For the rubber match with Hayes, Dorando returned to the embrace of New York's Italian community and worked indoors at the 69th Regiment Armory. Johnny and Hjertberg trained along the Coney Island cycle path and in Prospect Park, often joined by Svanberg. The promoters and the newspapers played up the Italian–Irish rivalry, with Hayes emerging as the consensus favorite.

Two days before St. Patrick's Day, Celtic Park and Little Italy were well represented in the standing-room-only crowd at the Garden.[21] Two bands entertained before the start, one American, the other "from the sunny country where the Mafia and earthquakes provoke a reign of terror," according to the *Sun* newspaper.[22]

Johnny broke with Dorando, and they roared through the first mile in 5:06, more than twenty seconds faster than their previous meeting. They racked up five miles in 27:38, the fastest ever at the Garden.

Johnny employed frequent surges—it was obvious he had worked on his speed—and took the lead in the sixth and seventh miles, only to have Pietri answer. They sailed through the tenth mile in 56:46, another Garden record.

"Pass him again, Johnny," came the cry from the stands.

In the thirteenth mile, Hayes broke through again, and the Irish roared with delight. But Dorando fought back and, passing Johnny, smirked at him. The Italian band began playing the country's national anthem.

During the sixteenth mile, Pietri sprinted ahead. When Johnny lagged, Dorando applied more pressure, passing the seventeenth mile in yet another record. He gained a lap on Johnny, then a second.

There was no response. Dorando had, finally, broken Johnny Hayes. The pent-up tension in the Garden was punctured. The Italian coasted to the finish, the victory assured after mile twenty. He ran side by side with Hayes for a couple of laps, grinning and gesticulating at Johnny in Italian as the American stoically plodded onward. The humiliation continued when Dorando took off in a mad sprint with two laps to go and fell into the arms of his countrymen. They carried him off on their shoulders.

It was Dorando Pietri's most convincing victory since coming to America. By taking the rubber match, his cumulative earnings were, by one estimate, $30,000. He was a very wealthy man and ready to return to Italy with his riches.

But Pat Powers had yet another challenge.

TWENTY

P at Powers had jump-started the professional marathon craze, but he soon realized that the one-on-one format was imperfect. The pool of legitimate drawing cards was small, and the stars could perform at their peak only so often. Fans quickly tired of the same matchups because they knew the runners' tendencies so well.

In search of a second wind, Powers decided to schedule a "four-cornered" tilt at the Garden that would, in effect, determine the world's best professional marathoner. He signed up Dorando, Hayes, and Shrubb, but Tom Longboat was the lone holdout. He claimed his body needed rest after competing in three marathons in less than two months. And, after the shenanigans with Flanagan, he was adamant about taking control of his career.

"These men think I am a running machine, and [that] they can make me run as often as they like without giving me time to get into condition," he said. "I have got to have time to train for these races and I think I can do better by managing my own affairs."[1]

Powers cancelled the race and journeyed to Canada to plead with Longboat to participate in the championship. When that didn't work, he threatened legal action if Tom refused to honor their contract. Longboat reluctantly agreed to participate.

With spring coming and interest high, Powers shifted the race uptown and outdoors to the Polo Grounds, home to the New York Giants, at 155th Street by the Harlem River. The wooden ballpark would soon be replaced; construction of modern sports stadiums had moved apace after the London Olympics, with Major League Baseball's first concrete-and-steel stadium, Shibe Park in Philadelphia, opening that very month. But the horseshoe-shaped Polo Grounds was plenty big, with a roomy outfield and seating for upward of 35,000 fans (not counting the impecunious regulars who stood atop Coogan's Bluff and peered down at the action).

The athletes welcomed the change as none had enjoyed the indoor experience at the Garden, with its tight turns, the smoke-and dust-filled air, and the interminable lap counts. Powers added two newcomers to the mix, Irish-born Matthew Maloney and Frenchman Henri St. Yves, to enhance the international flavor of what he dubbed "The Marathon Derby."[2] The $10,000 purse got the public's and the newspapers' attention.

Each of the four names approached the race with added incentive. Dorando, eyeing a return to Italy, hoped to go out on top. Driven to even the score with Dorando, Hayes relished the opportunity to engage his personal rival. Longboat wanted to prove that he could win without Tom Flanagan. And Alf Shrubb coveted his first victory at the marathon distance.

For the two newcomers, the Derby offered a chance to become headliners. Sturdy Matthew Maloney had immigrated to New York a few years previous. He took up marathoning with Brooklyn's Trinity Athletic Club in the wake of Johnny Hayes's success, and his amateur mark of 2:36:26 was the fastest ever recorded (although naysayers believed that the Rye-to-Columbus Circle course was shorter than advertised).

Little was known about Henri St. Yves except that he had won a marathon in Scotland. Many newspapers identified him as a waiter, but he was actually a mechanic. He was only twenty-one, slightly chubby, and even smaller than Hayes and Dorando. He arrived three weeks before the race and trained at Princeton University under

Coach Al Copland. The school's runners watched his tireless chopping stride, never more than six inches off the ground, and were convinced that he was something special.

On the afternoon of April 3, more than 30,000 spectators braved dun skies and leaden clouds. Thousands more stood on Coogan's Bluff, where bettors had established Longboat as the betting favorite, with Dorando the second choice. Copland and his students, as well as pioneering hot dog concessionaire Harry M. Stevens, quietly placed wagers on St. Yves at 10:1 odds.

The rains and sodden outfield turf augured a muddy race. The six-laps-per-mile track was outlined by a white cord stretched over wooden stakes upon which were attached miniature American flags. With the towering grandstands as backdrop, each runner had a private encampment inside the stadium: Dorando in left field, Hayes at home plate, Longboat near first base, Shrubb in center field, St. Yves in right, and Maloney at third, near the finish. The Vitagraph company set up cameras to film the action.

St. Yves, wearing a red-white-and-blue sleeveless jersey, effortlessly skimmed to the front, with Dorando, Longboat, and Shrubb following as if hitched to a team and Maloney trailing the quartet. Hayes reverted to his strategy of hanging back in the hope that he could prey on the leaders in the latter stages of the race.

Shrubb pushed the pace and tucked behind St. Yves. The crowd initially chuckled at the "sturdy little Gaul" and his pitter-patter footsteps, but as mile after mile passed and he refused to give way, they applauded his courage. He covered the opening ten miles in 57:16 as the rains sputtered out. Dorando was in third behind Shrubb, with Longboat laboring to keep up. Hayes harbored his resources, but he had fallen well behind.

St. Yves continued to toy with the field, allowing Shrubb, Longboat, and Dorando to catch up to him before drawing ahead. Shrubb gamely made a race of it, engaging the Frenchman in a series of spurts that separated them from the pack. They reached mile fifteen in 1:26:23.

Hayes lagged. Longboat halted to change his shoes and lost valuable laps to the leaders. His handlers pushed him back onto the course, but his lack of fitness was clearly showing.

St. Yves regained the advantage in mile nineteen with a madcap sprint that dusted Shrubb and brought the huge crowd to its feet. Longboat stopped once more, and soon he was through for the afternoon. Dorando was stuck in third, with Hayes one mile behind.

The little Frenchman motored on, passing mile twenty in 1:57:25. Shrubb was now in distress. He began to walk and retreated to his quarters for a brisk massage. He struggled back to the fray, but quit after twenty-three miles, again overwhelmed by the daunting distance of the marathon. Dorando claimed second as Hayes, belatedly, made up ground.

By then, St. Yves was coasting to the finish. He completed the rout with a quarter-miler's kick that sparked the band into a stirring version of "La Marseillaise," his time of 2:40:50 setting a new professional record. The victory netted him $5,000.

Five minutes later came Dorando, with second worth $2,500. Another four minutes back was Hayes, frustrated in his third consecutive attempt to vanquish his adversary. He earned $1,500. Maloney was fourth for $1,000.

ST YVES WINS THE GREATEST MARATHON EVER HELD IN AMERICA, was the headline in the *Herald*.

Perhaps the biggest winners on the day were Al Copland and his Princeton students, who returned to New Jersey with a small fortune by betting on St. Yves.

On the heels of St. Yves's upset victory, Powers scheduled a second $10,000 Derby for May 8. Dorando and St. Yves signed up, but

Longboat and Hayes decided to sit this one out. Powers expanded the field by importing several 1908 Olympians—Canada's Simpson, England's Appleby, Sweden's Svanberg, America's Morrissey—and reached to Cuba for Félix Carvajal, the fourth-place finisher at the 1904 Olympics.

The large contingent of Princeton students in attendance at the Polo Grounds did not find such good odds on this day, with St. Yves sent off as the heavy favorite. And with good reason: The Frenchman romped again after setting a torrid pace that caused several runners to collapse well before the finish. He collected another $5,000 for his efforts. Svanberg was second, while Dorando faded to sixth (and $500).

The race drew about 10,000 fans, an indication that New York City was sated with the marathon. The derby then hit the road, with St. Yves, Hayes, and Longboat, along with Svanberg, Appleby, and Simpson clashing at Chicago's Comiskey Field in late May.[3] In his third marathon in less than two months, St. Yves's punishing schedule caught up with him as he was forced to quit in the fifteenth mile because of blisters. Hayes took second behind Svanberg, while Longboat dropped out in the fourteenth mile after suffering a sunstroke attack.

By then, Dorando and Ulpiano had left for Italy.[4] In a six-month tour of North America, Pietri had raced a remarkable eight marathons, winning four of them, and competed in at least a dozen other matches at distances ranging from ten to fifteen miles. He was now a wealthy man, but his body needed rest.

Their return set off another round of wild celebrations that left Dorando as exhausted as if he had run twenty miles. He had enough energy for at least two more major events. In August, he married his love, Teresa Dondi, and they soon moved into a villa that he built with earnings from his U.S. races. In November, King Victor Emmanuel III summoned him to Pisa, where he discussed training methods with the Italian ruler and gave a running demonstration that delighted the King's children.

As his body healed, he started jogging on the familiar roads around Carpi. He appeared in select races in Italy, greeted everywhere as the conquering hero. The money wasn't anything like he had made in the States, but the contests kept him in decent shape.

TWENTY-ONE

The three derbies of 1909 represented the culmination of marathon mania. Professional distance racing remained popular, but the stakes and the scale diminished. Instead of competing in venues like the Polo Grounds, the runners circuited roller-skating rinks and minor league baseball stadiums. In August 1910, when Johan Svanberg became the first man to break the 2:30 barrier for the marathon, few newspapers bothered to carry the news.

Marathoning's most famous personalities carried on. Tom Longboat's two subpar performances at the derbies led Pat Powers to sell his contract for $700 to Sol Mintz, a sportsman from Hamilton. The press was merciless, led by his old pal, Lou Marsh. "The Onondaga hasn't got it left in him. He had it once, but he hasn't got it now and I seriously doubt if he will ever get it again. I think his sun has set. . . . The greatest factor in his defeat was his swelled head. With his cranium enlarged by several victories, which his common sense should have told him were sheerest luck, he thought he could neglect even the rudimentary rules of training and defeat any man in the world."[1]

Longboat shrugged it off. He had earned buckets of money—some $17,000[2] by one estimate—and he used this to build a two-story home for his mother and family on the Six Nations Reserve. He continued to run for a living and soon proved he was anything but washed-up. In the summer of 1909, after losing to Shrubb at fifteen miles in Montreal, he bounced back with a decisive victory at twenty miles, when the Englishman quit at the fifteen-mile mark.

The two barnstormed across Canada and the United States, in Winnipeg, Toronto, Boston, Pittsburgh, and Stratford, racing at distances from twelve miles to twenty, for purses large and small. The rivalry between the tall, dark Native Indian with the easy smile and the scrawny, pale Brit with the focused stare turned into a relationship of mutual respect.

"You beat me, but I beat you next time," Tom would say as the two shook hands after yet another hotly contested contest.[3]

He kept his own counsel on training, allowing for long walks and plentiful rest. He was no longer the dominant force, but when he was feeling right nobody could beat him. In 1912, he went overseas for two races at Edinburgh's prestigious Powderhall track. He dropped out of the marathon, but later set the professional fifteen-mile record in 1:20:04. He was credited with another world's record the next year, but the track at Madison Square Garden turned out to have been incorrectly measured.

Offtrack incidents, however, continued to overshadow his career. He was arrested twice for drunkenness, once in Toronto and once in New York.[4] The press began to stereotype him as an alcoholic. One Montreal columnist called for a "Society for the Promotion of Temperance and Long Distance Running Among Indians."[5]

Tom never denied being a social drinker. After all, part of the running scene revolved around the taverns and bars where sportsmen like Tom Flanagan gathered daily to meet with other promoters and make race arrangements. But he wasn't a drunk, as his friends attested.

"We all took a drink," a longtime friend from the Reserve, Frank Montour, later told a reporter. "Usually we curbed it; there's times we might have had one or two too many, but it never done no damage or harm."[6]

. . .

N ow twenty-four and married, Dorando Pietri resumed his career in London in December 1909. His return to the city of his infamous Olympic defeat was precipitated by a challenge from *Sporting Life* to take on Charlie Gardiner, considered to be Britain's crack professional marathoner, with £100 to the winner and £50 for the loser.[7] The site was Royal Albert Hall, the famous concert arena, on a narrow track topped by a fine coconut matting. Squeezed in between the stalls, the 88-yard oval required 20 laps per mile, or 524 laps in total. Ropes were strategically placed to keep the runners from colliding with a staircase rail at one end.

His professional status in the land that venerated the amateur made him a curiosity, not a major attendance draw. The partisan crowd of about 2,000 spectators hooted for Gardiner and waved Union Jacks, but greeted Dorando with warm applause. An original composition was played while the race was on: "Dorando," a march composed by Lilla Saitta and dedicated to Queen Alexandra. Neither monarch appeared at Royal Albert Hall, but King Edward VII earlier paid tribute by naming one of his racehorses after the Italian.

The Hall's tight configuration didn't slow the pair as they zoomed through the first mile in 4:39. Gardiner took the lead in the second mile, and the pair stayed neck and neck for the initial ten miles, clocking an astonishing 51:58.

Gardiner pressed the pace in the second half of the contest. The breaking point came when Dorando was forced to stop to change from a pair of new shoes to low boots, to relieve his bloody and blistered feet, before continuing. Limping, Dorando trailed by multiple laps before calling it quits during mile twenty-three. Dorando had faltered in London again.

He and Ulpiano sailed for the United States, then crossed the continent by railroad to take on a familiar foe, Johnny Hayes, this time in San Francisco.[8] Johnny and his Olympic gold medal were still a big draw. He was second to Pat Dineen in a marathon in Burlington, Vermont, and lost to Hans Holmer in Lowell, Massachusetts. In October 1909, at a marathon in Seattle underwritten by millionaire Robert Guggenheim, he took third as St. Yves raced to a new world's record in 2:32:39. In December, he chewed on a quill toothpick while cantering to victory over Con Connolly, the top marathoner on the west coast, at the Ocean Shore grounds in San Francisco (although the course was later found to be more than one mile short).

By the time Johnny and Dorando clashed again, on the afternoon of January 30, 1910, Hayes's professional running résumé had only one hole: since the London Olympics, he still had not finished a race ahead of Dorando Pietri.

They met in Recreation Park, a wooden baseball stadium built after the 1906 San Francisco earthquake to house the Seals of the Pacific Coast League. In a city of vibrant ethnic enclaves, and the birthplace of such standout athletes as Lefty O'Doul, Ping Bodie (née Francesco Stefano Pazzolo), Tony Lazzeri, and the DiMaggio brothers, it was the perfect spot to resume the Irish–Italian rivalry.

Their third and final one-on-one race was their most competitive. Never separated by more than a yard for the entire race, one man breathing on the other's shoulder, the pair ran as if they were twin shadows. They prodded and pushed and elbowed around the ten-laps-per-mile track, Hayes desperate to conquer Dorando without any question or controversy, the Italian desperate to stave off the American.

After 2½ hours and nearly 26 miles, Johnny had Dorando exactly where he wanted him when he had run the race in his head, over and over again. Dead even, 385 yards remaining. The crowd of 8,000 rose in anticipation.

Side by side they raced around the track as Dorando unleashed a furious, closing kick. Hayes was ready and answered, edging past Pietri slightly. Then, in a rush, Dorando swept by, opening a gap of ten, twenty, now thirty yards, and on to the finish, once more holding the upper hand. His time was 2:41:39, with Hayes trailing by 10 seconds.

Dorando was mobbed and borne from the field on his countrymen's shoulders. Dejected and spent, forgotten again in the adulation for the Italian, Johnny was escorted to a waiting automobile.

A rematch was scheduled for the end of February, with St. Yves and four others added to the mix. Moments before the start of the race, Dorando appeared at Recreation Park with a doctor's certificate stating that he was suffering from bronchitis and could not run. He was booed from the stadium by the 4,000 spectators who had braved the rain to see the contest.

"He is through so far as San Francisco is concerned," harrumphed the *Call* newspaper. "He gave the Marathon game a black eye and spoiled himself as a drawing card here."

Hayes waded through the mud to gain the triumph in 2:44:55, a sweet victory made bitter because of Dorando's hasty departure. It would be Johnny's last victory in a marathon.

Dorando and Ulpiano embarked on a mini-tour of the United States, whipping Tom Longboat and St. Yves, then traveled to South America to race and perform exhibitions in Argentina and Brazil. In May 1910, in Buenos Aires, Dorando entered his final marathon and won it in a time of 2:38:48, the fastest time he ever recorded. He ran his final professional contests in 1911, primarily in Italy.

By then, he and Ulpiano had plowed the profits earned from Dorando's legs into a new venture. They bought two parcels of land in

Carpi, along the same plaza where Dorando had once worked, and built a four-story, fifty-four-room luxury hotel.[9] The Grand Hotel Dorando was modeled after the fine establishments they had stayed at in the States, complete with a bar, a restaurant, and a garage with a car-for-hire service. Photographs of Dorando during his running career, in London, Rome, and New York City, lined the walls. Everything on display—the linens, the tablecloths, the silverware, the ceramic dishes—was marked UDP, for "Ulpiano Dorando Pietri." (This was nicknamed *utile dei piedi,* or "good with his feet.") The once-impoverished baker's boy was now a successful entrepreneur in his hometown.

Hayes and Dorando never met again after their race in San Francisco. But Johnny never gave up trying to track down his rival. In 1911, he and Mike Ryan went to Europe for several months. On a lark, they swooped into Italy to find Dorando and arrange another match. Instead, they were thrown into jail for not having proper railroad tickets. They never did locate "Ol' Pete," as Hayes took to calling him.

Johnny placed second in a marathon in Berlin in 1912, then retired from competitive racing not long afterward. That summer, he served as the marathon trainer for the U.S. Olympic team under head coach Mike Murphy. The Americans arrived in Stockholm to defend Hayes's gold medal with a twelve-man contingent, led by several holdovers from 1908: Ryan (the winner of that April's Boston Marathon), Louis Tewanima, and Joe Forshaw (appearing in his third Olympics).[10]

South Africa's Kennedy McArthur, a pipe-smoking policeman born and raised in Ireland, navigated the short course, which measured only 24.98 miles (or 40.20 kilometers), to win the gold medal, with countryman Christian Gitsham second. The big surprise was Gaston Strobino, an Italian-born, naturalized citizen from Paterson, New Jersey. He was a last-minute addition to the squad and finished third; the U.S. placed a total of ten runners in the marathon's top eighteen, including Native American Andrew Sockalexis fourth, Forshaw tenth, and Tewanima sixteenth, just six days after the Hopi took second in the 10,000 meters and set an American record that would stand for fifty-two years. (Tewanima's buddy from the Carlisle Indian School, Jim Thorpe, captured the decathlon and pentathlon gold medals.)

In a repeat of London, the runners had to deal with high temperatures. Sadly, Portugal's Francisco Lázaro collapsed during the race and died the next day. Hayes and others blamed the afternoon start time. "I think that marathons should start in the cool of the evening and not in the full heat of the day," he told the New York Times. "Today's race was nothing but a brutal exhibition, the men being badly burned."[11]

When Johnny returned to the States, he helped train runners at his old club, St. Bartholomew's. He found work as a sportswriter for the Hudson Dispatch newspaper and continued to support his younger siblings, with help from his bride-to-be, Anna Reilly. The two were married in 1914, and the birth of their only daughter, Doris, soon followed. Later, he coached the cross-country team at Columbia University.

Hayes visited President Taft at the White House, but he threw his support behind Teddy Roosevelt's unsuccessful Progressive Party bid to recapture the presidency in 1912. The two occasionally corresponded—Johnny once requested a job recommendation from Roosevelt—and in his 1913 autobiography, Roosevelt identified Johnny as "one of my valued friends and supporters," and an example that, "any young man in a city can hope to make his body all that a vigorous man's body should be."[12]

TWENTY-TWO

The outbreak of World War I in 1914 abruptly ended Marathon Mania (and forced the cancellation of the 1916 Olympics). Several 1908 Olympians lost their lives, including Wyndham Halswelle, the winner of the controversial 400 meters, who was killed by a sniper at the Battle of Neuve Chapelle. The two eldest sons of Lord and Lady Desborough, Julian and Gerald William Grenfell, perished within a three-month span. Gold-medal-winning rower F. S. Kelly died at the Battle of the Somme. Henri St. Yves, who used his marathon winnings to build a monoplane and barnstorm across the country, was severely wounded at Verdun and poisoned with gas. He had shrapnel in his legs for the remainder of his life.

Dorando Pietri had previously served in the military. He was mobilized to fight against Austria, but he was eventually dismissed for medical reasons. His heart, which had gotten him through so many races in such a brief window of time, was too damaged.[1]

Johnny Hayes sat out the war, reportedly because of color blindness.[2] (His brother, Willie, fought.) Later, with the Knights of Columbus, Johnny went to France and assisted with the athletic entertainment and training of U.S. troops.

In February 1916, Tom Longboat volunteered with the 37th Haldimand Rifles squad of the Canadian Over-Seas Expeditionary Force.[3] On his attestation papers, he gave as his trade or calling: "Professional Runner." His old friend, Tom Flanagan, arranged for him to be transferred to the 180th Sportsmen's Battalion, a unit that provided athletic entertainment for the troops. As one newspaper put it, "Private Longboat left his wife and wigwam . . . and is extremely proud of his first real 'war paint.'"[4]

He was sent overseas in 1917 with the 107th Pioneer Battalion made up of Native soldiers, and raced in England and France against British and Canadian runners. In Europe, he saw action as a dispatch carrier, shuttling messages and orders between the trenches and the command posts behind the lines. He liked to recount the time he was escorting a general to the front at a fast pace. The Englishman, unable to keep up, demanded: "For God's sakes, who do you think I am? Tom Longboat?"

"No, sir," replied Tom with a straight face. "That's me."[5]

Tom needed every ounce of humor to survive the war. He used his athleticism to navigate through what can only be described as hell on earth. Machine guns, mortars, and German Big Bertha howitzers exploded around him. The heavy artillery left the cries of the wounded and the dying echoing across the front. Churned-up fields of liquid mud and barbed wire made footing treacherous, while poisonous gas attacks polluted the air.

According to one account, he was wounded twice. Another report stated that he was buried in a trench for six days. While it's difficult to separate truth from myth, what is true is that, on at least two occasions, Longboat was reported to have been killed.[6]

St. Yves, who was serving as a dispatch bearer for the French Army, told a reporter, "I hear that poor old Tom Longboat has been killed with the Canadians up near Lens [a town in France]. Well, Tom was a wonderful runner, but no man ever lived that can run as fast as the Boche bullets."[7]

Tom may not have outrun a bullet, but he was decidedly not dead. Or, as the headline in the *New York Times* put it, INDIAN VERY MUCH ALIVE. The article, from October 1917, reprinted a letter that he wrote: "No doubt you will be surprised to hear from the really original, mysterious Longboat. . . . I was over to the front lines last night, and I was sweating like an old horse. I was covered with mud from head to feet, and I don't know how many times I fell in the shell holes over the wires. They cut me all up. Everything was flying around, high explosives, shrapnel, whizz bangs, coal boxes, rum jars, oil drums."

Longboat survived unscathed. Finally, he returned to Canada in 1919. He ran his final race for the military in Toronto, at the Grand Army of Canada Sports Show, and with a final surge that brought the crowd of 4,000 to their feet, nipped American Bill Queal in a three-miler.[8]

A fter World War I, the Olympics resumed in Antwerp in 1920. The marathon course was the longest in Olympic history— more than 26½ miles (or 42.750 kilometers). The discrepancies over the marathon distance persuaded track-and-field officials to take action. In 1921, at the fifth IAAF Congress in Geneva, they standardized the length for Olympic marathons at the "London distance" of 26 miles, 385 yards (42.195 kilometers), the measurement that Jack Andrew concocted in 1908. Non-Olympic marathons followed suit, with the Boston Marathon lengthening its course in 1924, which shifted the start to the town of Hopkinton.

In 1920, few spectators were able to travel to the Belgian port city for the Games. The local organizing committee went bankrupt, and the so-called "aggressor" nations—including Germany, Austria,

Hungary—were barred from this barebones competition. But Pierre de Coubertin and his Olympic Movement had survived the Great War, even if the nationalistic fervor that led to it gave lie to the baron's vision of athletic harmony. (Coubertin's bitter rival, James Sullivan, had died suddenly in 1914 after attending the AAU championships.)

The Olympics endured in large part because of the 1908 London Games. They resuscitated the Olympics after the "farcical Games" of 1900 and 1904, when many believed that Coubertin's Olympics were destined for dissolution. Bracketed by the unofficial 1906 Games and the well-organized 1912 Games, London 1908 served as the blueprint for subsequent Olympics. They were the first to involve national squads (as opposed to a collection of individual athletes). They were the first to have an Opening Ceremony, with each country's team marching en masse, and the first to feature a newly built, state-of-the-art stadium. They were the first to be extensively photographed and filmed and, with the inclusion of figure-skating events, they were the first to bring winter sports into the Olympic fold.

The many disputes over Britain's officiating in London led to the introduction of a pool of neutral judges at the 1908 Olympics. And the sermon by Bishop Talbot at St. Paul's Cathedral inspired Coubertin to coin the Olympic creed: "The most important thing in the Olympic Games is not to win but to take part, just as the most important thing in life is not the triumph, but the struggle. The essential thing is not to have conquered but to have fought well."

The significance of the London Games goes beyond mere words. The 1908 Olympics was the first sporting event that was both major and modern. The Games featured exhaustive press coverage, larger-than-life celebrity athletes and personalities, fierce international rivalry, and daily controversy—the currencies that continue to drive popular interest in sports. Indeed, as the Olympics prepare to return to London in 2012, it's noteworthy that the issues that arose in 1908 still resonate today: performance-enhancing drugs, disputes about officiating, racism, gambling, the marketing and image of star athletes, media saturation, and the construction of expensive sporting facilities.

EPILOGUE

As the wealthiest and most famous professional athlete in Italy, Dorando Pietri expected to live out his days in comfort in Carpi. But he met with several setbacks.[1] The hotel that he and Ulpiano built went bust after the war and the collapse of Carpi's hat-manufacturing business. He lost most of the fortune that he had earned in America. He fell back on the car service.

In the early 1920s, he and Teresa moved to Sanremo, a town on the Mediterranean Coast. He made a living as a driver, operating a Fiat with a rumble seat. His name was a conversation starter among the tourists who flocked to the Italian Riviera. Always, they asked him about that sweltering July day in London: Did he remember collapsing in the Stadium? Could he have finished without any help? What was it like to meet the Queen? Who was better: him or Tom Longboat?

Dorando and Teresa never had children, but they found contentment with their quiet, modest life. He returned once to England, what he described as "the unforgettable land," to start a pre-Olympic marathon in London in 1924. Later, having joined an early incarnation of the Fascist Party under Benito Mussolini, he was knighted and received a small salary from the government as a marathon consultant.

The long hours sitting behind the wheel and the lack of exercise turned the svelte, muscle-bound athlete into a middle-aged man with a large paunch. His sharp features became puffy and almost unrecognizable. He died of a heart attack on February 7, 1942, at age fifty-six. He asked to be buried in a black shirt, emblematic of the Fascist regime, along with the scarf from his first national championship, won at Vercelli in 1905.

Dorando was fated to live like he competed: running beyond exhaustion, refusing to quit even when his next breath was nearly his last. So, too, he plunged headlong through the obstacles he encountered, from extreme poverty in childhood to crushing athletic disappointment in London to nonstop competition as a professional runner to the business misfortune with his brother, never retreating until, finally, the very muscle that had taken him to the pinnacle of Olympic glory, his heart, gave out.

His legacy is inextricably tied to that fateful afternoon in 1908. He was the first athlete to become globally famous because of the Olympics. His gallant defeat brought him more notoriety than any gold medal, his courage and misfortune repaid through eternal glory. He remains the most celebrated loser in Olympic history.

The gold cup given to Dorando by Queen Alexandra more than a century ago sits in a bank vault in Italy. A small street is named for him in London, Dorando Close, near where Imre Kiralfy's Stadium once stood. White City Stadium, as it became known, was demolished in 1985. The site itself is now home to the BBC Media Village; outside, on the sidewalk, a marker indicates the location of the finishing line of the marathon.

A bronze statue of Dorando, complete with a pair of flaming red running shorts, was erected in Carpi in 2008. The city hosts an annual marathon in his memory every fall. The now-classic photograph of him at the finish has been displayed in art museums and reproduced on everything from postage stamps to lithographs.

In 1960, the Olympic Games finally came to Rome, some fifty-two years after Italy bowed out of hosting the 1908 Games. In the first Olympics to be widely televised, Ethiopian marathoner Abebe Bikila ran barefoot over the Eternal City's streets and highways, finishing at night under the Arch of Constantine. He repeated his gold-medal-winning performance four years later (this time wearing sneakers). Bikila was the first black African to win Olympic gold, and his success foreshadowed Africa's dominance of long-distance racing and marathoning.

At the 1988 Seoul Olympics, some eighty years after Dorando faltered in London, Gelindo Bordin surged past the fading leaders in the closing stages to take home Italy's first Olympic gold medal in the marathon. Bordin also captured the Boston Marathon in 1990, becoming the first male Olympic champ to turn that trick.

In 2004, the Olympic Games returned to Athens after a ninety-eight-year absence. The marathon course, which began in the village of Marathon and concluded at Panathenaic Stadium, the site of Spiridon Louis's inaugural victory in 1896 and Billy Sherring's win in 1906, was lengthened to modern standards. This time, Stefano Baldini triumphed, becoming Italy's second Olympic marathon winner.

To date, no marathoner from Great Britain has won the Olympic gold medal. No Canadian marathoner has won since Sherring did so in 1906. No Greek runner has won since 1896. Marathon organizers now schedule the start in the morning so as to avoid the midday heat.

Tom Longboat returned from World War I intending to resume his life. He discovered that his wife, Lauretta, apparently believing the published reports of his death overseas during the war, had remarried. Mystery surrounds the exact nature of this event. According to one biographer, "the small available evidence suggests that Lauretta may never have re-married and may even have reclaimed her maiden name."[2]

Whatever the truth, Tom moved on and married another woman, Martha Silversmith, a Cayuga Indian from the Six Nations Reserve. The couple had four children: Tom Jr., Ted, Phyllis, and Clifford. With a family to support, Tom moved west and tried farming in Alberta. When that didn't pan out, he returned to Toronto and earned $3 a day at the Dunlop Rubber factory. Then, he worked at the Bethlehem steel mill in Buffalo. By the late 1920s, he was employed by the city of Toronto as a street cleaner and garbageman.

His "friends" dubbed him a failure. "If anyone ever writes the history of Tom Longboat, I beg to suggest a title: 'Corn Pone—Caviar—Corn Beef,'" wrote Lou Marsh in the *Toronto Daily Star*. "He started on corn pone, worked up to caviar and now he is tickled to get his corn beef regularly."

Marsh lamented that "the man who was the Babe Ruth and the Man O' War and the Paavo Nurmi of his day" didn't fare better. "Why isn't Tom Longboat on easy street? Because he does not have a white man's business brain. He was headstrong and unreliable. You couldn't keep track of him without handcuffs, leg irons, a straight jacket, and a regiment of [Pinkertons]. He was as hard to train as a leopard and harder to watch than a chunk of loose lightning."[3]

Tom shrugged off the criticism. He told reporters that he was satisfied to have a regular paycheck during the Depression years, one that allowed him to take care of his wife and children and work outdoors. He held on to the job for the next nineteen years and said that he didn't understand the fuss. "I'm just happy, that's all," he said. "It's a good way to be."[4]

He occasionally competed in old-timers' races at exhibitions and festivals. In the late 1920s, he won a used car by beating Sherring and Charles Hefferon in a five-miler in Hamilton. He liked to take Martha and the children out to the Reserve on weekends and visit with old friends like Frank Montour.

"I proudly speak perfect Onondaga, my father's language, because he taught it to me as a boy," his son, Tom Jr., recalled in the early 1980s. "Dad was a real Indian, loyal to his ancestral traditions thousands of years old. He remained true to these ways even while on his excursions into the other world of fast talk and big money, the white man's world. . . . What kept him going, especially during some difficult times in his life, was the knowledge that he was always a part of his people."[5]

Indeed, disquieting incidents continued to interrupt Tom's life. He reportedly went broke and had to pawn his medals and trophies for cash.[6] For years, a man masquerading as Longboat cadged free drinks at local saloons, perpetuating the image of Tom as a drunk. Fed up with the "cheap, two-bit imposter," he protested that "this man has been capitalizing on my famous name for the past 15 or 20 years and I think it's high time I put an end to it, once and for all."[7] Finally, believing that an evil spirit was attacking him, he visited a medicine man on the Reserve to clear up the problem.

The worst moment came in 1932, after an appearance at the Canadian National Exhibition. Tom watched as his youngest son, five-year-old Clifford, was struck and fatally injured by a car.[8] He and Martha never got over that sadness.

After World War II, he retired to live on the Reserve with Martha. He was slowly dying of diabetes, his thick mane of black hair now entirely white. He had a smile for everyone and still went on long strolls, invigorated by the familiar scents and undulating roads, many of them now paved and busy with automobile traffic. Every Wednesday, he walked to the market at Hagersville, fourteen miles round-trip.

He died at Lady Willingdon Hospital in Ohsweken on January 9, 1949, at age sixty-two.[9] His body was prepared for burial, clothed in tribal colors, according to tradition. On the feet that had propelled him to so many victories, and had taken him around the world, were a new pair of moccasins made of buckskin, fringed and beaded.

Martha and the children helped lay him to rest in the burial grounds behind the Onondaga Longhouse, his grave marked by a two-foot-high wooden marker. On a bleak and gray winter day, former opponents and managers attended the ceremony, including Sol Mintz and Billy Sherring.

"He was erratic, but when he was good, he was a wow," Johnny Hayes said from New York upon hearing the news.[10]

The spirit of Tom Longboat found peace, but even in death he could not escape the poisonous pen. In 1956, *Maclean's* magazine ran a long feature about Tom that shaped public opinion for years to come. "The rise and fall of Tom Longboat" was "a Horatio Alger story in reverse," the article read. "He worked his way to the bottom. Literally, his was a story of Public Hero to Garbage Collector."

As usual, the last word went to Tom Flanagan, a critic still at age seventy-seven. "He was a better man as an Indian than he was trained as a white man," he said. "I often thought if we could have kept him on the reservation and brought him out just to run, what he could have done would have been even more remarkable."[11]

Tom Longboat lived, raced, and died underappreciated by mainstream Canada. His career and reputation were subject to the racist ideology of the times and plagued by a paternalistic group of trainers and managers who thought they knew what was best for him. He was judged and written about solely from their perspective. Was he naïve? Probably. Exploited? At times. Misunderstood? Definitely.

Much of the anguish about Longboat dates from 1908 and his

ill-fated performance at the London marathon. The most famous athlete at the Games entered the race as the odds-on favorite; the entire nation of Canada (not to mention his handlers) was counting on him. His failure was considered inexplicable—was he drugged? Did he overtrain? Did the injury he suffered while in Ireland hold him back? The enduring image of Longboat became someone whose enormous potential went unfulfilled.

With the passage of time has come a reappraisal of Longboat's achievements. His record-smashing run at the 1907 Boston Marathon, and his "Marathon Mania" wins over Dorando and Alf Shrubb, rank him as the first superstar marathoner and one of the all-time greats. He was also among the first nonwhite athletes to achieve sports success in the modern era, a pioneering role that paved the way for others, beginning with Jim Thorpe and swimmer Duke Kahanamoku at the 1912 Olympics.

Today, Longboat is a member of the Canada Sports Hall of Fame, and a plaque pays tribute to his accomplishments on the Six Nations Reserve. The Tom Longboat trophy is awarded annually to the outstanding Native athlete in Canada. In 1998, in a survey of the most important Canadians in history, Maclean's awarded Longboat the number-one ranking in its "Stars" category,[12] above Wayne Gretzky, Marshall McLuhan, Lorne Michaels, and Celine Dion.

In 1979, University of Toronto professor and distance runner Bruce Kidd discovered that the city had apparently never paid Longboat the $500 it had pledged to the runner's education fund after his 1907 Boston Marathon victory.[13] Kidd's sleuthing prodded the mayor and the city council to take action. They voted to distribute the sum of $10,000 to Tom's three surviving children at the time, Phyllis, Ted, and Tom Jr.

· · ·

Johnny and Anna Hayes, with daughter Doris, settled in Woodcliff Lake, New Jersey.[14] He remained the responsible one, helping out his siblings when they needed him and raising a family out of the spotlight. After the war, he worked with his brother, Willie, for the California Peach & Fig Growers Association to spread the gospel of American figs. His most formidable competitor? Figs grown in Italy, of course.

He branched out and started his own food brokerage business, his office decorated with a print of "The Reaper." He dabbled in coaching, advising heavyweight champ Gene Tunney during his training sessions. The Depression wiped out his company and the small fortune he had accumulated during the racing years. He worked for his old outfit until he got back on his feet and again opened his own food brokerage company on Hudson Street in lower Manhattan. He lived like he ran marathons: in control and steady to the end.

Johnny watched sports boom in the United States during the 1920s and 1930s, the stadiums ever bigger and the heroes more famous. Babe Ruth took baseball and New York by storm and Red Grange did the same for college football. Golf, tennis, swimming became major activities. Track and field flourished, except for the marathon, which returned to its cultish roots—an amateur's affair with small fields of hardy men. Parts of Asia, Scandinavia, and Africa developed into marathon hotbeds, but only the Boston Marathon preserved the tradition in the States. Johnny Hayes became remembered as the answer to a trivia question: Who was the last American to win the Olympic marathon?

The Madison Square Garden that Johnny and Dorando and Longboat sold out was torn down and replaced by an uptown edition on Eighth Avenue between 49th and 50th Streets. Celtic Park, the pride and joy of the Irish-American Athletic Club, was sold in 1930 and the land developed into housing units. Today, the Celtic Park

Apartments in Queens stand where the world's greatest athletes met in competition.

Johnny stayed in touch with old friends and rivals, including Mike Ryan, Joseph Forshaw, Tom Morrissey, and Matt McGrath. In 1932, he visited his brother Willie in California and attended the Los Angeles Olympics when, for the first time, each country was limited to three marathoners. Another teammate, A. C. Gilbert, mentored pole-vaulters and served as the *chef de mission* for the U.S. team in 1932. Gilbert became rich and famous for another reason: He invented the Erector Set.

In 1954, Johnny was reunited with Louis Tewanima when the Helms Foundation named the pair to the all-time U.S. Olympic team. After graduating from Carlisle as a tailor, Tewanima returned to the Hopi pueblo of Shungopovi in northeastern Arizona, where he farmed and tended his sheep. En route to New York City for the award ceremony, Louis smoked a cigar during the flight. He was taken to the top of the Empire State Building, and he looked down at New York and said, "Not enough land for sheep."[15]

Johnny's wife, Anna, died in 1954, at age sixty-five. Shortly after her death, he returned to Ireland.[16] He visited with his uncle, Martin Hayes, in Nenagh and was amazed by how much had changed since 1908 and by how much was still the same in County Tipperary. Not long afterward, commuting from his home in North Bergen, he was mugged on the subway in New York, the very system that he helped to build as a sandhog at the turn of the century.

His health went downhill after that. His daughter, Doris Hale, took care of him during his final years in Spring Lake Heights, on the "Irish Riviera" of the Jersey shore, near Asbury Park. He spent summer days on the beach, a bandy-legged old man in glasses who needed help with the deck chairs and whom nobody recognized as an Olympic champion. He died on August 25, 1965, at age seventy-nine.

Doris took to wearing Johnny's gold medal, a pendant as tiny as he was, as a bracelet around her wrist. She became a fierce defender of his legacy. When *Time* magazine identified Dorando as having "finished the marathon first," she complained in a letter to the editor that, "my father . . . finished the race and broke the tape on his feet like the courageous man he was, not like Pietri being dragged across by hypocritical Olympic officials."[17]

Her well-meaning efforts were futile. To this day, her father does not receive proper credit. The slights come even from experts who know the facts of the race. Martin Polley, a University of Southampton professor, has published numerous scholarly articles on the 1908 Games. About the marathon he recently wrote, "[Dorando's] heroic victory was short-lived, as the U.S.'s officials rightly complained about the physical assistance that Pietri had received. John Hayes of the U.S., second over the line on the day, was given the race."[18]

Hayes was not "given" anything. He won the 1908 marathon fairly. But it explains why Dorando Pietri will never be forgotten, and why "Little Johnny" Hayes remains but an afterthought.

After Doris Hale died, she left her father's trophies (including the gold medal), photographs, letters, and his well-worn autograph book to the Shore Athletic Club in New Jersey. Johnny was inducted into the Long Distance Running Hall of Fame in Utica, New York, in 2008. A life-sized bronze statue of him stands in Nenagh, alongside those of the town's other Olympic champs, Matt McGrath and Bob Tisdall. The wording on Hayes's plaque reads: SPEED IN HIS LEGS.

From 1920 through 1968, only one American marathoner medaled at the Olympics: Clarence DeMar, third in 1924. That changed in 1972, when Frank Shorter cruised to the gold medal in

Munich (with teammate Kenny Moore fourth). For his efforts, Shorter was awarded the James E. Sullivan Award, named for the former head of the AAU, as the best amateur athlete in America. Four years later, Shorter took the silver medal in the marathon at the Montreal Olympics.

"I was the first American since Johnny Hayes, in 1908, to have won it," Shorter commented. "I was proud of that, of 'winning for America.' I felt I'd earned some respect for American distance running, which was considered inferior in the international athletics community."[19]

His success was perfectly timed. He and a generation of brilliant distance runners—including Moore, Amby Burfoot, Steve Prefontaine, Bill Rodgers, and Alberto Salazar—sparked the second marathon boom in the United States, one that continues to the present day. This is a very different marathon mania than the Dorando–Hayes–Longboat version. Prodded and inspired by fitness advocates Dr. Kenneth Cooper (author of *Aerobics*) and Jim Fixx (*The Complete Book of Running*), legions of weekend warriors have joined the elite runners to make marathoning a participatory sport.

Bill Bowerman, the longtime track coach at the University of Oregon (and mentor of Moore and Prefontaine), used his wife's waffle iron to craft a unique rubber sole for running sneakers. With another of his athletes, Phil Knight, Bowerman created a company called Nike that is a latter-day Spalding's and, along with adidas, ASICS, New Balance, and others, produced comfortable, lightweight, affordable sneakers. An old word, "jogging," took on new meaning.

In 1970, Fred Lebow organized the first modern-day New York City Marathon, with all of 127 runners entered. By 1976, Lebow had expanded the race to reach into the five boroughs of New York City, a populist twist that soon attracted over 30,000 runners and millions of spectators annually. That spawned an industry of festival marathoning in places like Berlin, Chicago, London, Tokyo—and even in Boston, which retains the title as the world's oldest annual marathon.

The days of using strychnine and brandy for energy are long gone, replaced by mountains of scientific and medical knowledge about human physiology, diet, and training methodology. Today's marathoners benefit from sophisticated advances in sports medicine and nutrition, fields that did not exist at the turn of the twentieth century. Magazines devoted to marathoning dole out expert advice, and even novice marathoners know about endorphins, oxygen debt, and carbo-loading.

These and other changes have aided the corps of elite athletes who race marathons for a living—the direct heirs of Dorando, Longboat, and Hayes. With rules barring professionals from the Olympics having long been eliminated, today's top runners earn six-figure incomes through prize money and bonuses, sneaker and other endorsement deals, and personal appearances. Their workouts differ radically from those used at the turn of the century. They log as many as 125 miles per week, train at altitude, and integrate weight lifting, yoga, deep-tissue massage, and other regimens. Periods of rest are built into their schedules; they put their bodies through no more than two or three competitive marathons per year. The fastest time recorded for a marathon to date is 2:03:02, by Kenya's Geoffrey Mutai at the 2011 Boston Marathon (the 115th edition of the race).

The two manias differ in one other significant way. For much of the twentieth century, women were not allowed to compete in distance running. The dubious (some would say ignorant) argument was that endurance sports were damaging to their health (and, especially, their reproductive ability). As recently as 1968, the longest Olympic race for women was 800 meters.

Runners outraged at this policy began to take action. Merry Lepper unofficially completed the 1963 Western Hemisphere Marathon in Culver City, California. At the 1966 and 1967 Boston Marathons, Roberta "Bobbi" Gibb hid behind a bush near the start before jumping out to join the men and unofficially finish both races.

One K. V. Switzer also registered for the 1967 Boston Marathon.[20] Unlike Gibb, K. V. Switzer received an official bib (number 261). Her full name was Kathrine Switzer, and she was a twenty-year-old student at Syracuse University. She started the race without hassle, but a couple of miles from the start, Jock Semple, the longtime co-director of the Boston Marathon, jumped from the media truck and attempted to rip the number from Switzer's gray sweatshirt. Semple was elbowed aside by a companion of Switzer's, and number 261 was able to complete the marathon, finishing an hour behind Gibb.

The heroics of Lepper, Gibb, Switzer, and other women runners led to change. In 1972, the Boston Marathon officially admitted women, with Nina Kuscsik winning the distaff division. The first all-women's marathon was held in Waldniel, Germany, in 1973. As women marathoners' times plummeted, Miki Gorman (two-time winner at both Boston and New York), Joan Benoit (two-time Boston winner), and Norway's Grete Waitz (nine-time winner in New York) emerged as stars.

The IOC finally added a women's marathon to the Olympic program in time for the 1984 Los Angeles Games. Benoit cruised through Los Angeles to defeat Waitz in a time of 2:24:52. The memory of Dorando Pietri resonated shortly after Benoit completed the race, when Switzerland's Gabriele Andersen-Scheiss came into view on the track at the Los Angeles Coliseum. She swooned and staggered and nearly replicated Dorando's famous collapse. But she waved off medical help and managed to complete the final lap unassisted, finishing in thirty-seventh place.

Like Dorando Pietri, she recovered. And the marathon, the race known as the "great grind," added another dramatic chapter to its storied history.

POSTSCRIPT

In 1948,[1] when London hosted the Olympic Games for the second time, the city was in far different shape than in 1908, when Imre Kiralfy had an unlimited budget to build the first-ever modern sports cathedral and Lord Desborough and his colleagues donned tails and top hats for their nightly banquets.

Forty years later, blocks of London lay in ruin from German bombing raids during World War II. Food, clothing, fuel, and other supplies were rationed. These were "Make Do and Mend" times, and austerity was the byword for the shoestring-budget Games. No new facilities were constructed, and organizers asked visiting nations to supply their own food.

In the run-up to the Games, the *Evening News* published photographs of a plump, nondescript man pouring tea while wearing a trilby hat, a vest, and a cheeky grin. It was, the paper said, Dorando Pietri, the long-lost hero from 1908. The newspaper detailed that the Italian had taken a British wife and settled in the city of Birmingham. There, he owned a pub called The Temperance.

The reemergence of Dorando Pietri jolted a nation enervated by war. His very name, "Dorando," conjured up a halcyon moment from the Edwardian era, an age when mighty Britannia was the reigning superpower and the world was in its proper order. Plans were made to honor the roly-poly tavern owner, described by one columnist as "a figure of lively local distinction," in conjunction with the upcoming Olympic marathon.

Italian sports authorities, including the president of *La Patria*, Pietri's former sports club in Carpi, smelled a rat. After all, they had buried their friend in 1942. They journeyed to Birmingham to confront this Dorando and, in short order, exposed him as an imposter. He spoke little Italian—and not the local dialect from Carpi—and possessed no trophies from his running career, not even the special cup personally presented to him by Queen Alexandra. In fact, he was a sixty-three-year-old named Pietro Palleschi, who physically resembled the real Dorando.[2]

In the days before wall-to-wall television coverage, it would have been easy to perpetuate such a fraud. Dorando had lived quietly in Sanremo, and word of his death did not spread much outside of Italy during the war. But it's equally accurate to say that Londoners who had survived The Blitz and now faced daily hardships wanted to believe that Dorando was still alive. He had shown such nerve not to give up, even when he was lying unconscious on the track. He was the man who received not the gold medal but, instead, the true prize, eternal hero status. Those old enough to remember saw in his mettle the same determination, the same never-say-die pluck that they saw in themselves. Who even recalled the name of the American who was "awarded" the race?

"Today, as he was 40 years ago, Dorando is a burning issue," wrote *Boston Globe* columnist Red Smith, who interviewed the faux Pietri while sitting in the stands at Wembley Stadium. "Dead or alive, he remains the most celebrated loser in the long catalogue of international high-jinks."[3]

The proposal to recognize Dorando was cancelled, and an apology extended to his widow. On August 7, the Olympic marathon started with a lap inside Wembley, then looped north through London suburbs before returning to the track. (No portion of Jack Andrew's route from 1908 was used.) On a warm and windy Saturday afternoon, Etienne Gailly entered Wembley with a slim lead. He had only to cover 500 yards to win the gold medal. But the mustachioed Belgian had nothing left. He slowed to a tottering crawl along the track. In close pursuit were not one but two competitors, Delfo Cabrera and Tom Richards. Olympic officials stood and watched from the infield, opting not to proffer any assistance.

Wrote the *London Times* the next day:

A figure fully as tragic as Dorando's emerged from the tunnel. It was the Belgian, Gailly, so sore of foot and weary of leg and soul that he could hardly make any progress at all. Suddenly, quite close behind him, appeared another figure, that of the strongly built Cabrera, who doubtless was tired too, but looking a fresh and lively sprinter by comparison. The Argentinean passed his man in a few strides and set off to complete a lap that must have seemed like 5 miles to the poor tottering Belgian.

Gailly once very nearly pulled up dazed and hopeless with the appalling distance of 60 yards still between him and the tape. Already other gallant runners were appearing, and it was in no grudging spirit that one breathed again when Gailly at long last staggered into third place. He then collapsed and was carried off on a stretcher.[4]

As tens of thousands of spectators witnessed an exhausted and courageous athlete struggle beyond the limits of the human body, the specter of Dorando Pietri, the real Dorando Pietri, loomed in the thoughts of everyone gathered inside Wembley Stadium.

For a brief moment, 1908 felt like yesterday.

ACKNOWLEDGMENTS

It's an overused analogy but in this case appropriate: Researching and writing a book is like running a marathon. I've been fortunate to lean on many individuals in the course of this journey. Thanks to my agent, Robert Wilson, for his unwavering belief in this project and for stewarding the book to St. Martin's. My editor there, Rob Kirkpatrick, prodded the manuscript into shape, while Nicole Sohl helped me throughout the publication process.

In London, historian-author Bob Wilcock of the Society of Olympic Collectors was generous with his time, his encyclopedic expertise, and his amazing photographic collection related to the 1908 Olympic marathon. Information about organizing the 1908 Olympics came from the British Olympic Association's archives located at the University of East London, where librarian Caroline Lam and archivist Paul Dudman ably assisted me. At the University of Westminster, which houses the archives of the Polytechnic Institute at its historic building on Little Titchfield Street, Elaine Penn and Anna McNally facilitated my research about Jack Andrew. At the British Film Institute, Steve Tollervey showed me the entirety of motion picture footage from the 1908 Games, while Dr. Luke McKernan, curator of the Moving Image, British Library, answered other questions. Staff at the British Library at King's Cross, the British Newspaper Library in Colindale, and the Camden Library were also helpful. I could not have managed in London without the gracious hospitality of my cousin, Diana Shaw Clark, and her husband, Simon Clark, as well as family friends John Reed and German Angulo.

From their home in Nenagh, Nancy Murphy and her husband, Donal, eased my way in Ireland. Nancy provided me with invaluable information about Johnny Hayes's roots and shared the contents of letters written by his late daughter. Nancy took the time to show me every Hayes-related site in town (including his grandfather's former home and the town's famous statues), escorted me to the Tipperary Studies locale in Thurles, and introduced me to local experts Ger Ryan, Sean Naughton, and Matt McGrath (nephew of 1908 Olympian Matt McGrath), while Donal patiently explained the lure of track and field in Nenagh and throughout Ireland. Nancy and Donal left me in the capable hands of Ronnie Long, who drove me to the old Flanagan farm and places where Tom Longboat trained before the 1908 Games, along the way introducing me to Pat McGrath, Robert O'Sullivan, Joseph O'Connor, and Donal Madden. Kevin McCarthy, author of *Gold, Silver and Green: The Irish Olympic Journey: 1896–1924*, was equally accommodating; he drove me from Nenagh to Dublin, introduced me to scholars Cyril White and Larry Ryder, and eased my way at the National Library of Ireland. Cezanne Flanagan Toccini and her son, Steve, in the United States introduced me to their relatives in the Blackrock area of Dublin; there, Mary Flanagan Nolan, the nonagenarian niece of John and Tom Flanagan, regaled me with tales about her uncles, and her children, Donal, David, Austin, Tonette, and MaryBeth, presided over a memorable evening of song, stories, and food. A special "cheers" to Donal for his patience and for allowing use of one family photograph. Finally, Beth Lonergan with the Manuscripts branch of the National Library of Australia in Canberra provided information about rower-poet F. S. Kelly.

In Toronto, Dr. Bruce Kidd was gracious enough to meet with me at his office at the University of Toronto and to speak with me about the life of Tom Longboat. So, too, Arden Herbert, curator at Canada's Sports Hall of Fame, shared the Hall's vaults on Longboat. The Toronto Public Library was a great source for material on and about Longboat, with the added bonus of housing the Arthur Conan Doyle Collection. Thanks to librarian Peggy Perdue, who answered all my questions and put me in contact with scholar Clifford Goldfarb. In Brantford, inside the very building where Tom Longboat lived while a student at the Mohawk Institute, Virve Wiland helped me with research about the Iroquois at the Woodland Cultural Centre. Six Nations Parks & Recreation Office director Cheryl Henhawk and Tourism Manager Edith Styres assisted my research. The International Centre for Olympic Studies at the University of Western Ontario contains a treasure trove of Olympic and sports reference material, and Dr. Robert Barney and Dr. Janice Forsyth generously allowed me to access the collection and answered my numerous queries.

For information about Dorando Pietri, I turned to my uncle and fellow journalist, Antonio Cirino. He eloquently translated articles from Italian-language newspapers published in the States, helped explain the mindset of Italian immigrants, and encouraged this project from day one. My cousin Mark Cirino provided great advice and tracked down an elusive manuscript. Another cousin, Sally Berman, based in Rome, located a translator for the Dorando portion of the story. That translator, Neal Putt, patiently answered all my queries via telephone, Skype, and e-mail. Finally, Augusto Frasca, author of *Dorando Pietri*, confirmed facts about Dorando's life through e-mail.

Closer to home, the legendary David Smith opened doors at the New York Public Library and elsewhere. David steered me to Maira Liriano, of the Milstein Division of U.S. History, Local History & Genealogy, who gave invaluable assistance about Irish-immigration patterns in the nineteenth century and Johnny Hayes's early years in

New York City. John Devlin and Meaghan Doherty facilitated research at the American Irish Historical Society, while papers at the Municipal Archives in downtown Manhattan provided evidence about the Hayes family. Carey Stumm, archivist at the New York City Transit Museum, was helpful for information about the construction of the New York City subway system. Tom Quinn was my knowledgeable guide at the New York Athletic Club, while Percy Preston Jr. and Roz Dimon at St. Bartholomew's Church provided background information about Hayes's career with St. Bart's Athletic Club. John Favareau, reference librarian at the Yonkers Public Library, uncovered articles about the 1907 Yonkers Marathon from the *Yonkers Herald* newspaper. In New Haven, Mary Caldera, archivist of the Manuscripts and Archives at Yale University, helped me access A. C. Gilbert's papers at the Sterling Library, which offered an insider's view of the U.S. Olympic team. Mary Frances Ronan, with the National Archives in Washington, D.C., and Barbara Landis, with the Cumberland County Historical Society, provided articles and information about the life and career of Louis Tewanima. Jean Knaack, executive director of the Road Runners Club of America, helped me locate articles about the history of the marathon from her organization's archives.

From headquarters within the Celtic Park Apartments in Queens, historian-archivist Ian McGowan has done yeoman's work to celebrate the long-forgotten history of the Irish-American Athletic Club and Celtic Park. As the executive director of the Winged Fist organization, Ian has generously shared his vast knowledge and introduced me to a merry crew of experts, including the aforementioned Kevin McCarthy, Dave Johnson, Alan Katchen (author of *Abel Kiviat*), Steve Cottrell, Joe Keaney, Mark Will-Weber. Thanks especially to Walter Kehoe for his expertise in finding and explicating genealogy and government papers and to Dr. Bill Mallon, whose groundbreaking research is the gold standard for Olympic historians.

In Spring Lake, New Jersey, Wayne Baker of the Shore Athletic Club is the go-to source for material on and about Johnny Hayes. He and Walter MacGowan personally showed me the many medals and trophies won by Hayes; I treasure the experience of holding Johnny's Olympic gold medal in my hands. Wayne also introduced me to Elliott Denman, a classy writer whose track-and-field knowledge is unsurpassed. Thanks to Joan Spindel and Milan Vaclavik for facilitating my stay in New Jersey.

In Boston, Gloria Ratti and T. K. Skendarian of the Boston Athletic Association generously opened their voluminous Boston Marathon files for me. Nearby their offices, the Boston Public Library yielded a trove of material about the early races. Stephen Plotkin and Sharon Kelly at the John F. Kennedy Presidential Library and Museum gave assistance about Rose Fitzgerald Kennedy. My Beantown family came through; thanks to my aunt, Donna Davis, and my cousins, Connie and Giles Moore and Liz, Ned, and Adam Hazen, for their hospitality. Bill Bunke, as always, was there for me.

In Chicago, archivist Daniel Meyer and librarian Julia Gardner helped me access the Amos Alonzo Stagg papers at the University of Chicago Library's Special Collections Research Center. University of Illinois librarian Geoff Ross was kind enough to forward *Daily Illini* articles about the 1908 Olympics. Thanks to my niece, journalist Delaney Hall, and Ryan Keisler, for making my stay in Chicago a memorable one.

Participants in the 1908 Olympics and Marathon Mania have long since passed away, but surviving relatives were extremely helpful. Eldredge Welton, the son of Alton "Roy" Welton (fourth in the 1908 Olympic marathon), and his lovely wife, Virginia, invited me into their home and allowed me to browse Roy's scrapbooks. Robert Ryan, the son of Mike Ryan, spoke with me about his father's friendship with Johnny Hayes; Mike's grandson, Paul Ryan, encouraged me throughout the process of the book and his wife, Paulette, shared the family's photo collection. Christy Forshaw O'Shaughnessy, the granddaughter of Joseph Forshaw, took time from a summer vacation to share personal memories of her grandfather and her collection of memorabilia (including his bronze medal). John Garrels spoke with me about his grandfather, hurdler John Garrels, as did Donald Murray, the Olympian's son-in-law. JoAnne Russo and Mary-Ellen Russo-Jasinski, cousins of Johnny Hayes, answered my queries about their family. With assistance from author Roger Robinson, I spoke and corresponded with Alain St. Yves, the grandson of Henri St. Yves, from Ottawa. Finally, Graham Owen provided valuable material about his great-great-great grandfather, Imre Kiralfy, and the construction of White City Stadium.

I could not have completed this work without the advice and encouragement from many writers, scholars, editors, and former colleagues (many of whom I also call friends): Donnell Alexander, Emily Green, Lynell George, Kateri Butler, Kit Rachlis, Karen Wada, Pamela Klein, Ron Rapoport, Bert Sugar, Vince Beiser, Steve Kettmann, Julian Rubinstein, Joe and Kit Reed, Mack Reed, Jason Levin, Paul Feinberg, Bruce Bebb, Daniel Shaw, Randy Williams, Randy Harvey, David Wallechinsky, Al Martinez, Nicole Laporte, Amby Burfoot, Roger Robinson, Rob Hadgcraft, the late John Kelley, Marc Bloom, Dr. Edward Kozloff, and Dr. Matthew Llewellyn.

I am forever indebted to two scribes-angels: journalist Susan Reifer, based in British Columbia, who dug out numerous articles about Tom Longboat in Canada and made expert edits on the first draft, and novelist-screenwriter Kate Maruyama, who helped in every step of the process, from sketchy outline to first draft to Web site design.

I'm fortunate to live in Los Angeles, not least because it allows me access to the invaluable resources of the LA84 Foundation. The LA84 Foundation has one of the finest sports and Olympic research centers in the world—many photos in the book came from here—as well as an amazing Web site. Its most treasured resource is its staff, and I'm thankful to Wayne Wilson, Michael Salmon, Patrick Escobar, and the indefatigable Shirley Ito for their collective expertise, unflagging patience, and enthusiastic support.

My parents, Andy and Jessie Davis, have been in my corner since 1962. My dad and I journeyed to the Olympics in 1980, in Lake Placid, New York, the first of many such trips. My sister, Jennifer Davis Hall, has provided encouragement and love, and I could not have managed without my extended family in southern California, in particular Lucy Ito and Rob Corn, Hugo Ito, Eric and Rose Harmon, Regino Chavez, Sally Hudson, and Tony Shaw.

Finally, to Flora: my eternal gratitude and love.

NOTES

When I started to research this book, I wondered whether I'd be able to find enough material about the three protagonists. After all, they were long dead. On the plane ride home from England and Ireland, my suitcase packed with enough archival documents to wallpaper a large home, I could only marvel at my naïveté.

Newspapers in the first decade of the twentieth century were like blogs today: Every town had one—and large cities had multiple newspapers, oftentimes with multiple editions. These accounts form the core of the book's narrative.

Unfortunately, there was no press coverage of the three runners before they started competing at an elite level. I took some creative liberty in describing their formative years, backed with as much factual information (census reports, contemporary books, historical analysis, other biographical accounts) as I could find. Any errors are my responsibility.

I accessed material from the following archives and libraries:

A. C. Gilbert collection, Yale University

Amos Alonzo Stagg papers, University of Chicago

A. Roy Welton scrapbooks

Boston Athletic Association archives

Boston Public Library

British Film Institute

British Library

British Library Newspapers—Colindale

British Olympic Association archive, University of East London

Canada's Sports Hall of Fame

"Chronicling America," Historic American Newspapers, Library of Congress, accessed online http://chroniclingamerica.loc.gov/

Clarence DeMar scrapbook

International Centre for Olympic Studies, University of Western Ontario

LA84 Foundation archives and Olympic collection

Los Angeles Public Library

National Library of Ireland

New York Municipal Archives

New York Public Library

New York Transit Museum

Polytechnic Institute archive, University of Westminster

Sports Illustrated Vault (online)

Tipperary Studies, Thurles

Toronto Public Library

Woodland Cultural Centre, Brantford

Among the newspapers and magazines I read were: *American Magazine, Architectural Record, Architectural Review, Asbury Park Press, Arizona Republic, Athletics Weekly, Bally's Magazine, Bell's Life, Birmingham Evening Despatch, Black & White, Black Country Bugle, Boston Globe, Boston Herald, Boston Journal, Brantford Courier, Brantford Expositor, Brooklyn Eagle, The Bystander, Carlisle Arrow, Century Magazine, Chicago Daily Tribune, Collier's, Cork Examiner, Cork Sportsman, Corriere della Sera, Country Gentleman, Courier Journal, Cycling, Daily Chronicle, Daily Express, Daily Graphic, Daily Mail, Daily Mirror, Daily News, Daily Telegraph, Dublin Evening Mail, Empire, Evening News, Evening Standard, Evening Sun, Evening Telegram, Evening World, The Field, FootNotes, Freeman's Journal, Gaelic American, Glasgow Herald, The Graphic, Hamilton Herald, Hamilton Spectator, Harvard Magazine, Il Progresso, Illustrated London News, Indian Craftsman, International Journal of the History of Sport, Irish America Magazine, Irish Independent, Irish News, Irish World, Journal of Olympic History, Journal of Sport History, La Stampa, Lady's Pictorial, Limerick Leader, London Standard, London Times, Los Angeles Times, Lowell Sun, Maclean's, Manchester Guardian, Marathon & Beyond, Montreal Star, Nenagh Guardian, Nenagh News, News of the World, New York American, New York Globe, New York Herald, New York Herald Tribune, New York Press, New York Sun, New York Times, New York Tribune, New York World, The New Yorker, The Observer, Outing Magazine, Outlook, Olympika, Pall Mall Gazette, Peterborough Examiner, Philadelphia Bulletin, Philadelphia Ledger, Pittsburgh Leader, Polytechnic Magazine, The Red Man, Review of Reviews, Revue Olympique, Runner's World, San Francisco Call, The Standard, The Scotsman, Sinn Fein, St. Louis Post Dispatch, Sporting Chronicle, Sporting Life, Sporting Times, Sports Illustrated, The Sportsman, Stadion, Star Phoenix, Strand Magazine, The Tatler, Toronto Daily Star, Toronto Globe, Toronto Telegram, Track Stats, Truth, Victoria Daily Colonist, Wall Street Journal, Washington Post, Weekly Freeman, Westminster Gazette,*

Windsor Express, Windspeaker, Winnipeg Free Press, New York World, World Sports, Yonkers Herald.

ENDNOTES

These notes are incomplete because, in many cases, newspapers and magazines from the late nineteenth and early twentieth centuries did not include bylines. Oftentimes, articles that I quoted from personal scrapbooks and archives did not include the date of the article, the publication name, or both. I've also tried, whenever possible, to credit those secondary sources that quoted the articles used in the text.

1.   Quoted in an article by Bill Cunningham, from the Clarence DeMar scrapbook at the Boston Public Library.
2.   *All That Glitters Is Not Gold: The Olympic Game*, by William O. Johnson, p. 19.

Introduction

1.   *Boston Marathon: The First Century of the World's Premier Running Event*, by Tom Derderian, p. xxiv.

One

1.   Quoted (in English) by James Connolly in "The Shepherd's Bush Greeks," *Collier's*, September 5, 1908, pp. 12–13.

Two

1.   English-language accounts of Dorando Pietri's childhood are wildly divergent. For this, I relied on Augusto Frasca's biography, *Dorando Pietri: La Corsa del Secolo*, published in Italian and translated for me by Neal Putt, as well as Dorando's own words in various interviews.
2.   *Chicago Daily Tribune*, January 17, 1909.
3.   *Dorando Pietri*, by Augusto Frasca, p. 52.
4.   Census reports.
5.   *How the Other Half Lives: Studies Among the Tenements of New York*, by Jacob Riis, p. 43.
6.   Ibid., p. 210.
7.   Census, interviews, and visit.
8.   *Beyond the Golden Door*, by William O'Dwyer, p. 67.
9.   Irish-American experience: Census reports; *The New York Irish*, edited by Ronald Baylor and Timothy Meagher; *Making the Irish American: History*

and Heritage of the Irish in the United States, edited by J.J. Lee and Marion Casey.

10.   *The Catholic Church in the United States of America,* p. 305.

11.   Tom Longboat background: Interviews, personal visit to the Six Nations Reserve, contemporary newspapers. Secondary sources: *The Man Who Ran Faster Than Everyone,* by Jack Batten; *Tom Longboat,* by Bruce Kidd; *Boston: The Canadian Story,* by David Blaikie; *The People of the Longhouse,* by Edward-Mauon Chadwick; *A Narrow Vision: Duncan Campbell Scott and the Administration of Indian Affairs in Canada,* by E. Brian Titley; *Aboriginal Ontario: Historical Perspectives on the First Nations,* edited by Edward Rogers and Donald Smith.

12.   Longboat's Attestation Paper was accessed from the Web site of the Library and Archives, Canada, http://www.collectionscanada.gc.ca/premiereguerre/025005-3200.002.01-e.html.

13.   *Toronto Telegram,* April 24, 1907.

14.   Annual Report of the Dept. of Indian Affairs 1897, p. 292.

15.   *Indian Helper,* March 18, 1898.

16.   *History of the New England Company,* p. 307.

17.   *The Mush Hole: Life at Two Indian Residential Schools,* edited by Elizabeth Graham, p. 25.

18.   See www.wherearethechildren.ca/en/school/classroom.html.

Three

1.   Johnny Hayes's background: Published interviews with Hayes, including *New York World,* August 23, 1908 and *New York American,* July 30, 1908. Hayes also self-published a booklet entitled "The Marathon Race of 1908." Secondary sources include: *Making the Irish American: History and Heritage of the Irish in the United States,* edited by J. J. Lee and Marion Casey. *The Marathon Makers,* by John Bryant.

2.   Sports in the Industrial Age: Secondary sources include: *America's Sporting Heritage: 1850–1950,* by John Rickard Betts; *A History of Recreation: America Learns to Play,* by Foster Rhea Dulles; *A Sporting Time: New York City and the Rise of Modern Athletics,* by Melvin Adelman; *Spalding's World Tour: The Epic Adventure That Took Baseball Around the Globe—and Made It America's Game,* by Mark Lamster; *A. G. Spalding and the Rise of Baseball: The Promise of American Sport,* by Peter Levine; *American Sports: From the Age of Folk Games to the Age of Televised Games,* by Benjamin Rader; *Patriotic Games: Sporting Traditions in the American Imagination, 1876–1926,* edited by S. W. Pope.

3.   *The Industrial Revolutionaries: The Making of the Modern World, 1776–1914,* by Gavin Weightman.

4.   Sports media: "Media Made Sport: A History of Sports Coverage in the United States," by Robert McChesney in *Media, Sports, & Society,* edited by Lawrence Wenner.

5.   *Beyond the Melting Pot: The Negroes, Puerto Ricans, Jews, Italians, and Irish of New York City*, by Nathan Glazer and Daniel Moynihan, p. 246.

6.   Twain probably spoke these words in 1889; the text later appeared in *Mark Twain's Speeches*.

7.   *The Mush Hole*, edited by Elizabeth Graham, p. 100.

8.   "Runner of Messages," from *To Run with Longboat: Twelve Stories of Indian Athletes in Canada*, by Brenda Zeman, p. 13.

9.   From *Gospel of the Red Man*, by Ernest Thompson Seton, quoted in "An Historical Overview of Twentieth Century Native American Athletes," *Indian Historian*, 1979.

10.   "Running to Nowhere," by Bertram Gabriel, *Sports Illustrated*, November 26, 1979. Secondary source: *Indian Running*, by Peter Nabokov.

11.   From *Lacrosse: A History of the Game*, by Donald Fisher.

12.   *Toronto Daily Star*, January 5, 1909.

13.   *Lacrosse: The National Game of Canada*, by W. G. Beers, pp. 32–33.

14.   *Chicago Daily Tribune*, January 17, 1909.

15.   Cycling history: *Hearts of Lions: The History of American Bicycle Racing*, by Peter Nye.

16.   Conan Doyle quoted in *Scientific American*, January 18, 1896.

17.   *Dorando Pietri* by Augusto Frasca, p. 44, 46, 48.

18.   Pierre de Coubertin biography and the formation of the modern Olympics: From Coubertin's *Olympic Memoirs* and *Olympism: Selected Writings* and other writings (books, magazines, letters). Secondary sources: *This Great Symbol: Pierre de Coubertin and the Origins of the Modern Olympic Games*, by John MacAloon; *The Modern Olympics: A Struggle for Revival*, by David Young; *The Olympics: A History of the Modern Games*, by Allen Guttmann; *The First Modern Olympics*, by Richard Mandell; *The Modern Olympic Games*, by John Lucas; *Making the American Team: Sport, Culture, and the Olympic Experience*, by Mark Dyreson.

19.   World's fair background: *Historical Dictionary of World's Fairs and Expositions, 1851–1988*, edited by John Findling.

20.   Coubertin quoted in MacAloon, *This Great Symbol*, p. 167.

21.   Coubertin quoted in Mandell, *The First Modern Olympics*, p. 91.

Four

1.   *The Olympic Marathon: The History and Drama of Sport's Most Challenging Event*, by David Martin and Roger G. H. Gynn, p. 6. See also, "Michel Bréal—the Man Behind the Idea of the Marathon," by Norbert Muller, *Pathways: Critiques and Discourse in Olympic Research*, 2008.

2.   Battle of Marathon: *History of the Greek and Persian War*, by Herodotus, translated by George Rawlinson; "A History of the Marathon Race, 490 B.C. to 1975," by John Lucas, *Journal of Sport History*.

3.   *This Great Symbol*, by John MacAloon, p. 208.

4.   1896 Olympics: Coubertin's writings; *1896 Official Report*; *The 1896 Olympic*

Games: Results for All Competitors in All Events, with Commentary, by Bill Mallon and Ture Widlund; *The Complete Book of the Summer Olympics,* by David Wallechinsky; *The Modern Olympics,* by David Young.

5.   1896 Marathon: *1896 Official Report; The 1896 Olympic Games;* "That Memorable First Marathon," by Anthony Bijkerk and David Young, *Journal of Olympic History; The Modern Olympics,* by David Young; *The Complete Book of the Summer Olympics; This Great Symbol* by John MacAloon; *The Olympic Marathon,* by David Martin and Roger G. H. Gynn.

6.   *This Great Symbol,* by John MacAloon, p. 227.

7.   "High Hurdles and White Gloves," by Thomas Curtis, *The Sportsman,* July 1932, quoted in *This Great Symbol,* by John MacAloon, p. 217.

8.   "The Olympian Games at Athens," by Charles Waldstein, *Harper's Weekly,* April 18, 1896, quoted in "That Memorable First Marathon," p. 12.

9.   "The Olympian Games," by E. Burton Holmes, quoted in "That Memorable First Marathon," by Anthony Bijerk and David Young, p. 9.

10. *The Olympic Marathon,* by David Martin and Roger G. H. Gynn.

11. "First American Marathon," by Pamela Cooper, *FootNotes,* p. 14. Cooper's book, *The American Marathon,* was an excellent source.

12. *New York Times,* September 20, 1896.

13. First Boston Marathon: "The Marathon Race," *Boston Post,* April 18, 1897; *Boston Marathon,* by Tom Derderian; and *Boston: A Century of Running,* by Hal Higdon.

14. "The Course," by Brian MacQuarrie, *Boston Globe,* April 17, 1992.

15. *Boston Post,* April 18, 1897.

16. *Boston Daily Globe,* April 20, 1897, quoted in *Boston Marathon,* by Tom Derderian, p. 6.

17. Ibid.

18. *Hamilton Spectator,* April 20, 1897, quoted in *Boston Marathon,* by Tom Derderian, p. 18.

19. "Athletics and the Stadium," by James Sullivan, *Cosmopolitan,* September 1901, p. 506.

20. *A Complete System of Treatment for the General Care of the Body,* by J. R. Judd, p. 151, http://books.google.com/books?oe=UTF-8qid=fyDkp9QSxs Cqg=long-distance+runner#v=snippet&g=long-distance%20runner& f=false.

21. *Olympic Memoirs,* by Pierre de Coubertin, p. 37.

Five

1.   *Dorando Pietri,* by Augusto Frasca.

2.   *Chicago Daily Tribune,* January 17, 1909.

3.   *Boston Globe,* April 20, 1901.

4.   *Toronto Telegram,* April 24, 1907.

5.   Municipal records.

6.   Published interviews with Johnny Hayes, 1908; St. Bartholomew's Parish yearbooks, 1906–1907.
7.   "What We Can Expect of the American Boy," by Theodore Roosevelt, *St. Nicholas Magazine*, May 1900, p. 574.
8.   Prof. Shailer Mathews quoted in *The Hundred Yard Lie: The Corruption of College Football and What We Can Do to Stop It*, by Rick Telander, p. 32.
9.   Theodore Roosevelt telegram, quoted in *America's First Olympics: The St. Louis Games of 1904*, by George Matthews, p. 107.
10.   1904 Olympics: *The Olympic Games, 1904*, by Charles Lucas; *The Olympic Marathon*, by David Martin and Roger G. H. Gynn; *America's First Olympics*, by George Matthews; "The 1900 & 1904 Olympic Games: The Farcical Games," by Reet Howell and Maxwell Howell; *The 1904 Anthropology Days and Olympic Games: Sport, Race, and American Imperialism*, edited by Susan Brownell.
11.   *Spalding's Official Athletic Almanac for 1905*, edited by James E. Sullivan, pp. 257, 259, http://www.la84foundation.org/6oic/OfficialReports/1904/1904Spal.pdf.
12.   *The Olympic Games, 1904*, by Charles Lucas, p. 52.
13.   Ibid., p. 53.
14.   As advertised in *Outing*, September 1896.
15.   *A History of Drug Use in Sport, 1876–1976*, by Paul Dimeo, p. 22.
16.   *The Olympic Games, 1904*, Lucas, p. 51.
17.   "Chief Sullivan's Opinion of the Marathon Race," *St. Louis Republic*, August 31, 1904, quoted in *The American Marathon*, by Pamela Cooper.
18.   "The 1900 & 1904 Olympic Games," by Reet Howell and Maxwell Howell.
19.   Sullivan quoted in "Entrepreneurs, Structures, Sportsgeist," by Stephen Hardy, in *Essays on Sport History and Sport Mythology*, p. 66.
20.   Sullivan–Coubertin correspondence, June 26, 1906, from the Avery Brundage papers, viewed on microfilm.
21.   *Olympic Memoirs*, by Pierre de Coubertin, p. 43.

Six

1.   *Dorando Pietri*, by Augusto Frasca, pp. 52, 54.
2.   Ibid., p. 54.
3.   Ibid, pp. 60–64.
4.   *New York Times*, November 25, 1904.
5.   Municipal records.
6.   Letter written by Doris Hayes to Nancy Murphy, dated June 25, 1997. I contacted the Blauvelt facility and was unable to verify that the Hayes children were placed at this particular orphanage.
7.   *The National Cyclopedia of American Biography, Volume XIV*, by James Terry White, p. 122.

8. *The City Beneath Us: Building the New York Subway*, by The New York Transit Museum and Vivian Heller, p. 21.
9. *Brooklyn Daily Eagle*, March 27 and 28, 1905.
10. *Tom Longboat*, by Bruce Kidd and *The Man Who Ran Faster Than Everyone*, by Jack Batten.
11. *Toronto Telegram*, April 24, 1907.
12. *Boston Globe*, April 19, 1906; *Boston Marathon*, by Tom Derderian, pp. 35–37.
13. *The Marathon Makers*, by John Bryant, p. 78.
14. *Dorando Pietri*, by Augusto Frasca, p. 87.
15. *Dorando Pietri*, by Augusto Frasca, p. 72.
16. Ibid., pp. 72–73.
17. "The Vesuvius Eruption of 1906," by Frank Perret, *Nature*, April 1906.
18. *The Olympic Games at Athens, 1906*, by James E. Sullivan, p. 137.
19. *The 1906 Olympic Games: Results for All Competitors in All Events, with Commentary*, Bill Mallon, p. 7.
20. *The Olympic Marathon*, by David Martin and Roger G. H. Gynn, p. 58.
21. "Joseph Forshaw, Marathon Runner," by Christine Forshaw O'Shaughnessy, *Journal of Olympic History*, May 2004; and interview.
22. *The Olympic Marathon*, by David Martin and Roger G. H. Gynn, p. 61. "The History of the Marathon in Canada," by Marion Raycheba, *Marathon & Beyond*, May–June, 2005.

Seven

1. Dorando in Athens: *Dorando Pietri*, by Augusto Frasca; *The Olympic Marathon*, by David Martin and Roger G. H. Gynn; *The Marathon Makers*, by John Bryant.
2. *The Olympic Games at Athens, 1906*, by James E. Sullivan, p. 37.
3. *London Daily Mail*, May 2, 1906.
4. *Dorando Pietri*, by Augusto Frasca, pp. 74–76.
5. *The Olympic Games at Athens, 1906*, by James E. Sullivan, p. 37.
6. "Joseph Forshaw, Marathon Runner," by Christine Forshaw O'Shaughnessy.
7. *The Olympic Games at Athens, 1906*, by James E. Sullivan, p. 97.
8. *Evening World*, May 2, 1906.
9. *The Olympic Games at Athens, 1906*, by James E. Sullivan, p. 45.
10. Rome to London: Material at the British Olympic Association archives; *The Evolution of the Olympic Games, 1829–1914*, by F. A. M. Webster; *The First London Olympics, 1908*, by Rebecca Jenkins; *Olympic Follies: The Madness and Mayhem of the 1908 London Games*, by Graeme Kent; *The 1908 Olympic Games: Results for All Competitors in All Events, with Commentary*, by Bill Mallon and Ian Buchanan.
11. *New York Times*, May 23 and July 15, 1906.
12. Around the Bay: *Brantford Courier*, October 19, 1906; *Tom Longboat*, by Bruce Kidd; *The Man Who Ran Faster Than Everyone*, by Jack Batten.

13.   *Tom Longboat*, by Bruce Kidd, p. 16.
14.   "Tom Longboat: Canada's Outstanding Indian Athlete," by Wilton Littlechild, p. 9.
15.   *Profiles in Canadian Literature 7*, edited by Jeffrey Heath, p. 60.
16.   Toronto and Rosenthal background: *The Man Who Ran Faster Than Everyone*, by Jack Batten, pp. 18–19.
17.   Ibid., p. 22.
18.   CAAU: "Tom Longboat," by Wilton Littlechild; *Tom Longboat*, by Bruce Kidd; *The Man Who Ran Faster Then Everyone*, by Jack Batten; and "The Longboat Incident of the 1908 Olympics: A Study in International Sporting Relations," by Dan Reid.
19.   *Brantford Courier*, March 20, 1907, quoted in Littlechild, p. 13.
20.   *Toronto Daily Star*, April 12, 1907, quoted in Reid, p. 28.
21.   Ibid., April 15, 1907, quoted in Reid, p. 29.
22.   Ibid., February 21, 1907, quoted in Reid, p.21.
23.   *New York Times*, September 8, 1907.
24.   See "Amateur Athletes Exposed," *Physical Culture*, December 1908, p. 488, and "The Hegemonic Rule of the American Amateur Athletic Union 1888–1914: James E. Sullivan as Prime Mover," by John Lucas, *Stadion*, December 1994, p. 360.
25.   "The Capitalization of Amateur Athletics," by James Connolly, *Metropolitan*, July 1910, p. 450.
26.   "Spiked Shoes and Cinder Paths: An Athlete's Story," by Melvin Sheppard, *Sport Story Magazine*, May 1924, p. 107.

Eight

1.   *Boston Post*, April 19, 1907.
2.   *Toronto Daily Star*, April 19, 1907.
3.   Ibid., April 20, 1907.
4.   *Boston Journal*, April 20, 1907, and newspaper accounts from Boston, New York, Toronto, Brantford; *Boston Marathon*, by Tom Derderian, pp. 38–43.
5.   *Boston Globe*, April 20, 1907.
6.   Ibid.
7.   Ibid.
8.   Ibid.
9.   *Brantford Courier*, April 20, 1907.
10.   *Boston Globe*, April 20, 1907.
11.   *Toronto Telegram*, April 24, 1907.
12.   *Toronto Daily Star*, April 25, 1907.
13.   Ibid.
14.   *Brantford Courier*, April 20, 1907.
15.   *Montreal Gazette*, April 20, 1907.
16.   *Toronto Daily Star*, 1907, quoted in Kidd, p. 25.
17.   *Toronto Globe*, July 10, 1907.

18.   *Boston*, by David Blaikie, http://www.davidblaikie.com/david_blaikie/bos ton/baa_aut.htm.

19.   Flanagan quoted in *A Text-Book of True Temperance*, edited by M. Monahan, pp. 57–58 (accessed online, 2010: http://books.google.com/books? id=1VgLAQAAIAAJ&pg=PA57&Ipg=PA57&dg=%22flanagan%22+ %22true+temperance%22&source=bl&ots=GlweO1kb0K& sig=XjSBDEIQ8tLzy6EO1ChZ1x62uWM&hl=en&ei=gma9Tt_IBafjiAK Plg38Ag&sa=X&oi=book_result&ct=result&resnum=1& ved=0CBsQ6AEwAA#v=onepage&g&f=false.

20.   *Dorando Pietri*, by Augusto Frasca, p. 87.

21.   *Vanity Fair*, July 15, 1908.

22.   Lord Desborough background: *The Olympic Century: The Official History of the Modern Olympic Movement*, Volume 5, p. 22.

23.   Taplow Court, *Pall Mall Gazette*, *Empire*, *Black & White*, June and July, 1908.

24.   Imre Kiralfy: Interview with Graham Owen; "The Spectacle Plays," by Brendan Edward Gregory.

25.   *Review of Reviews*, May 1908.

26.   Letter from Percy Fisher, December 17, 1906, BOA Archives.

27.   Hague: *The 1908 Olympic Games*, by Bill Mallon and Ian Buchanan, pp. 6–7.

28.   British sport: See *Empire Games: The British Invention of Twentieth Century Sport*, by Roger Hutchinson; *The Age of Empire 1875–1914*, by Eric Hobsbawm; *Empire: The British Imperial Experience from 1765 to the Present*, by Denis Judd; *Sport: A Cultural History*, by Richard Mandell.

29.   *Making the American Team*, by Mark Dyreson, p. 135.

Nine

1.   *New York Times*, November 29, 1907.

2.   *Yonkers Herald*, November 29, 1907, p. 8.

3.   Ibid., November 30, 1907, p. 8.

4.   Ibid., November 29, 1907, p. 8.

5.   *New York Times*, June 28, 1931.

6.   *Beyond the Golden Door*, by William O'Dwyer, p. 96.

7.   "Spiked Shoes and Cinder Paths," by Melvin Sheppard, Part IV, p. 5.

8.   Ibid., Part III, p. 7.

9.   Irish-American Athletic Club: Interview and correspondence with Ian McGowan; *Abel Kiviat: National Champion*, by Alan Katchen; *Gold, Silver and Green: The Irish Olympic Journey, 1896–1924*, by Kevin McCarthy. See also: www.wingedfist.org.

10.   Hayes interview in *The New Yorker*, July 4, 1936, p. 21; *All That Glitters Is Not Gold*, by William O. Johnson.

11.   *The Man Who Ran Faster Than Everyone*, by Jack Batten, p. 38.

12. Victoria *Daily Colonist*, November 19, 1907.
13. Telegram from Hugh Graham, reprinted in "Tom Longboat," by Wilton Littlechild, p. 39.
14. *Boston*, by David Blaikie, http://davidblaikie.com/david_blaikie/boston/baa_aut.htm.
15. *New York Times*, November 13, 1907.
16. *New York Times*, December 21, 1907.
17. Athletic War: *The Struggle for Canadian Sport*, by Bruce Kidd; "The Longboat Incident of the 1908 Olympics," by Dan Reid.
18. *Mind and Body*, June 1907, http://books.google.com/books?id=l_afAAAA-MAAJ&pg=PA145&dq=tom+longboat&lr=&cd=44#v=onepage&q=tom%20longboat&f=false.
19. "Tom Longboat," by Wilton Littlechild, p. 53.
20. *Dorando Pietri*, by Augusto Frasca, p. 68.

Ten

1. *America 1908: The Dawn of Flight, the Race to the Pole, the Invention of the Model T, and the Making of the Modern Nation*, by Jim Rasenberger, p. 1.
2. *New York Times*, February 20, 1907.
3. *New York American*, n.d.
4. *Toronto Daily Star*, n.d.
5. *Montreal Star*, May 16, 1907.
6. *Boston Globe*, April 21, 1908.
7. "The Marathon Race of 1908," by John J. Hayes.
8. Article from Welton archive, n.d.
9. *The Red Man*, n.d.
10. Quoted in many places, including "Footrace in the Desert," by Edward Abbey, from Abbey's *Down the River*.
11. Several biographies of Jim Thorpe mention this alleged incident.
12. Dorando's 1908 trials: *Dorando Pietri*, by Augusto Frasca, p. 90.
13. *Montreal Star*, June 12, 1908.
14. *Evening World*, July 15 1908.
15. Ibid.
16. *The Man Who Lives in Paradise*, by A. C. Gilbert, p. 93.
17. "The Marathon Race of 1908," by John J. Hayes.
18. *Irish News*, July 8, 1908.
19. *Limerick Leader*, July 8, 1908.
20. *Cork Sportsman*, July 18, 1908.
21. *Nenagh Guardian*, July 22, 1908.
22. *Toronto Daily Star*, n.d.
23. *Cork Sportsman*, July 18, 1908.
24. *Dorando Pietri*, by Augusto Frasca, p. 91.

Eleven

1. *The Guardian,* June 3, 1908, quoted in "Art, Politics and Society at the Franco–British Exhibition of 1908," by Paul Greenhalgh, *Art History,* December 1985, p. 439.
2. "The Franco–British Exhibition," *Architectural Record,* August 1908.
3. *Sports Grounds and Buildings: Making, Management, Maintenance and Equipment,* by F. A. M. Webster, p. 110.
4. *The First London Olympics, 1908,* by Rebecca Jenkins, p. 50.
5. Marathon course: Research about Jack Andrew's course came from the Polytechnic Harriers' archives. Additional details came from *The 1908 Olympic Games, the Great Stadium, and the Marathon: A Pictorial Record,* by Bob Wilcock; "The 1908 Olympic Marathon," by Bob Wilcock, *Journal of Olympic History,* March 2008; "From Windsor Castle to White City: The 1908 Olympic Marathon Route," by Martin Polley; *London Journal,* July 2009.
6. *Polytechnic Magazine,* May 1908.
7. "Marathon Trial Race program, 1908."
8. "Athletics Programme, Rules and Conditions of Competition, 1908," p. 10.
9. "The 1908 Olympic Marathon," by Bob Wilcock, p. 32.
10. Ibid., pp. 44–45.

Twelve

1. *Evening News,* July 13, 1908.
2. Opening Ceremonies: London newspaper reports; *Dorando Pietri,* by Augusto Frasca.
3. *Daily Illini,* October 1, 1908.
4. *Detroit News-Tribune,* Aug. 6, 1908.
5. "To No Earthly King . . . ," by Bill Mallon and Ian Buchanan, *Journal of Olympic History,* September 1999; "'This Flag Dips for No Earthly King': The Mysterious Origins of an American Myth," by Mark Dyreson, *International Journal of the History of Sport,* February 2008; "This Flag Dips to No Earthly King: The 1908 Olympic Opening Ceremony, Fresh Evidence," by Bob Wilcock, *Journal of Olympic History,* March 2011.
6. *Sporting Life,* July 18, 1908.
7. Article from LA84 Foundation archive, n.d.
8. *Daily Chronicle,* July 17, 1908.
9. *Daily Mail,* n.d.
10. *The Field,* July 18, 1908.
11. *Daily Telegraph,* July 16, 1908.
12. Article from Stagg archive, n.d.
13. *Sporting Life,* July 15, 1908.
14. *Chicago News,* n.d.

15. Article from LA84 Foundation archive, n.d.
16. *Chicago News*, July 14, 1908.
17. *Brooklyn Citizen*, n.d.
18. Quoted from "Ethelbert Talbot: His Life and Place in Olympic History," by Ture Widlund, *Citius, Altius, Fortius: Journal of the Society of Olympic Historians*, May 1994, p. 11.
19. *Daily Mail*, July 24, 1908.
20. *The Truth*, July 29, 1908.
21. *Sporting Life*, n.d.
22. *Pall Mall Gazette*, July 21, 1908.

Thirteen

1. *Pall Mall Gazette*, July 24, 1908.
2. *Sporting Life*, July 23, 1908.
3. Article from LA84 Foundation archive, n.d.
4. *Sporting Life*, July 11, 1908.
5. *New York Press*, July 20, 1908.
6. *Sporting Life*, July 24, 1908.
7. *Sportsman*, July 18, 1908.
8. *Philadelphia Examiner*, n.d.
9. *New York Press*, July 19, 1908.
10. *Star*, July 24, 1908.
11. *Evening Sun*, July 20, 1908.
12. *Running and Cross-Country Running*, by Alf Shrubb.
13. *Evening News*, July 23, 1908.
14. *Toronto Daily Star*, August 8, 1908.
15. Article from LA84 Foundation archive, July 24, 1908.
16. Dorando interview in *La Stampa*, n.d, translated by Antonio Cirino.
17. *London Times*, July 25, 1908.

Fourteen

1. The race action and scenes are drawn from eyewitness accounts (including interviews given by and/or articles written by Dorando, Hayes, Longboat, Forshaw, Hatch, Welton, Hefferon, and other marathoners in the race); photographs and motion pictures; and articles that appeared in American, British, Canadian, and Italian newspapers. I used references sparingly so as not to interfere with the narrative. Mile-split times came from *The 1908 Olympic Games*, by Bill Mallon and Ian Buchanan.
2. Diary of F. S. Kelly, n.p.
3. Article from LA84 Foundation archive, n.d.

Fifteen

1. Again, I relied on eyewitness accounts (including those given by Dorando, Hayes, Longboat, Forshaw, Hefferon, Welton, Hatch, and others); photographs and motion pictures; and articles that appeared in American, British, Canadian, and Italian newspapers. The accounts are contradictory; I've tried to be as accurate as possible.
2. *Sea-Borne: Thirty Years Avoyaging*, by James Connolly, p. 149.
3. Quoted in *The 1908 Olympic Games*, by Bill Mallon and Ian Buchanan, p. 402.
4. Article from LA84 Foundation archive, n.d.
5. *London Times*, July 25, 1908.
6. *Birmingham Evening Despatch*, July 25, 1908.
7. *Extra-Special Correspondent*, by G. Ward Price.
8. Coubertin quoted in *Official Report of the 1908 Olympic Games*, p. 793.

Sixteen

1. Headlines: From newspaper articles in the LA84 Foundation archive, Stagg papers, Gilbert papers, Welton scrapbook, and other sources.
2. *New York Times*, July 25, 1908.
3. *New York Tribune*, July 25, 1908.
4. *Daily Mail*, July 25, 1908.
5. *The Doctor and the Detective: A Biography of Sir Arthur Conan Doyle*, by Martin Booth, p. 275.
6. "Famous Sporting Photographs," by A. J. Wood and R. J. Maughan, *British Journal of Sports Medicine*, pp. 54–55.
7. Conan Doyle's own account appears in *Memories and Adventures*, pp. 223–25. See also "Arthur Conan Doyle and the Dorando Affair: How Rumours Become Facts," by Clifford Goldfarb, from *A Tangled Skein: A Companion Volume to the Baker Street Irregulars' Expedition to the Country of the Saints*, edited by Leslie Klinger, pp. 133–57.
8. *New York American*, August 8, 1908.
9. *New York Sun*, July 25, 1908.
10. Account of the medal ceremony taken from British and American newspapers; film footage.
11. *Daily Mail*, July 25, 1908.
12. *Memories and Adventures*, by Sir Arthur Conan Doyle, p. 225.
13. *Daily Mail*, August 11, 1908.
14. Carpi homecoming: *Daily Mail*, August 11 and 13.
15. *New York American*, August 3, 1908.
16. *Toronto Daily Star*, n.d.
17. "Report of the First Canadian Olympic Athletic Team," by J. H. Crocker, p. 12.

Seventeen

1. Croker visit: "The Marathon Race of 1908," by John J. Hayes.
2. Hayes's autograph book, Shore Athletic Club.
3. *Limerick Leader*, August 5, 1908.
4. *Cork Examiner*, July 27, 1908.
5. *Sinn Fein*, August 8, 1908.
6. Hayes in Nenagh: Interviews with Nancy and Donal Murphy; accounts in *Nenagh Guardian*, *Nenagh News*, and *Midland Tribune*.
7. "Exit Longboat," *Cork Sportsman*, August 8, 1908.
8. *New York Times*, August 30, 1908.
9. *Nenagh News*, n.d.
10. A. C. Gilbert papers.
11. From accounts in various New York newspapers; see also *Irish World*, September 5, 1908.
12. Shore Athletic Club.
13. *The World*, August 30, 1908.
14. "Heading the List," by Grantland Rice, *Sporting Life*, October 10, 1908.
15. Originally in the *Gaelic American*, reprinted in *Boston Globe*, September 24, 1908.
16. Articles from LA84 Foundation archive, n.d.
17. *New York Times*, September 3, 1908.
18. *New York Tribune*, n.d.
19. "Americans in Sport and Jingoism," by G. K. Chesterton, *London Illustrated News*, August 15, 1908.
20. *Olympism*, by Pierre de Coubertin, p. 425.
21. Quoted in "Coubertin and Americans: Wary Relationships, 1889–1925," by Robert Barney, in *Coubertin and Olympism: Questions for the Future, Proceedings of the Le Havre Congress, 1897–1997*, p. 57.
22. Letter from Caspar Whitney to Lord Desborough, July 31, 1908, BOA Archive.
23. Roosevelt letter, August 24, 1908, quoted in "Theodore Roosevelt and Baron Pierre de Coubertin," by John Lucas, *Stadion*, 1982–1983, p. 144.
24. *The Academy*, August 1, 1908.
25. Quoted in *A History of Drug Use in Sport*, p. 27.
26. "Report of the First Canadian Olympic Athletic Team," pp. 5, 11.
27. *Toronto Daily Star*, n.d.
28. *Pound/Williams: Selected Letters of Ezra Pound and William Carlos Williams*, edited by Hugh Witemeyer, p. 11.
29. "'Mr. Dooley' on the Olympic Games," by Finley Peter Dunne, *American Magazine*, October 1908.
30. "Community, Ethnicity, Status: The Origins of the Marathon in the United States," by Pamela Cooper, *International Journal of the History of Sport*, April 1992, p. 55.
31. Articles from LA84 Foundation archive, n.d.

32.   Connolly's comments were published after Longboat's victory in the 1907 Boston Marathon. His opinion echoed the viewpoint expressed by JAMA in 1903, quoted in "'Athlete's Heart': The Medical Debate over Athleticism, 1870–1920," by James C. Whorton, in *Sport and Exercise Science: Essays in the History of Sports Medicine*, p. 126.

33.   *New York Times*, February 24, 1909.

34.   This was the conclusion from studies of early Boston Marathon races conducted by Drs. Blake and Larrabee, quoted in "Athletes and Their Training in Britain and America, 1800–1914," by Roberta Park, in *Sport and Exercise Science: Essays in the History of Sports Medicine*, p. 92.

Eighteen

1.   Pat Powers and Marathon Mania: Background from "The Professional Marathon Craze in America, 1908–1909," by John Lucas, *Track Quarterly Review*, December 1968; "'Viva l'Italia! Viva l'Italia!' Dorando Pietri and the North American Professional Marathon Craze," by Matthew Llewellyn, *International Journal of the History of Sport*, May 2009; "The Fascinating Struggle," by Roger Robinson, *Marathon & Beyond*, March–April and May–June 2007.

2.   *Dorando Pietri*, by Augusto Frasca, p. 210.

3.   From census figures and "'Viva l'Italia! Viva l'Italia!'" by Matthew Llewellyn.

4.   Material from *La Stampa* and *Il Progresso Italo-Americano* newspapers, 1908–1909, translated by Antonio Cirino.

5.   Training and race details from New York City newspapers, including those serving the Irish-American and Italian-American communities.

6.   Madison Square Garden: Details from *Fifty Years at Ringside*, by Nat Fleischer.

7.   Dorando at Hammerstein's: "Reminiscences of Hammerstein's Victoria," by Loney Haskell, *New Yorker*, December 13, 1930, pp. 38–42.

8.   Longboat's race results in 1908: "Tom Longboat," by Wilton Littlechild and *Tom Longboat*, by Bruce Kidd, p. 34.

9.   *Tom Longboat*, by Bruce Kidd, p. 34.

10.   *Evening World*, December 7, 1908.

11.   Ibid., December 5, 1908.

12.   Ibid., December 15, 1908.

13.   Ibid., December 16, 1908.

14.   Race details and post-race comments from Toronto and New York City newspapers (including those serving the Italian-American community); see also "'Viva l'Italia! Viva l'Italia!,'" by Matthew Llewellyn.

15.   *Toronto Globe*, December 28, 1908.

16.   *New York Times*, December 27, 1908.

Nineteen

1.   Race details and comments from New York and Toronto newspapers.
2.   "'Viva l'Italia! Viva l'Italia!,'" by Matthew Llewellyn.
3.   Words and music by Irving Berlin. From *The Complete Lyrics of Irving Berlin*, edited by Robert Kimball and Linda Berlin Emmet. This includes Berlin's account of the making of "Dorando."
4.   "Effect of the Marathon Craze," by Charles Dana Gibson, *Collier's*, February 6, 1909, pp. 18–19.
5.   Advertisement in *New York Times*, August 25, 1908.
6.   *Mr. Dooley on Making a Will and Other Necessary Evils*, by Finley Peter Dunne, pp. 109–110.
7.   Theodore Roosevelt to Whitelaw Reid, letter dated January 6, 1909, *The Letters of Theodore Roosevelt*, edited by E. E. Morison, vol. 6, pp. 1465–66.
8.   *Washington Post*, December 6, 1908.
9.   Article from A. C. Gilbert papers, n.d.
10. Ibid.
11. *Running and Cross-Country Running*, by Alfred Shrubb, p. 64.
12. *Brantford Courier*, January 9, 1909, quoted in "Tom Longboat," by Wilton Littlechild, p. 72.
13. Longboat–Flanagan breakup (and reunion): Lou Marsh covered this in the *Toronto Daily Star* in January–February 1909. Also, see *Tom Longboat*, by Bruce Kidd, pp. 40–41.
14. "The Rise and Fall of Tom Longboat," by Fergus Cronin, *Maclean's*, February 4, 1956.
15. *The Man Who Ran Faster Than Everyone*, by Jack Batten, p. 69.
16. Race details and comments from New York City and Toronto newspapers. Shrubb background, see *The Little Wonder: The Untold Story of Alfred Shrubb, World Champion Runner*, by Rob Hadgraft.
17. *Toronto Daily Star*, February 6, 1909.
18. *Brantford Expositor*, February 6, 1909.
19. *Toronto Daily Star*, February 6, 1909.
20. *Tom Longboat*, by Bruce Kidd, p. 44.
21. Race details and comments from New York City newspapers, including those serving the Irish-American and Italian-American communities.
22. *New York Sun*, March 16, 1909.

Twenty

1.   "Tom Longboat," by Wilton Littlechild, p. 86.
2.   Marathon Derby I and II: Race details and comments from New York and Toronto newspapers; interview with Alain St. Yves; see also *Dorando Pietri*, by Augusto Frasca, pp. 234–40.
3.   Marathon Derby III: Race details from Chicago newspapers.
4.   Dorando's return to Italy: *Dorando Pietri*, by Augusto Frasca, pp. 242–44.

Twenty-one

1. *Toronto Daily Star*, April 5, 1909.
2. "Tom Longboat," by Wilton Littlechild, p. 96.
3. Ibid., p. 94.
4. Ibid., p. 95; *New York Times*, June 2, 1912.
5. *Tom Longboat*, by Bruce Kidd, p. 48.
6. *To Run with Longboat: Twelve Stories of Indian Athletes in Canada*, by Brenda Zeman, p. 18.
7. Race details from *Sporting Life* and *The Observer*.
8. Race details from *San Francisco Call* and *New York Times*; see also "'Viva l'Italia! Viva l'Italia!,'" by Matthew Llewellyn.
9. *Dorando Pietri*, by Augusto Frasca, p. 248.
10. 1912 Olympics: *The 1912 Olympic Games: Results for All Competitors in All Events, with Commentary*, by Bill Mallon and Ture Widlund; *The Olympic Marathon*, by David Martin and Roger G. H. Gynn.
11. *New York Times*, July 15, 1912.
12. *An Autobiography*, by Theodore Roosevelt, p. 50.

Twenty-two

1. *Dorando Pietri*, by Augusto Frasca, p. 262.
2. *The Marathon Makers*, by John Bryant, p. 290.
3. Attestation papers, Library and Archives Canada, http://www.collections canada.gc.ca/premiereguerre/025005-3200.002.01-e.html; Toronto newspapers, *New York Times*.
4. *Bally's Magazine of Sports & Pastimes*, May–June 1916.
5. *To Run with Longboat*, by Brenda Zeman, p. 19.
6. *New York Times*, October 28, 1917.
7. *Stevens Point Daily Journal*, December 15, 1917.
8. *Tom Longboat*, by Bruce Kidd, p. 54.

Epilogue

1. Dorando's final years: *Dorando Pietri*, by Augusto Frasca, pp. 264–70, pp. 282–84.
2. *The Man Who Ran Faster Than Everyone*, by Jack Batten, pp. 85–86.
3. *Toronto Daily Star*, December 1922.
4. Ibid., July 4, 1941.
5. Tom Longboat Jr. letter to Brantford *Expositor*, September 7, 1983.
6. *The Man Who Ran Faster Than Everyone*, by Jack Batten, p. 88.
7. Longboat letter to *Hamilton Spectator*, December 1947.
8. *Lethbridge Herald*, September 12, 1932.

9. Longboat's death and funeral: *Brantford Expositor*, January 12, 1949; *Toronto Globe*, January 12, 1949; *New York Times*, January 11, 1949.
10. *Olean Times Herald*, January 14, 1949.
11. "The Rise and Fall of Tom Longboat," by Fergus Cronin, p. 20.
12. *Maclean's*, July 1, 1998.
13. Interview with Professor Kidd, 2010.
14. Hayes's postrace career: Letters from Hayes's daughter; "Runner Outrun," *Time*, November 5, 1928; "Where Are They Now?," *New Yorker*, July 4, 1936; and "Johnny Hayes, Olympic Hero, Is Food Broker," by Al Laney, *New York Herald Tribune*, January 4, 1944.
15. *Arizona Republic*, September 8, 1968.
16. Ireland trip: Interview with Nancy and Donal Murphy.
17. Doris Hale letter to *Time*, August 12, 1996.
18. "'The Archive of the Feet': Field Walking in Sports History," by Martin Polley, *Journal of Sport History*, Spring 2010, pp. 144–45.
19. *Olympic Gold: A Runner's Life and Times*, by Frank Shorter, p. 85.
20. *Marathon Woman*, by Kathrine Switzer.

Postscript

1. 1948 Olympics: *The Complete Book of the Summer Olympics*, by David Wallechinsky, *The Austerity Olympics: When the Games Came to London in 1948*, by Janie Hampton.
2. Faux Dorando: "Dorando—The Immortal Loser," by Harold Abrahams, *World Sports*, February 1948; "Dorando—Alive or Dead?," *World Sports*, October 1954; "The Most Famous Marathoner of All: The Story of Dorando Pietri," by Peter Lovesey, *Athletics Weekly*, April 6, 1968; *The Marathon Makers*, by John Bryant, pp. xvi–xvii; *Dorando Pietri*, by Augusto Frasca, pp. 22–33.
3. "Dorando Pietri (Heesa Gooda for Not) Sees Marathon Finish—or Did He?," by Red Smith, *Boston Globe*, August 8, 1948.
4. *London Times*, August 8, 1948.

BIBLIOGRAPHY

Select Books

Abbey, Edward. *Down the River.* New York: Plume, 1991.

Adams, David Wallace. *Education for Extinction: American Indians and the Boarding School Experience, 1875–1928.* Lawrence, KS: Univ. Press of Kansas, 1995.

Adelman, Melvin. *A Sporting Time: New York City and the Rise of Modern Athletics.* Urbana, IL: University of Illinois Press, 1986.

Atkinson, Hugh. *The Games.* New York: Simon and Schuster, 1968.

Baedeker's Guide to London, 15th edition, 1908.

Baker, Keith. *The 1908 Olympics.* Cheltenham, UK: SportsBooks, 2008.

Bascomb, Neal. *The Perfect Mile.* Boston: Houghton Mifflin, Mariner Books edition, 2005.

Batten, Jack. *The Man Who Ran Faster Than Everyone.* Toronto: Tundra Books, 2002.

Baylor, Ronald, and Timothy Meagher, eds. *The New York Irish.* Baltimore, MD: Johns Hopkins Univ. Press, 1997.

Beaver, George. *Mohawk Reporter: The Six Nations Columns of George Beaver.* Ohsweken, Ontario: Iroqrafts, 1997.

Beers, W. G. *Lacrosse: The National Game of Canada.* Montreal: Dawson Brothers, 1869.

Berryman, Jack, and Roberta Park, eds. *Sport and Exercise Science: Essays in the History of Sports Medicine.* Champaign, IL: Univ. of Illinois Press, 1992.

Betts, John Rickard. *America's Sporting Heritage: 1850–1950.* Reading, MA: Addison-Wesley, 1974.

Blaikie, David. *Boston: The Canadian Story.* Ottawa: Seneca House Books, 1984.

Blom, Philipp. *The Vertigo Years: Europe, 1900–1914.* New York: Basic Books, 2008.

Bloom, Marc. *Run with the Champions: Training Programs and Secrets of America's 50 Greatest Runners.* Emmaus, PA: Rodale, 2001.

Booth, Martin. *The Doctor and the Detective: A Biography of Sir Arthur Conan Doyle.* New York: Thomas Dunne Books, 1997.

Brant, John. *Duel in the Sun: Alberto Salazar, Dick Beardsley, and America's Greatest Marathon.* Emmaus, PA: Rodale, 2006.

Brinkley, David. *Wheels for the World: Henry Ford, His Company, and a Century of Progress.* New York: Viking, 2003.

Brownell, Susan, ed. *The 1904 Anthropology Days and Olympic Games: Sport, Race, and American Imperialism.* Lincoln, NE: Univ. of Nebraska Press, 2008.

Bryant, John. *The Marathon Makers.* London: John Blake, 2008.

Buford, Kate. *Native American Son: The Life and Sporting Legend of Jim Thorpe.* New York: Alfred Knopf, 2010.

Burfoot, Amby. *The Runner's Guide to the Meaning of Life.* New York: Skyhorse Publishing, 2007.

Burlford, Thomas. *American Hatred and British Folly.* London: T.R. Burlford, 1911.

The Catholic Church in the United States of America. New York: The Catholic Editing Co., 1914, http://books.google.com/books?id=KL4YAAAAYAAJ&pg=PA305 &lpg=PA305&dg=%22glory+of+catholic+america%22&source=bl& ots=EvKzuhvyhZ&sig=XoD98OGgOOFmnTnd9CQyKowSBIQ&hl=en& ei=UHW9Tr6YCqfZiQKK29mtAw&sa=X&oi=book_result&ct=result&res-num=1&sqi=2&ved=0CBoQ6AEwAA#v=onepage&q=%22glory%20of %20catholic%20america%22&f=false.

Chadwick, Edward-Mauon. *The People of the Longhouse.* Toronto: The Church of England, 1897.

Cheever, Benjamin. *Strides: Running Through History with an Unlikely Athlete.* Emmaus, PA: Rodale, 2007.

Connolly, James. *Sea-Borne: Thirty Years Avoyaging.* Garden City, NY: Doubleday, Doran and Co., 1944.

Cook, Theodore. *The Fourth Olympiad: Being the Official Report of the Olympic Games of 1908 Celebrated in London Under the Patronage of His Most Gracious King Edward VII.* London: IOC, 1908.

Cooper, Pamela. *The American Marathon.* Syracuse, NY: Syracuse Univ. Press, 1998.

Coote, James, and John Goodbody. *The Olympics.* London: Robert Hale, 1972.

Coubertin, Pierre de. *Olympic Memoirs.* Lausanne, Switzerland: IOC, 1997.

———. *Olympism: Selected Writings,* ed. Norbert Muller. Lausanne, Switzerland: IOC, 2000.

Daniels, Roger. *Coming to America: A History of Immigration and Ethnicity in American Life.* New York: Harper Perennial, 1991.

DeMar, Clarence. *Marathon.* Brattleboro, VT: Stephen Daye Press, 1937.

Derderian, Tom. *Boston Marathon: The First Century of the World's Premier Running Event.* Champagne, IL: Human Kinetics, 1996.

Dimeo, Paul. *A History of Drug Use in Sport, 1876–1976.* London: Routledge, 2007.

Doyle, Sir Arthur Conan. *Memories and Adventures.* Boston: Little, Brown, 1924.

———. *Letters to the Press: The Unknown Conan Doyle.* London: Secker & Warbury, 1986.

Dulles, Foster Rhea. *A History of Recreation: America Learns to Play.* New York: Appleton-Century-Crofts, 1965.

Dumas, F. G., ed. *Franco–British Exhibition 1908 Illustrated Review.* London: Chatto & Windus, 1908.

Dunne, Finley Peter. *Mr. Dooley on Making a Will and Other Necessary Evils.* London: William Heinemann, 1920.

Dyreson, Mark. *Making the American Team: Sport, Culture, and the Olympic Experience.* Urbana, IL: Univ. of Illinois Press, 1998.

Emiris, Yannis. *Marathon Run: The History of a Sport*. Athens, Greece: 2004.

Everbach, Tracy. "Sports Journalism and the New American Character of Energy and Leisure," in Betty Winfield, ed. *Journalism 1908: Birth of a Profession*. Columbia, MO: Univ. of Missouri Press, 2008.

Findling, John, ed. *Historical Dictionary of World's Fairs and Expositions, 1851–1988*. Greenport, CT: Greenwood Press, 1990.

Fischler, Stan. *Uptown Downtown: A Trip Through Time on New York's Subways*. New York: Dutton, 1979.

Fisher, Donald. *Lacrosse: A History of the Game*. Baltimore, MD: Johns Hopkins Univ. Press, 2002.

Fleischer, Nat. *Fifty Years at Ringside*. London: Corgi Books, 1960.

Fleming, G. H. *The Unforgettable Season*. Lincoln, NE: Univ. of Nebraska Press, 1981.

Frasca, Augusto. *Dorando Pietri: La Corsa del Secolo*. Reggio, Italy: Aliberti Editore, 2007.

Gilbert, A. C. *The Man Who Lives in Paradise*. New York: Rinehart & Co., 1954.

Glazer, Nathan, and Daniel Moynihan. *Beyond the Melting Pot: The Negroes, Puerto Ricans, Jews, Italians, and Irish of New York City*. Cambridge, MA: MIT Press, 1970.

Graham, Elizabeth, ed. *The Mush Hole: Life at Two Indian Residential Schools*. Waterloo, Ontario: Heffle Publishing, 1997.

Guttmann, Allen. *The Games Must Go On: Avery Brundage and the Olympic Movement*. New York: Columbia Univ. Press, 1984.

———. *Games & Empires: Modern Sports and Cultural Imperialism*. New York: Columbia Univ. Press, 1994.

———. *The Olympics: A History of the Modern Games*. Urbana, IL: Univ. of Illinois Press, 1994.

Hadgraft, Rob. *The Little Wonder: The Untold Story of Alfred Shrubb, World Champion Runner*. Essex, UK: Desert Island Books, 2004.

Hampton, Janie. *The Austerity Olympics: When the Games Came to London in 1948*. Camden, UK: Aurum, 2008.

Hardy, Stephen. "Entrepreneurs, Structures and the Sportsgeist," in Donald Kyle and Gary Starks, eds. *Essays on Sport History and Sport Mythology*. College Station, TX: Texas A&M Univ. Press, 1990.

Herodotus. *History of the Greek and Persian War*. Translated by George Rawlinson. New York: Washington Square Press, 1963.

Higdon, Hal. *Boston: A Century of Running*. Emmaus, PA: Rodale, 1995.

History of the New England Company. London: Taylor and Co., 1871. http://books
.google.com/books?id=k6YNAAAAQAAJ&pg=PA5&lpg=PA5&dq=%
22history+of+the+new+england+company%22+%22gospel+of+christ%22+%
22heathen+natives%22source=bl&ots=TI_vcMTICe&sig=odPR12BnpEs_
h0Va3sqz9UW4FJc&hl=en&ei=EHi9TrXEPOfTiAL_o7D5Ag&sa=X&
oi=book_result&ct=result&resnum=2&ved=0CCcQ6AEwAQ#v-onepage&q&
f=false.

Hobsbawm, Eric. *The Age of Empire 1875–1914*. New York: Pantheon Books, 1987.

Hutchinson, Roger. *Empire Games: The British Invention of Twentieth Century Sport*. London: Mainstream Publishing, 1996.

Hymans, Richard. *The U.S. Olympic Trials for Track and Field, 1908–1992*. Indianapolis: USA Track & Field, 1996.

Isenberg, Michael. *John L. Sullivan and His America*. Urbana, IL: Univ. of Illinois Press, 1988.

Jenkins, Rebecca. *The First London Olympics, 1908*. London: Piatkus Books, 2008.

Johnson, William O. *All That Glitters Is Not Gold: The Olympic Game*. New York: G. P. Putnam, 1972.

Judd, Denis. *Empire: The British Imperial Experience from 1765 to the Present*. New York: Basic Books, 1996.

Katchen, Alan. *Abel Kiviat: National Champion*. Syracuse, NY: Syracuse Univ. Press, 2009.

Kent, Graeme. *Olympic Follies: The Madness and Mayhem of the 1908 London Games*. London: JR Books, 2008.

Kidd, Bruce. *The Struggle for Canadian Sport*. Toronto: Univ. of Toronto Press, 1999.

———. *Tom Longboat*. Markham, Ontario: Fitzhenry & Whiteside, 2004.

Kimball, Robert, and Linda Berlin Emmet, eds. *The Complete Lyrics of Irving Berlin*. New York: Applause Books, 2005.

Krise, Raymond, and Bill Squires. *Fast Tracks: The History of Distance Running Since 884 B.C.* Brattleboro, VT: The Stephen Greene Press, 1982.

Lamster, Mark. *Spalding's World Tour: The Epic Adventure That Took Baseball Around the Globe—and Made It America's Game*. New York: PublicAffairs, 2006.

Larson, Erik. *Devil in the White City: Murder, Magic, and Madness at the Fair That Changed America*. New York: Vintage Books. 2004.

Lee, J. J., and Marion Casey, eds. *Making the Irish American: History and Heritage of the Irish in the United States*. New York: New York Univ. Press, 2006. Two chapters were particularly useful: Larry McCarthy's "Irish Americans in Sports: The Twentieth Century" and Ralph Wilcox's "Irish Americans in Sports: The Nineteenth Century."

Levine, Peter. *A. G. Spalding and the Rise of Baseball: The Promise of American Sport*. New York: Oxford University Press, 1985.

Levy, E. Lawrence. *The Autobiography of an Athlete*. Birmingham, UK: J. G. Hammond, 1913.

Lucas, Charles J. P. *The Olympic Games, 1904*. St. Louis, MO: Woodward & Tiernan, 1905.

Lucas, John. *The Modern Olympic Games*. New York: A. S. Barnes, 1980.

Lycett, Andrew. *The Man Who Created Sherlock Holmes: The Life and Times of Sir Arthur Conan Doyle*. New York: Free Press, 2007.

MacAloon, John. *This Great Symbol: Pierre de Coubertin and the Origins of the Modern Olympic Games*. Chicago: Univ. of Chicago Press, 1981.

Mallon, Bill. *The 1900 Olympic Games: Results for All Competitors in All Events, with Commentary*. Jefferson, NC: McFarland, 1997.

———. *The 1904 Olympic Games: Results for All Competitors in All Events, with Commentary*. Jefferson, NC: McFarland, 1999.

————. *The 1906 Olympic Games: Results for All Competitors in All Events, with Commentary*. Jefferson, NC: McFarland, 1999.

Mallon, Bill, and Ian Buchanan. *The 1908 Olympic Games: Results for All Competitors in All Events, with Commentary*. Jefferson, NC: McFarland, 2000.

Mallon, Bill, and Ture Widlund. *The 1896 Olympic Games: Results for All Competitors in All Events, with Commentary*. Jefferson, NC: McFarland, 1997.

————. *The 1912 Olympic Games: Results for All Competitors in All Events, with Commentary*. Jefferson, NC: McFarland, 2002.

Mandell, Richard. *The First Modern Olympics*. Berkeley, CA: Univ. of California Press, 1976.

————. *Sport: A Cultural History*. New York: Columbia Univ. Press, 1984.

Maraniss, David. *Rome 1960: The Olympics That Changed the World*. New York: Simon & Schuster, 2008.

Martin, David, and Roger G. H. Gynn. *The Olympic Marathon: The History and Drama of Sport's Most Challenging Event*. Champagne, IL: Human Kinetics, 2000.

Matthews, George. *America's First Olympics: The St. Louis Games of 1904*. Columbia, MO: Univ. of Missouri Press, 2005.

McCarthy, Kevin. *Gold, Silver and Green: The Irish Olympic Journey: 1896–1924*. Cork, Ireland: Cork University Press, 2010.

McDougall, Christopher. *Born to Run: A Hidden Tribe, Superathletes, and the Greatest Race the World Has Never Seen*. New York: Alfred Knopf, 2009.

Meyer, Bruce. "Frank Prewett," in Jeffrey Heath, ed. *Profiles in Canadian Literature 7*. Toronto: Dundurn Press, 1981.

Moore, Kenny. *Best Efforts: World Class Runners and Racers*. Garden City, NY: Doubleday, 1982.

————. *Bowerman and the Men of Oregon: The Story of Oregon's Legendary Coach and Nike's Cofounder*. Emmaus, PA: Rodale, 2006.

Morison, E. E., ed. *The Letters of Theodore Roosevelt*. Cambridge, MA: Harvard Univ. Press, 1951.

Morris, Edmund. *The Rise of Theodore Roosevelt*. New York: Modern Library, 1979.

————. *Theodore Rex*. New York: Random House, 2001.

Murphy, Cait. *Crazy '08: How a Cast of Cranks, Rogues, Boneheads, and Magnates Created the Greatest Year in Baseball History*. New York: HarperCollins, Smithsonian Books edition, 2008.

Murphy, Michael. *Athletic Training*. New York: Charles Scribner's Sons, 1914.

Nabokov, Peter. *Indian Running*. Santa Barbara, CA: Capra Press, 1981.

New York Transit Museum and Vivian Heller. *The City Beneath Us: Building the New York Subway*. New York: W. W. Norton, 2004.

Nye, Peter. *Hearts of Lions: The History of American Bicycle Racing*. New York: W. W. Norton, 1989.

O'Dwyer, William. *Beyond the Golden Door*. New York: St. John's Univ. Press, 1987.

The Olympic Century: The Official History of the Modern Olympic Movement, volumes 1–6. Los Angeles: World Sport Research & Publications, 2000.

Oxendine, Joseph. *American Indian Sports Heritage*. Champagne, IL: Human Kinetics, 1988.

Pederiali, Giuseppe. *Il Sogno del Maratoneta: Il Romanzo di Dorando Pietri*. Milan, Italy: Garzanti, 2008.

Perret, Frank. *The Vesuvius Eruption of 1906*. Washington, D.C.: Carnegie Institution, 1924.

Pope, S. W., ed. *The New American Sport History: Recent Approaches and Perspectives*. Urbana, IL: Univ. of Illinois Press, 1997.

———. *Patriotic Games: Sporting Traditions in the American Imagination, 1876–1926*. New York: Oxford Univ. Press, 1997.

Price, G. Ward. *Extra-Special Correspondent*. London: George Harrap, 1957.

Rader, Benjamin. *American Sports: From the Age of Folk Games to the Age of Televised Games*. Englewood Cliffs, NJ: Prentice Hall, 1996.

Rasenberger, Jim. *America 1908: The Dawn of Flight, the Race to the Pole, the Invention of the Model T, and the Making of the Modern Nation*. New York: Scribner, 2007.

Riis, Jacob. *How the Other Half Lives: Studies Among the Tenements of New York*. New York: Charles Scribner's Sons, 1890, http://books.google.com/books?id=zhcv_oA5dwgC&printsec=frontcover&source=gbs_ge_summary_r&cad=0#v=onepage&q&f=false.

Rodgers, Bill. *Marathoning*. New York: Simon and Schuster, 1980.

Rogers, Edward, and Donald Smith, eds. *Aboriginal Ontario: Historical Perspectives on the First Nations*. Toronto: Dundurn Press, 1994.

Rosen, Daniel. *Dope: A History of Performance Enhancement in Sports from the Nineteenth Century to Today*. Westport, CT: Praeger, 2008.

Roosevelt, Theodore. *An Autobiography*. New York: Charles Scribner's Sons, 1913.

Roxborough, Henry. *One Hundred—Not Out: The Story of Nineteenth-Century Canadian Sport*. Toronto: Ryerson Press, 1966.

Rudd, J. R. *A Complete System of Treatment for the General Care of the Body*. New York; J. R. Rudd, 1891.

Samuels, Charles. *The Magnificent Rube: The Life and Gaudy Times of Tex Rickard*. New York: McGraw-Hill, 1957.

Scharf, Aaron. *Personal Choice: A Celebration of Twentieth Century Photographs*. London: Victoria and Albert Museum, 1983.

Sears, Edward. *George Seward: America's First Great Runner*. Lanham, MD: Scarecrow Press. 2008.

———. *Running Through the Ages*. Jefferson, NC: McFarland, 2001.

Sekunda, Nicholas. *Marathon 490 B.C.* Westport, CT: Praeger. 2005.

Shorter, Frank. *Olympic Gold: A Runner's Life and Times*. Boston: Houghton Mifflin, 1984.

Shrubb, Alfred. *Running and Cross-Country Running*. London: Health & Strength, 1908.

Stone, Norman. *Europe Transformed 1878–1919*. Great Britain: Fontana Paperbacks, 1983.

Sullivan, James E. *Marathon Running*. New York: Spalding Athletic Series, 1909.

———. *The Olympic Games at Athens, 1906*. New York: American Sports Publishing, 1906.

————, ed. *Spalding's Official Athletic Almanac.* New York: Spalding Athletic Series, 1909.

————, ed. *Spalding's Official Athletic Almanac for 1905.* New York: Spalding Athletic Series, 1905.

Switzer, Kathrine. *Marathon Woman.* New York: Carroll & Graf, 2007.

Telander, Rick. *The Hundred Yard Lie: The Corruption of College Football and What We Can Do to Stop It.* Champaign, IL: Univ. of Illinois Press, 1996.

Titley, E. Brian. *A Narrow Vision: Duncan Campbell Scott and the Administration of Indian Affairs in Canada.* Vancouver: UBC Press, 1995.

Wallechinsky, David. *The Complete Book of the Summer Olympics.* Woodstock, NY: Overlook Press, 2000.

Webster, F. A. M. *The Evolution of the Olympic Games, 1829–1914.* London: Heath, Cranton & Ouseley, 1914.

————. *Sports Grounds and Buildings: Making, Management, Maintenance and Equipment.* London: Sir Isaac Pitman & Sons, 1940.

Weightman, Gavin. *The Industrial Revolutionaries: The Making of the Modern World, 1776–1914.* New York: Grove Press, 2009.

White, G. Edward. *Creating the National Pastime: Baseball Transforms Itself, 1903–1953.* Princeton, NJ: Princeton Univ. Press, 1996.

Wilcock, Bob. *The 1908 Olympic Games, the Great Stadium, and the Marathon: A Pictorial Record.* Great Britain: The Society of Olympic Collectors, 2008.

Williams, Craig. *The Olympian: An American Triumph.* New York: iUniverse, 2010.

Witemeyer, Hugh, ed. *Pound/Williams: Selected Letters of Ezra Pound and William Carlos Williams.* New York: New Directions Books, 1996.

Young, David. *The Modern Olympics: A Struggle for Revival.* Baltimore, MD: The Johns Hopkins Univ. Press, 1996.

Zeman, Brenda. *To Run with Longboat: Twelve Stories of Indian Athletes in Canada.* Edmonton, Canada: GMS2 Ventures, 1988.

Select Articles

Abrahams, Harold. "Dorando—The Immortal Loser," *World Sports*, February 1948.

Bainbridge, John. "American Boy," *New Yorker*, December 20, 1952.

Barney, Robert. "Born from Dilemma: America Awakens to the Modern Olympic Games, 1901–1903," *Olympika: The International Journal of Olympic Studies*, 1992.

————. "Coubertin and Americans: Wary Relationships, 1889–1925," in *Coubertin and Olympism: Questions for the Future, Proceedings of the Le Havre Congress, 1897–1997*.

Bijkerk, Anthony, and David Young. "That Memorable First Marathon," *Journal of Olympic History*, Winter 1999.

Burroughs, W. G. "Burroughs Tells of the European Trip," *Daily Illini*, October 1, 1908.

Chesterton, G. K. "Americans in Sport and Jingoism," *London Illustrated News*, August 15, 1908.

Churchill, Ward, Norbert Hill, and Mary Jo Barlow. "An Historical Overview of Twentieth Century Native American Athletes," *Indian Historian*, 1979.

Connolly, James. "The Shepherd's Bush Greeks," *Collier's*, September 5, 1908.

———. "The Capitalization of Amateur Athletics," *Metropolitan*, July 1910.

Cooper, Pamela. "The First American Marathon," and "How the AAU Suppressed the Marathon," *FootNotes*, Fall 1983.

———. "Community, Ethnicity, Status: The Origins of the Marathon in the United States," *International Journal of the History of Sport*, April 1992.

Cosentino, Frank. "Afros, Aboriginals and Amateur Sport in Pre-World War One Canada," *Canadian Historical Society*, Booklet No. 26, 1998.

Coubertin, Pierre de. "American Ambitions," *Revue Olympic*, December 1908.

Cronin, Fergus. "The Rise and Fall of Tom Longboat," *Maclean's*, February 4, 1956.

"Dorando—Alive or Dead?" *World Sports*, October 1954.

Duggan, Eileen. "The Marathon from Hell," *Marathon & Beyond*, July–August 2004.

Dunne, Finley Peter. "'Mr. Dooley' on the Olympic Games," *American Magazine*, October 1908.

Dyreson, Mark. "America's Athletic Missionaries: Political Performance, Olympic Spectacle and the Quest for an American National Culture, 1896–1912," *Olympika: The International Journal of Olympic Studies*, 1992.

———. "'This Flag Dips for No Earthly King': The Mysterious Origins of an American Myth," *International Journal of the History of Sport*, February 2008.

Ecker, Tom. "The Birth and Early Survival of the Marathon," *Marathon & Beyond*, March–April 2000.

Goldfarb, Clifford. "Arthur Conan Doyle and the Dorando Affair: How Rumours Become Facts," in Leslie Klinger, ed. *A Tangled Skein: A Companion Volume to the Baker Street Irregulars' Expedition to the Country of the Saints*. New York: The Baker Street Irregulars, 2008.

"The Great Marathon Race, 1908," *Polytechnic Magazine*, 1908.

Greenhalgh, Paul. "Art, Politics and Society at the Franco-British Exhibition of 1908," *Art History*, December 1985.

Hawke, Edward. "The Olympic Games in London," *Review of Reviews*, July 1908.

Hayes, John J. "How I Won the Marathon Race," *Cosmopolitan*, December 1908.

Karlson, Kate. "Sir Arthur Picks a Winner in the Olympics of 1908," *Canadian Holmes*, 1980.

Kidd, Bruce. "In Defense of Tom Longboat," *Canadian Journal of History of Sport*, May 1983.

Laney, Al. "Johnny Hayes, Olympic Hero, Is Food Broker," *New York Herald Tribune*, Jan. 4, 1944.

Llewellyn, Matthew. "The Battle of Shepherd's Bush," *International Journal of the History of Sport*, April 2011.

———. "'Viva l'Italia! Viva l'Italia!' Dorando Pietri and the North American Professional Marathon Craze," *International Journal of the History of Sport*, May 2009.

Lovesey, Peter. "The Most Famous Marathoner of All: The Story of Dorando Pietri," *Athletics Weekly*, April 6, 1968.

Lucas, John. "American Involvement in the Athens Olympian Games of 1906," *Stadion*, 1980.

———. "A History of the Marathon Race, 490 B.C. to 1975," *Journal of Sport History*, 1976.

———. "Early Olympic Antagonists: Pierre de Coubertin Versus James E. Sullivan," *Stadion*, 1977.

———. "The Hegemonic Rule of the American Amateur Athletic Union 1888–1914: James E. Sullivan as Prime Mover," *Stadion*, December 1994.

———. "The Professional Marathon Craze in America, 1908–1909," *Track Quarterly Review*, December 1968.

———. "Theodore Roosevelt and Baron Pierre de Coubertin," *Stadion*, 1982–1983.

Mallon, Bill, and Ian Buchanan. "To No Earthly King . . .," *Journal of Olympic History*, September 1999.

Matthews, George. "The Controversial Olympic Games of 1908 as Viewed by the New York Times and the Times of London," *Journal of Sport History*, Summer 1980.

McChesney, Robert. "Media Made Sport: A History of Sports Coverage in the United States," in Lawrence Wenner, ed. *Media, Sports, & Society*. Newbury Park, CA: Sage Publications, 1989.

McDowell, Edwin. "Memories of a Forgotten Olympian," *Wall Street Journal*, August 11, 1972.

McGrath, Roger. "Running Rings 'Round the Empire," *Irish America Magazine*, September 1988.

McIntire, Matthew. "National Status, the 1908 Olympic Games and the English Press," *Media History*, April 2009.

———. "The Battle of Shepherd's Bush," *International Journal of the History of Sport*, April 2011.

Milvy, Paul, ed. "The Marathon: Physiological, Medical, Epidemiological, and Psychological Studies," *Annals of the New York Academy of Sciences*, October 1977.

Morrow, Don. "A Case Study in Amateur Conflict: The Athletic War in Canada, 1906–08," *British Journal of Sports History*, September 1986.

Muller, Norbert. "Michel Bréal—the Man Behind the Idea of the Marathon," from *Pathways: Critiques and Discourse in Olympic Research*, Univ. of Western Ontario: International Centre for Olympic Studies, 2008.

O'Shaughnessy, Christine Forshaw. "Joseph Forshaw, Marathon Runner," *Journal of Olympic History*, May 2004.

Polley, Martin. "From Windsor Castle to White City: The 1908 Olympic Marathon Route," *London Journal*, July 2009.

"The Polytechnic Marathon Trial Race," *Polytechnic Magazine*, 1908.

Pratt, Richard Henry. "Wants Indian Stories," *Indian Helper*, March 18, 1898.

Raycheba, Marion. "The History of the Marathon in Canada," *Marathon & Beyond*, May–June, 2005.

"Reminiscences of Hammerstein's Victoria," *New Yorker*, December 13, 1930.

Robinson, Roger. "The Fascinating Struggle," two-part series in *Marathon & Beyond*, March–April and May–June 2007.

Roosevelt, Theodore. "What We Can Expect of the American Boy," *St. Nicholas Magazine*, May 1900.

Sheppard, Melvin. "Spiked Shoes and Cinder Paths: An Athlete's Story," multipart series in *Sports Story Magazine*, 1924.

Smith, Red. "Dorando Pietri (Heesa Gooda for Not) Sees Marathon Finish—or Did He?" Boston *Globe*, August 8, 1948.

Sullivan, James E. "Athletics and the Stadium," *Cosmopolitan*, September 1901.

Thompson, Paul. "Historical Concepts of the Athlete's Heart," *Medicine & Science in Sports & Exercise*, March 2004.

"Tom Longboat, the Indian, and Jay Gould, the Millionaire," *Mind and Body*, June 1907.

Unwin, Peter. "Who Do You Think I Am? A Story of Tom Longboat," *Beaver*, April–May 2001.

"Where Are They Now? Little Johnny," *New Yorker*, July 4, 1936.

Whitney, Casper. "The View-Point," *Outing*, September and November 1908.

Widlund, Ture. "Ethelbert Talbot: His Life and Place in Olympic History," *Citius, Altius, Fortius: Journal of the Society of Olympic Historians*, May 1994.

Wilcock, Bob. "The 1908 Olympic Marathon," *Journal of Olympic History*, March 2008.

———. "This Flag Dips to No Earthly King: The 1908 Olympic Opening Ceremony, Fresh Evidence," *Journal of Olympic History*, March 2011.

"World's Champion Runner Now Sells Blue Ribbon," *Associated Grower*, September 1921.

Other Sources

"The 1900 & 1904 Olympic Games: The Farcical Games," by Reet Howell and Maxwell Howell, paper presented to the International HISPA Seminar, 1996.

"1908: The First True Olympics," docudrama film produced and directed by Anna Thomson, shown on BBC4, 2008.

"1908 Olympic Marathon"—http://www.nuts.org.uk/trackstats/1908marathon.htm—article on British marathoners from *Track Stats*. Accessed in 2010.

1908 London Olympic programs: Opening Day and Marathon.

2008 U.S. Olympic Marathon Trials, Media Guide.

British Olympic Association: Minutes and papers, 1906–1908.

Cook, Theodore. "The Olympic Games of 1908 in London: A Reply to Certain Charges Made by Some of the American Officials," BOA, 1908.

Crocker, J. H. "Report of the First Canadian Olympic Athletic Team," 1908.

"Dorando." Words and music by Irving Berlin.

Film clips from the 1908 Olympics, Pathé, 1908.

Gilbert, A. C. Letters and papers.

"The Irish American Athletic Club: Redefining Americanism at the 1908 Olympic Games," undergraduate paper by John Schaefer, New York University, 2001, http://www.nyu.edu/library/bobst/research/aia/newresearch/schaefer01b.pdf.

James E. Sullivan–Pierre de Coubertin correspondence, from the Avery Brundage papers, via microfilm.

"John Flanagan: His Life and Times," Memorial Tribute, 2001.

Kelly, F. S. Diary, July 24, 1908. Manuscripts Branch, National Library of Australia.

"The Longboat Incident of the 1908 Olympics: A Study in International Sporting Relations," thesis by Dan Reid, University of Western Ontario, 1988.

The Marathon, documentary directed by Bud Greenspan, 1974.

"The Marathon Race of 1908," by John J. Hayes, self-published booklet, 1908.

"The Olympic Games: An Answer to Mr. Francis Peabody Jr., and a 'Member of the British Olympic Committee,'" by A Member of the American Olympic Committee, 1908.

St. Bartholomew's Parish yearbooks, 1906–1907.

"The Spectacle Plays and Exhibitions of Imre Kiralfy," thesis by Brendan Edward Gregory, University of Manchester, 1988.

Theodore Roosevelt Papers, via microfilm.

"Thomas Longboat: A Great Canadian Sportsman," from the Proceedings of the Second Canadian Symposium on the History of Sport and Physical Education, University of Windsor, 1972.

"Tom Longboat: Canada's Outstanding Indian Athlete," thesis by Wilton Littlechild, University of Alberta, 1975.

"Tom Longboat's Attestation Paper," accessed from the Web site of the Library and Archives, Canada, http://www.collectionscanada.gc.ca/premiereguerre/ 025005-3200.002.01-e.html.

Wherearethechildren.ca, a Web site about the legacy of the Indian residential schools in Canada.

www.wingedfist.org/home.html, a Web site about the Irish-American Athletic Club and Celtic Park.

INDEX